Software Company

Software Company

Advice on how to start, grow and exit
a software company

David Cornwell

www.softwarecompanybook.com

First Published 2020

Published by Beaten Metal Books Ltd

Edition: 1.1 – Print*

ISBN: 978-1-913678-00-5

Cover Cartoon by Mark Wood.

* v1.1: Minor typos and formatting errors corrected

Disclaimer

The book contains the opinion of the author and is not intended to be an exhaustive examination of the subject matter. It is designed to provide helpful information on the topics considered and is therefore presented solely for educational and entertainment purposes. It is provided 'as is' without warranty either expressed or implied.

In no event will the author or the publisher be held liable to any person or entity for any decision made or action taken based on the information contained in this book. This includes any incidental or consequential loss or other damages caused or alleged to have been caused, directly or indirectly, by the information contained herein.

PLEASE NOTE: The author is not qualified to provide formal legal, accountancy or other professional services advice and this book does not provide such advice. The book explains the author's layman understanding of such matters in the hope that it will help the reader's understanding. Any reliance you place on the author's understanding is entirely at your own risk. You should undertake your own research and due diligence as relevant legislation and the business environment constantly changes.

In summary, you are responsible for your own decisions and actions and therefore results and your use of the information in this book is at your own risk.

Trademarks

All product names, brands, trademarks and registered trademarks are the property of their respective owners and used for identification purposes only. Neither the author nor the publisher is affiliated any of the companies mentioned herein.

Acknowledgements

Thanks to my wife of 37 years who has always supported me in my career and provided a voice of reason during difficult times. Having a supportive spouse is one of the key ingredients of success.

Thanks to the individuals mentioned by name in this book. They have all taken the time to read the sections in which they are mentioned and have confirmed that they are happy with or, at least, do not violently object to my inclusion of them and what I've said about them. A special thanks to Clare Beazley who has been a constant source of rational thought and personifies calm efficiency. In a presentation to aspiring entrepreneurs we once described Clare as my 'pooper scooper' coming behind me cleaning up the mess I'd left behind as I impetuously forged ahead. Everyone needs a Clare!

Thanks to my niece, Jessica Trappe (www.jessicatrappe.com), for providing editorial services for this book. However, I'd stress that while she provided valuable input, I didn't accept all her proposed changes as I like to think that my writing style is unique. Therefore all mistakes, grammatical inconsistencies and peculiarities are mine and mine alone.

Thanks to the beta readers who read an initial copy of this book and provided feedback. Their feedback certainly enhanced the final prose!

Finally, I'd like to thank all the 'business friends' I've made and kept in touch with over the years. Many of them are ex CDC alumni and went out of their way to support me during my time running PleaseTech. Others have been helpful throughout the years I've known them and have been very generous in their entertainment and support.

Table of Contents

Foreword

It is a matter of public record that on 23rd March 2017 it was announced via the London Stock Exchange that PleaseTech Ltd was to be acquired by Ideagen Plc for £10million + £2million on a cash free, debt free basis. The deal completed one week later on 28th March 2017.

For me, other than the significant cash injection to my personal bottom line, this meant that I was no longer running a software company - something I'd done more-or-less continuously since 1994. After the six month earnout, I'd be unemployed and have to think of something else to occupy my time.

I fell into running software companies by chance. My wife and I had established a home in South Wales and were busy bringing up a young family. I was working in business development for a small systems integration/custom software shop in Swindon (Kinesis Computing) but recognised that the time had come to move on. Despite energetic attempts, it transpired that no one was minded to offer me a decent job within an hour's drive of the Severn Bridge and so, given the paucity of other options, it was time to be in charge of my destiny.

With Kinesis I'd been working in the fledgling document management industry and had come across a US document management system called DCS-PowerNET[1] developed by a company called Mystic Management Systems (MMS)[2] based in Mystic, CT. I'd also established that they didn't have any UK representation. This was useful as it become clear that I was about to be made redundant as Kinesis had produced a new organisation chart which lacked one crucial element – my name!

The day after I officially left Kinesis I was on my way across the Atlantic to meet with MMS. I flew into Boston, took the train down to Mystic and had my first, of what would turn out to be many, night in The Whaler's Inn. The important thing was that a day or so later I emerged with an agreement for

---

[1] The only reference I can now find to DCS-PowerNET is in ComputerWorld dated 10th April 1995 in an article entitled 'The CW Guide to Document Management' where it is listed under 'Library Managers'. It's proof it existed! View the entry here: https://tinyurl.com/y8az3ua8

[2] Mystic Management Systems appears to now be called 'DocXellent' (www.docxellent.com).

the exclusive UK re-sale rights (and non-exclusive European rights) of DCS-PowerNET. My entrepreneurial career had commenced.

I had no grand ambitions. I wanted to be able to live where I lived, earn a living and, if I got lucky, to pay off the mortgage.

An external observer would have almost certainly concluded that my chances of achieving even these modest objectives were slim. I'd never run a company, never had any line management responsibilities and had no financial reserves. Yet my company, Computerised Document Control (which later became CDC Solutions) went on, with me at the helm, to raise over £11m in venture capital and have sales all over the world. It was, by any measure, a very successful business.

After I left CDC in 2002, the thought of working for someone else again didn't appeal so I did the only thing I really knew how to do and that was set-up another software company, Kcentrix Software - which was later renamed PleaseTech Ltd. The very same PleaseTech Ltd which, approximately 15 years later, was acquired by Ideagen plc. PleaseTech was another very successful business.

Shortly after the earnout was complete and I was unemployed and getting bored of painting the bedroom, I contacted Bath University (my MBA alma mater) and was invited to give a presentation to their MBA program on my experience of entrepreneurship. Putting together the presentation was tough. Trying to cram 23 years of experience into a 40 minute talk was problematic to say the least! After all, I could witter on for 40 minutes on any one of the bullet points! This experience gave me the belief that I had enough interesting material for a book on the subject. The positive reaction to my presentation suggested that my knowledge was worth sharing.

So this book documents my experience and learnings and gives advice based on over 23 years of starting, running and exiting two very successful software companies. It covers set-up, first steps, hiring, firing, growth, culture, development culture, the Agile Methodology, offshoring development, selling to the USA, selling to Europe, software licensing, patent trolls, marketing, sales, partnerships, venture capital investors, bootstrapping, the analyst game, professional advisors and the exit process. In short, it's a brain dump that I hope some people will find useful and which will support the next generation of entrepreneurs.

Obviously I draw heavily on my experience at CDC and PleaseTech but my knowledge extends beyond these two organisations. Over the years I've spoken with a lot of people from all levels within companies, been asked for advice and witnessed the rise and fall of companies and individuals. Late night conversations at the convention hotel bar are always very revealing – you get the reality as opposed to the PR newspeak. People discuss their 'challenges' whether that be the crap they are getting from their investors, staffing woes or other pressing matters. Conversations are not limited to their own companies. It has to be said that people passing on the dirt on their competitors is always very interesting!

Whilst the book is written from a UK perspective because I'm British and both my companies were set-up and were based in the UK, I do have experience of what goes on in American companies and bring that to bear. Of course, the general principles are common wherever you are based and, when you consider that 95% of PleaseTech's sales were export (75% to the USA), you'll soon realise that enterprise software is a global business and you need to think globally to succeed.

I think it necessary to note that this book is not, and is not intended to be, an autobiography. By way of background, you can download 'The CDC Story' and 'The PleaseTech Story' from the website (www.softwarecompanybook.com). Whilst these stories are an integral part of the narrative in so far as they are the basis of my experience, it's not necessary to read them to benefit from the wisdom I'm trying to impart. However, I hope some people find them a useful, interesting read that places the rest of the book in context!

Introduction

Some people are desperate to become entrepreneurs. They have an idea which they are convinced will change the world. Others, like me, fall into it as it is the next logical step for whatever reason. I've never considered myself to be an 'entrepreneur', it's a label others apply to me and what I do. I'm just an ordinary bloke who, because he couldn't get a decent job within an hour's commute, set-up a company which was moderately successful and then, because he needed something else to do, set-up another one. Simple really.

There are many misperceptions regarding entrepreneurs. A chap called Antony Buck, of REN Cosmetics, summed it up beautifully when he said[3]:

"Everyone assumes entrepreneurs are like Alan Sugar or the dragons in the Dragon's Den. They think you have to be suit-wearing, self-obsessed, aggressive bastards; someone who wants other people to lose; sees business as confrontation and toughness as crucial. There's a total lack of humanity – what about collaboration and enjoying what you do?"

This sums up my thoughts pretty almost precisely. People who set-up businesses, especially software companies, are generally passionate about something and it's generally not making money. In fact, I'd go as far as to say that if making money is your sole objective, running a software company may not be the career to which you are most suited. Consider becoming a Venture Capitalist (VC).

Making money is the sole objective of VCs. It's their stated aim and it attracts people interested in spreadsheets and dilution ratios and other such financial stuff. As we will discover, VCs are not interested in your business except as a means to invest, exit and earn. They'd play the stock market but believe that the returns in backing higher risk start-up companies are healthier. It's just another asset class. That's fine when they are not masquerading as anything else.

Over the years, I've come to realise that money is how you keep the score[4]. It's purely a measure of the success (or otherwise) of your business. Clearly

---

[3] In a 2007 Times Newspaper article "The Antipreneurs" (aka the new "caring, sharing entrepreneurs")

[4] Attributed to Ted Turner.

you need it to function but your focus should be on making your product or service the best it can be, managing the business to make it the best it can be, and working hard for your clients. These attributes are the basis of success and a natural consequence of success is value. The company ownership structure determines who collects that value.

Another key point to make at this early stage is that this book is not going to tell you how to set-up the next Google, or Amazon or eBay. It will help you start a software business which could, of course, turn into a unicorn and if the book helps you on your way to this then I'll be delighted for you. However, the crucial point is that you don't need to create a unicorn to have a very successful company and to make money. Both the businesses I founded sold for less than £20million (~US$30million)[5]. So it becomes a percentage game.

You are very unlikely to ever own 100% of your business as there are key staff you'll have to motivate, but the percentages are meaningful. Owning 60% of a business worth £20million should make you a very happy person. Owning 1% of the same business is 'only' worth £200,000 but, if one of your employees had EMI[6] stock options around that figure, they'd probably not be that unhappy! Stock is valuable.

Setting up and running a successful niche businesses can be very lucrative. Both the companies I ran operated in a niche. We, the team and I, didn't set out with a grand vision to change the world in any meaningful way. We set-out to survive and, once that had been accomplished, to make our products the best option for customers in our chosen market. We were absolutely passionate about our products but we were under no illusion we were anything but a software vendor; a bloody good software vendor, but a software vendor nonetheless.

Selling into a niche can be quite efficient. There is a clearly defined set of customers to address, a means to address them and you've got a better chance for recognition (especially when you are the standout vendor in the niche) which equates to a reduction in marketing costs.

---

[5] For ease, throughout this book, except when covering historical documented figures, I've used the exchange rate of £1 = US$1.50.
[6] Enterprise Management Incentive, a tax advantageous UK share option scheme designed for small companies.

It goes further than that. When you are struggling to get your first couple of customer reference sites, you need to consider the risks the customer is running. If you are trying to sell the customer an enterprise system which requires a step change in a fundamental business process and or a significant financial commitment you are stacking the odds against yourself. However, if you are offering to make a small but vital piece of the puzzle more efficient and there is a good fall back plan for the customer (i.e. revert to do it the way they currently do it), you are lowering the risk for the customer and maximising your chances of a successful sale.

So, for anyone who is bored and wants to stop reading now, the one bit of advice I'd give is: think globally and become the best in your chosen niche.

The other point I should mention is that my experience is all business to business (B2B). I've been successful selling software into businesses, specifically large, multi-national businesses. These companies can be hard taskmasters but they do spend a lot of money on software. In the early days of PleaseTech we did run a public subscription service and found it wasn't worth it. In other words, the effort exceeded the income by a long way. I know less about business to consumer (B2C) and, whilst most of the issues I discuss in these chapters will be relevant, I'm basing my advice and recommendations on B2B.

Whether you are a techie or a salesperson looking to do your own thing or you are already running a software business, we are going to look at how to start, how to grow and how to exit. There are occasions I do step back and look at the bigger picture but, if you keep reading, I'm confident you will find a considerable amount of practical advice in areas outside your current area of expertise.

How to Start

THE HARD YARDS

How to Start

Did you know that Microsoft started out life as a bootstrap?

What about Oracle? Cisco? Dell? eBay? FaceBook? GoPro?

These companies and many more started out life in a variety of guises but all have one thing in common, they were all doing business successfully without external funding before they received external VC investment[7] and spent that investment on growing their businesses and, in some cases, becoming household names.

It is possible to come up with a good idea, make a few presentations and get a VC seed investment purely on the basis of your track record and some PowerPoint slides[8]. It is, however, the exception rather than the norm and therefore the high probability is that you'll be bootstrapping.

The Investopedia website has a pretty good article on bootstrapping[9] which is rather annoying as it covers a lot of what I would have said. They define it as follows:

"Bootstrapping is a process whereby an entrepreneur starts a self-sustaining business, markets it, and grows the business by using limited resources or money – this is accomplished without the use of venture capital firms or even significant angel investment."

If you've read the appendices, you'll know both my businesses were bootstrapped. With CDC we bootstrapped via a redundancy payment, a couple of loans and a resale agreement into a profitable, successful business before taking venture capital. With PleaseTech I was able to bootstrap from my personal funds until we were profitable and cash generative which allowed us to grow steadily without the hassles of external investment.

---

[7] Microsoft took only £1million to get a VC on their board. Source: Question and answer with Bill Gates at the launch of the Harvard Campaign, 2013: https://youtu.be/cBHJ-8Bch4E

[8] I know someone who did exactly this. They reckoned they raised about £20K per PowerPoint slide!

[9] Companies That Succeeded With Bootstrapping on Investopedia: https://tinyurl.com/y8bpjn85

The key point about bootstrapping is that the company is started with no outside funding (except perhaps family, friends and a very understanding spouse) and grown primarily via internal cash flow. Personally, I'd consider loans as falling into the definition of bootstrapping because the company's equity is not at stake. The equity will continue to be held by the founder(s) and, as the company grows, by a controlled set of key employees.

Clearly, when you are bootstrapping, breaking even or being profitable is an absolute necessity unless you have unlimited personal funds or an extremely generous set of relatives and or friends. In principle, however, you have to make a bit to spend a bit.

Bootstrapping is a raw experience. There is no cushion. It's pure survival. You will have to run very lean and very mean. You'll find out the value of cash. How hard it is to get money in and how easy it is to spend it.

It's also the ultimate in test marketing – except it's for real. You'll soon find out if the market does really want what you are offering. As I found out with the first product we tried to sell at PleaseTech, whilst lots of people may say lots of nice things about your offering, the acid test is whether they are willing to pay real, actual money for it. To do this they will have to justify it and so it will need to demonstrate a clear return on investment (ROI).

Even if one company is willing to pay real, actual money for your product, remember that 'one swallow does not a summer make'. You need many swallows for the summer and therein lies the challenge.

Assuming you have one or two clients spending real money, the next question is: is what you do or offer sustainable and repeatable with multiple different customers? In other words, is there a wider market into which you can grow the business?

However, before you get to this stage you need to take the first step and that is setting up a company and getting on with it.

First Steps

Setting up a company is really easy. In the UK it currently costs £40 (or £100 if required on the same day) and is really a matter of filling in some forms. You can do it yourself or pay an accountant to do it for you. You'll also want to register for VAT[10]. Again, do it yourself or pay an accountant[11]. Once you have your company formed you'll need a bank account and then you are good to go.

Before you do all that, one of the more important decisions is the name of your business. Personally I advocate having a name which 'does what it says on the tin'. For example, I wouldn't have called my company Google, I'd have called it 'EZSearch' or 'WebSearch' or something similar!

You will also want the top level '.com' domain name. This may push you towards a unique 'new word'. Be careful. If you have to explain people how to pronounce it (Kcentrix, you say the letter 'k' and then add 'centrix') or explain what it means (Kcentrix stands for Knowledge Centric XML) you are probably being too clever.

We cover the topic of branding under the Marketing section, but, when considering the domain, at least get the basics right. As noted above, you'll mainly be interested in the '.com' domain and I'd suggest you avoid punctuation or hyphens – however that is a subject of legitimate debate. Obviously, it's up to you whether you feel sufficiently strongly to pay a domain squatter for a domain you want. I never have, but I've been lucky. When I decided to write this book the first thing I did was register the domain! I've followed my own rules with softwarecompanybook.com.

Having said all that, both my companies have changed their name as their focus changed, so it's best not to get too hung up about it!

Once you've established the basics you'll then need to offer something to the market i.e. have something to sell. The key point in having something to sell is that it gives you a focus and an excuse to reach out and talk to people. You're unlikely to get far calling someone and saying: 'Hi I'm Dave, I've just set up a software business and don't really have a focus. What can I sell you?'.

---

[10] Value added Tax. The equivalent of Sales Tax in the USA.

[11] Note that company set-up and VAT registration comes with commitment. You will need to submit regular returns of various types. It's not register and forget!

However, if you call them, offer your product/service and get a 'No', ask a follow-up of 'do you mind me asking what is currently on your agenda' or 'what's the focus of your budget at the moment'?

The worst you can get is the equivalent of 'Yes, I do mind telling you'! However, you may well get some valuable marketing feedback which helps you establish what is selling to your target market or even that your target market is wrong!

Whether you are like me in my first company and don't have a grand plan, or whether you have spotted a niche and want to occupy it before someone else does, unless you have venture funding, you'll have to do the hard yards.

The Hard Yards

The Urban Dictionary[12] defines 'The Hard Yards' as *"Difficult, irksome, tedious, boring and unglamorous work or effort needed to achieve success in a business venture, sport or study"* and I reckon that's a pretty good description.

If you are really bootstrapping you're unlikely to be taking a salary, you'll be funding company purchases on your personal credit cards and watching cash flow like a hawk. It's always harder to earn a bit than spend a bit.

BTW; if you are tempted to set-up your new company as a moonlight operation, be sure to review your employment contract. If your employment contract has been drawn up properly, it is likely to have two key clauses which prevent such activity: (i) a clause preventing you undertaking any other work, paid or otherwise, whilst in employment; and (ii) a clause which assigns all intellectual property (IP) you create whilst employed to your employer.

It goes without saying that you cannot simply copy your employer's IP as a basis for your own to give you a fast start. I'd describe that as 'very naughty'. The lawyers have a different description for it and it isn't pleasant.

If you did any of the above and were employed by a company I was running, I'd have the lawyers all over you before you could say 'oh dear me, I've screwed up'. You really don't want to start your entrepreneurial career fighting a lawsuit with money which, if you have it, was probably earmarked

---

[12] https://tinyurl.com/y8yfcpbr

to cover your expenses for a couple of months/quarters. At worst, it not only means your entrepreneurial career is over before it started but you've lost your house and are no longer particularly employable.

In such circumstances, coming down on you like a ton of bricks wouldn't make me a bad person. I would simply be defending my company, its IP and setting an example to the rest of the staff. You'll see it differently when you're in the driving seat defending the company you've worked hard to get off the ground!

So, best keep it clean. Resign, work out your notice period ensuring that you are not using your employer's time or equipment for your personal business, then, once you have left you can set-up your company and get cracking. Note that you may have some non-compete clauses on your employment contract to honour.

I'm not sorry for introducing the concept of contracts, lawyers and threatened litigation at this early stage of proceedings. One of the first lessons one needs to learn in business is that contracts are very important and lawyers are your friends, expensive friends, but friends none the less.

Let's go back to the hard yards. How are you going to bring in that all important cash in the first few months? That's the key. Have a plan for this. What are you going to do on day one, day 10, day 20, etc.?

At PleaseTech it took over a year from the conception of PleaseReview to its delivery as a beta and then another six months before we sold a license and then another couple of months before we got paid (i.e. received the cash due). You will have a similar gap which will need to be funded.

Oracle started as database consultancy and managed to get a customer (the CIA) to pay for the development of its initial RDBMS. If you are lucky or smart enough to follow Oracle's lead and can swing it so that a client is paying for the development of your product from the get go, then you will have two challenges: (i) having a contract that assigns your company the IP in the developed software (don't assume anything - make it explicit) and (ii) ensuring that the software meets the client's unique requirements whilst keeping it generic enough to sell to others.

A top tip for keeping the IP (this is expanded upon later in the book as it's very important) is not to sell it as a custom development but as a software license for your new product. As the first licensee the customer is getting the equivalent of a custom developed solution for the cost of a standard software license, is buying into the maintenance and upgrades of the same and, as a bonus, they get to define the functionality critical to them. What's not to like?

In the event you are lucky enough to get a flying start as described the trick is to ensure that you get enough cash from the customer (think stage payments) to keep the business running whilst you develop the product. Larry Ellison is on record as saying that in the early days Oracle was once one week away from not being able to make the payroll and pay its employees[13].

You will also need to have a very clear definition of when the product is delivered so you can close the project out and not get caught in an endless development cycle. Ideally you'll have an agreed specification and stage payment schedule approved by both parties.

If you can't swing such a sweet deal, be sure to have a plan whether it be contract software development, systems integration, consultancy, acting as a reseller or whatever on which to focus on day one.

Running Lean and Mean

When you are in the start-up years slogging through the hard yards, it's cash that will make or break your business. You need it to be able to meet your financial commitments. It's cash that you use to pay bills, employees, sub-contractors, etc.

To generate cash you'll need sales and you will need to be profitable. To be profitable you need to keep your overheads low. The financial position needs to be constantly monitored and controlled.

In the Finance section I explain that these days the use of an accountant or of a self-employed part time book keeper, and an accounting package is more or less mandatory. However, in addition to the formal accounts which record financial history, you need to maintain a simple cash flow forecast spreadsheet. Money you know you are getting in against money you know you going to have to pay out month by month. Be realistic as to when you are likely to receive payments from clients. They may say thirty days but, in

---

[13] My source is eWeek.com. Read the article here: https://tinyurl.com/w9djq7k

reality, it's likely to be sixty or ninety. So, in principle, assume that cash out happens instantly and cash in happens at least two months after it's due.

Even if you are not taking a salary, make sure you are formally completing and submitting expense sheets for the expenses you've incurred on your personal credit cards, etc. You may only be submitting them to yourself for future payment when the company can afford it, but the key point is you are creating that important documentation trail which, if the nice people from the tax office decide to audit you (and they do from time to time), will stand you in good stead. Include all travel expenses. The Inland Revenue has a reasonably generous £/mile allowance for travel by private car on company business[14]. Use your expense sheet to record all these trips as they add up and, when you can afford to pay yourself back some expenses, they make for a nice tax free bonus.

In principle, regardless of the size of your company you should run it in a manner as if it is about to be audited tomorrow. If you are successful and make it to the exit stage you will discover that a thing called 'due diligence' is a critical part of the exit process. Having formal, consistent, detailed financial, licensing and other such records from day one will make for a much easier and less costly process.

There is a great saying which goes as follows: revenue is vanity, profit is sanity and cash is reality. Cash is king. Cash is the lifeblood of your company and never more so than in the start-up phase.

Keeping an Eye on the Ultimate Prize

When bashing away at the coalface in those early months and years it can be very easy to lose sight of the ultimate aim. As the saying goes: when you are up to your arse in alligators it's difficult to remember the objective was to drain the swamp!

The immediate aim is, of course, survival, profitability and getting to a point where you are paying yourself a salary, have paid back the Directors loans you made to the company, and are starting to build a cash balance in the company itself. To do this you will, by definition, need to be making a profit!

---

[14] Be sure to update your car insurance to include using it for your business purposes.

However, the ultimate aim is to set-up a software company not a consultancy, VAR or any other such 'means to an end' initial focus. You want to develop your own IP, your own product – that's where the true value is. Even if you didn't have a clue what IP that may be when you started out, the fact that you are out there talking to people and, most importantly listening to them, means you are getting the best market intelligence there is.

In my opinion there is no such thing as a wasted sales call. Every conversation, and you really need to think of it as a conversation not as a pitch, is an opportunity for market research. What is the pain people are really feeling? What would they happily spend money on if only they could find the tool/product/service which addressed said pain? What is their view of the market? How do they see the other vendors? Not everyone will tell you but a lot of people will be happy to give their opinion.

The challenge is, of course, not to get too comfortable in doing your consultancy or VAR business. If it's going well you may decide not to invest in creating your own IP and be quite happy building a business based on reselling a third party tool with some added services and ticking over nicely. You can even grow the business to a decent size. Of course, it won't have the exit value of a company which has its own IP and, to some extent, your success will be dependent on the third party software you've chosen to resell or consult around.

If you get to this stage and decide that the immediate lifestyle is more important than the long-term goal, then it's not a bad decision and I, for one, will have nothing but admiration for you. You've done the hard yards, got the business started and simply taken a different fork in the road. Running a business is hard, software development is way beyond hard and therefore you may well have selected the sensible lower risk choice which maximises the net worth/lifestyle equation.

It's difficult to make the decision to pay yourself less and re-invest the money, for which you've worked so hard, back into the company to recruit more staff to develop a product. The course of product development rarely runs smoothly.

Conversely, if things aren't going that well initially, to give you faith, it's a well-documented fact that companies rarely make a success of the thing they first start out with and it's the second phase product/service/offering which is successful. There are many examples. PayPal started life as a company called Confinity which developed an application to beam payments securely between Palm Pilots. At least, with PayPal you can understand the natural progression. Twitter came out of a podcast start-up which realised it would never be able to out-gun the major players and changed direction.

The concept that companies don't make money (or just about keep their heads above water) on their initial offering is certainly true in my experience. CDC, my first business, started out re-selling a US document management product and developed publishing technology to help itself compete and give itself an edge in a competitive market. It soon became apparent that our publishing technology was unique and much sought after. Therefore the obvious way forward was to port the publishing technology onto other DMS offerings. We caught the Documentum wave and 'on a rising tide all boats go up'. We certainly did.

PleaseTech started out doing something different (XML publishing) and, through that, found itself in document review. Personally, I'm not convinced it is possible to get it 'right first time'. However, you have to be out there demonstrating and listening. Or, to put it another way, you have to be in the game.

The choice of the words 'demonstrating' and 'listening' was not accidental. You need to be demonstrating because people generally can't visualise from textual descriptions and listening because your visualisation acts as a catalyst for them to discuss what really is causing them pain.

Pain is the critical ingredient. The equation is simple: Pain = pain solution = revenue = business success.

Company Structures & Ownership

I made no apology for introducing the concepts of contracts and lawyers and thereby company structure early in the proceedings and I make no apology for stressing its importance once again.

My strong advice to you is to never rely on good will and personal relationships as they go out of the window when cash is involved.

Don't for a minute believe that these rules don't apply to you and that your relationships are somehow different. You may be setting up a business with your good mates (not recommended – see below) with the best of intentions but things change. People change. People's priorities change. Promises made when nothing was at stake suddenly become distant memories when it matters and cash is involved.

It is a fact of life that business partners, in much the same way as life partners, fall out all the time. Harvard Business School professor Noam Wasserman's book 'The Founder's Dilemmas', quotes a 1989 study[15] which found that 65% of start-ups fail as a result of co-founder conflict. You may be inclined to dismiss this as an old historic study of no relevance in today's business environment, I disagree. Given the inherent pressures involved in a start-up I'm sure a more up-to-date study would have similar findings!

If you read the business press you'll come across regular stories of ex business partners suing each other and that's just the high profile ones! For more evidence, examine the histories of some of the successful companies already mentioned[16]. Of course, it's not just those in high profile companies who fall out, I have first-hand experience in this department.

Early in the CDC days we were involved in a joint venture company set-up to develop Adobe Acrobat plug-ins. We went in naively based on personal relationships and trust and, when the personal relationships rapidly failed, we paid the price in legal fees to extract ourselves. Furthermore, whilst thankfully not ending in break-up, the relationships between the key players in CDC itself went through periods of extreme tension.

The fact is that the hard yards are, by definition, hard and therefore there is plenty of scope for disagreement between even the closest of business partners. Not all co-founders stay the course. Some leave voluntarily, others in a swirl of ligation and settlements which are a major distraction from the job in hand.

Therefore thinking about this in advance can save an awful lot of heartache and, perhaps more importantly, disruption and cash.

---

[15] A study by Gorman and Sahlman which asked VCs the main reason why their portfolio companies which had failed (or were failing) had done so.
[16] If you want to study an extreme example of company founders falling out just search for information on the Transperfect Inc litigation between the founders who each owned 50% of the company.

Company Ownership

It is critical to get company ownership right early on. This doesn't mean that you need, at this early stage, to spend vast sums of money with lawyers but it does mean you need to think about who has what and what happens if it all goes pear-shaped.

If you hold a clear majority of all stock then life is relatively nice and simple. You are in control and can get on with it. A simple off the shelf company with standard articles should be adequate. Standard Articles of Association (the rules which govern the company) can normally be changed with the agreement of 75% of the shareholders. So if you control more than 75% of the voting shares so you are effectively in control although it's better to be safe than sorry so carry on reading!

However, if you are setting up with business partners you need to consider things like: Who is the boss? Who is the key driver? Whose company is it? Who is investing the most? Is that investment in cash or in kind? If in kind, how is it valued?

I'd advise that splitting the shares 50/50 is a poor idea. If the two shareholders reach an impasse there is no way forward. With three founders a three way split means, of course, that any two can out vote the third. They may not be able to change the articles but standard off-the-shelf articles are pretty generic. If this is your company, your brainchild, your passion, do you really want to be in a position where the people you brought along for the ride can out-vote you and take over your business?

If you think this won't happen to you I'd reiterate that 65% of start-ups fail as a result of co-founder conflict and, I'm sure, that none of these failures were set-up with that objective! So, if you are going to invest your time, money and sanity in a venture make sure that there is the equivalent of a pre-nuptial agreement.

In business this is called a shareholders agreement and, unlike a pre-nup, it is legally binding[17]. Shareholder agreements can cover almost anything and, as with all contracts, are extremely useful when people fall out. In my opinion, as a minimum, the critical thing you should anticipate and cover is

---

[17] In the UK pre-nuptial agreements are currently not legally binding.

the eventuality of one or more of the shareholders wanting out or being forced out.

You don't need to spend a fortune on lawyers (although a good lawyer will assist) as there are plenty of websites dedicated to creating all types of business and corporate documents including shareholder agreements. So, as a minimum, whether you hold a controlling 75% or not, you need to have a shareholders agreement or similar contract which specifies what happens if someone with stock decides to leave or you have to fire them.

Do they have to sell their shares back? If so, at what value?

My strong suggestion is that, yes, leavers have to sell their shares back. The last thing you want is to have shares held by those not participating in the business. You don't want to be slogging away on the hard yards with the knowledge that x% of your effort is rewarding someone who didn't stay the course and is potentially in a nice corporate job with a healthy salary!

I'm aware of a company set up by a group of techies who, despite my advice, gave a small percentage to a 'sales consultant' who they wanted to do the selling for them. There were no conditions attached. Apparently there was a misunderstanding. They thought the sales consultant was going to actually do something useful - like selling. The consultant had understood the brief as being to teach them how to sell (i.e. to provide sales consultancy/training services)! They went their separate ways. The sales consultant retained his percentage. The company is doing rather well. Lucky sales consultant!

As to the value placed on the shares, in my opinion, it's simple - it's the face value of the shares. If they've been issued 100 shares at £0.01 per share (for which they should have paid £1 into the company), they get that money back. These shares can then be used to motivate others who are participating in the hard yards.

If you are feeling generous, you may consider purchasing them back at the accounting book value of the company. In the early years that will be zero (due to all the Director's loans you and potentially others will have made and any other loans) and therefore it's back to the issue price. If you've had a few years of profit and have paid back the loans, the accounting book value of the company will be based on your cash and other assets.

The key point is that a shareholders agreement will specify on what basis the shares are bought back (or retained[18]) and therefore nullify any arguments and thus minimise the disruption to the business.

It's worth noting that I've never founded a business with a founders team already in place. I've always been the prime mover founding the company and have then invited people to join. So, for example, at CDC I'd founded the company, negotiated a resale relationship with an American company and started a marketing programme before seeking a technical counterpart. At PleaseTech, I'd purchased the assets of a bankrupt software company and formed a company before inviting/persuading Clare (the CFO with who I'd previously worked at CDC) to help with the finance and administration and join me as a founder. We then set about attracting a founding techie.

This gave me control and there was never any doubt as to the identity of the lead player. If you are considering founding a company with other people from the get go, you could do worse than read The Founder's Dilemmas, the previously referenced book, by Noam Wasserman. It covers all the scenarios including why it's a really bad idea to set-up a company with family and or friends!

Percentages

So how much of your company do you give away? That is, if you are successful, the multi-million dollar question!

Clearly, you want to give up as little equity as possible but enough to attract and then motivate the staff you want. You may think equity is an easy way to attract people because, in the early days, it's cheap and broadly worthless. However, never forget, it's potentially very valuable and, as the company grows, there will be increasing demands for it as you recruit more people. Senior new staff will expect stock options. Indeed, stock options may well be the key deciding factor in growing your business with the right staff. So, look to the future and not just the here and now.

---

[18] If you do have equity scattered around, make absolutely sure that you have 'drag along' (aka 'tag along') rights in place. Such rights prevent a minority shareholder blocking a sale by refusing to sell their stake.

It's also worth noting that, if you are founding with a team and all the authorised shares are issued to the founders[19], that everyone understands (in writing) that the company will need to create more shares, and thus dilute the founders, as it grows.

In all honesty, I don't think there is any clear answer to the question of how much you give away. Each circumstance is different. It is, obviously, a completely different ball game if VCs get involved, so I'm only considering founder or early-stage equity here.

I think it depends on how much the others are giving up or contributing financially. Are they taking a salary from the business? If so, is the salary a market salary (i.e. the going rate for the job) or are they taking a reduced salary in lieu of equity? Are they full time or part time? If they are taking a reduced salary, is there 100% attention focused on the business or are they permitted to moonlight to make up for the reduction?

If it all goes wrong, can they simply resign and go and get another job leaving you to sort out the mess – even if they were one of the key reasons it went wrong? If you close your eyes you can imagine them in the interview for their new job: 'Yes, I did take a chance and go and work for XYZ Ltd but, despite my best endeavours, the founder wasn't able to deliver, and wasn't able to pay me, so here I am. I'm looking forward to working for a stable company again.'

In short, how much skin do they have in the game? When the brown sticky stuff hits the fan, can they just walk away and wash their hands of it?

Whatever the position, my advice is to be parsimonious with your equity![20]

There are, of course, many ways to give staff a stake in the business other than issuing 'founder equity' straight away. Shares can vest over time

---

[19] In the UK, a company can have an authorised share capital not all of which is immediately issued (i.e. given to people). So, for example, PleaseTech Ltd had an authorised share capital of £1,000 divided into 100,000 ordinary shares of £0.01p each. Of this authorised share capital, initially only 95% was actually issued.

[20] If you are really interested in what I did and the associated percentages, the information is available from the companies house website. Simply search for the companies, examine the filings and it's easy to work out the exact number of shares each person had and therefore their percentage!

against clearly identifiable targets, be they time (i.e. length of service) or specific milestones. However, one needs to consider what, if any, are the advantages of such vesting over simply issuing the shares with an appropriate buy-back clause in a shareholders agreement.

If, for political reasons, there is no buy-back clause then vesting could be an option. It's not something I've ever used or have experience of (except with share options – see below). If doing this, I'd take legal advice as there could well be tax implications.

One of the advantages of founder equity is it is, to all intents and purposes, worthless. The company has no intrinsic value and therefore there are no tax implications. If you issue 100 shares at 0.01p per share (i.e. worth £1) then the shares are worth exactly that, £1. If you issue those same shares at the same price when the company has a net asset value then there will be a tax implication.

Share Options

As the business develops, share options are typically the way to reward staff.

A share option is a contract that allows someone to purchase a share at an agreed price at an agreed point in the future if certain conditions are met. The conditions under which an individual has the right to purchase the option are known as the 'vesting conditions' and, if the conditions are met, the shares are 'vested'. So, you may give someone the option to purchase 100 shares at 5p per share but restrict it to 20 shares per year i.e. the options vest in equal stages over a five year period.

The main point, of course, is that the recipient hopes or expects to be able to sell the share for a lot more than they paid for it. Typically, for a non-quoted company, the scheme is setup so that the employee never parts with any money and the purchase of the shares is only exercised upon exit. The options typically lapse, even if vested, if the employee leaves the company for whatever reason. This prevents the dilution of the shareholder base and the associated complications.

Upon exit the employee gets the difference between the purchase price per share paid for the business and the option exercise price, which, if you've got it right, should be a significant bonus. If the options scheme is approved by HMRC[21] under the very tax-efficient Enterprise Management Incentives (aka EMI) the bonus is much more valuable.

Note: It is my understanding that, in the USA, the equivalent to the UK EMI scheme is the Incentive Stock Option (ISO) scheme. However, I'm not a share options expert and know close to nothing about the USA tax regime!

The main takeaway is that shares options will only come into play as the business grows. By the stage you are issuing share options I'd expect you to have sales and be successfully growing the business. The business will have value and you'll need to get HRMC's agreement on the share valuation. In order to set-up the scheme, get the best (i.e. lowest) initial valuation and ensure that your option holders get the significant tax benefits, you'll need to take specialist advice. This advice will cost money. So it's just as well you've managed to move the business from being valueless to being valuable!

As I see it, there are two primary reasons for implementing a share options scheme.

The first is to lock-in good staff who don't have founder equity (i.e. golden handcuffs).

The second is to attract and then retain senior staff. If you need senior, highly experienced staff they will have multiple employment alternatives and your share option scheme will be one of the aspects which enables you to attract them.

My advice would be not to offer share options to everyone. Ask yourself: Can you attract the staff you need without offering share options? If so, do that. Keep the options for the really important people and the people who have proven their worth. We'll discuss in the employment/recruitment section what makes a job attractive. Not everyone will value the share options. If everyone has them, they become just another perk and aren't necessarily as special.

You must bear in mind that, at various times, especially during decent growth phases, you'll look around the company and think: 'we'd be stuffed if [insert name] leaves'. You may not want or be in the position to offer that

---

[21] The equivalent to the IRS (Internal Revenue Service) in the USA.

person a higher salary (it may not be their prime motivator), but that's where stock options come into play. Stock options will provide more than a simple monetary reward, they provide a sense of ownership and belonging – especially if not everyone has them. The employee becomes part of the inner circle with a stake in the success of the business. That can be a very high motivator.

The simple fact is that some of your staff will always go the extra mile and or be the lynchpins which keep the whole show on the road. It's these you want to ensure that you keep and reward. Share options are one of the tools you can deploy to this end.

Next the question on 'how much to give' raises its ugly head. And, as always, there is no clear answer. It depends on the person, their value to you and their expectations. The number of options you have to offer if you are trying to attract a senior sales VP[22] will be different from those offered to lock-in some of your key technical employees.

If it's any help, here's what we did when we were dishing out options to the lynchpin staff at PleaseTech: Firstly we formed a good idea of the valuation HMRC would accept (i.e. the option price) and then took a view on how much the business may sell for in three years' time (using standard industry metrics against projected growth). We then offered share options which broadly equated to a gain of a defined percentage of the person's gross annual salary. Clearly the percentage can be altered to reflect the perceived importance of the individual. It wasn't an exact science but at least it was a consistent methodology that seemed to work.

Finally, it's worth noting that options issued under the EMI scheme have a 10-year validity. Therefore think carefully about timing as their issue implies an exit within 10 years. If you haven't exited in 10 years the tax benefits lapse, and the options are worth considerably less to the individual!

---

[22] VP = Vice President. Most international software businesses adopt American job titles as America is the biggest software market in the world.

Running the Business

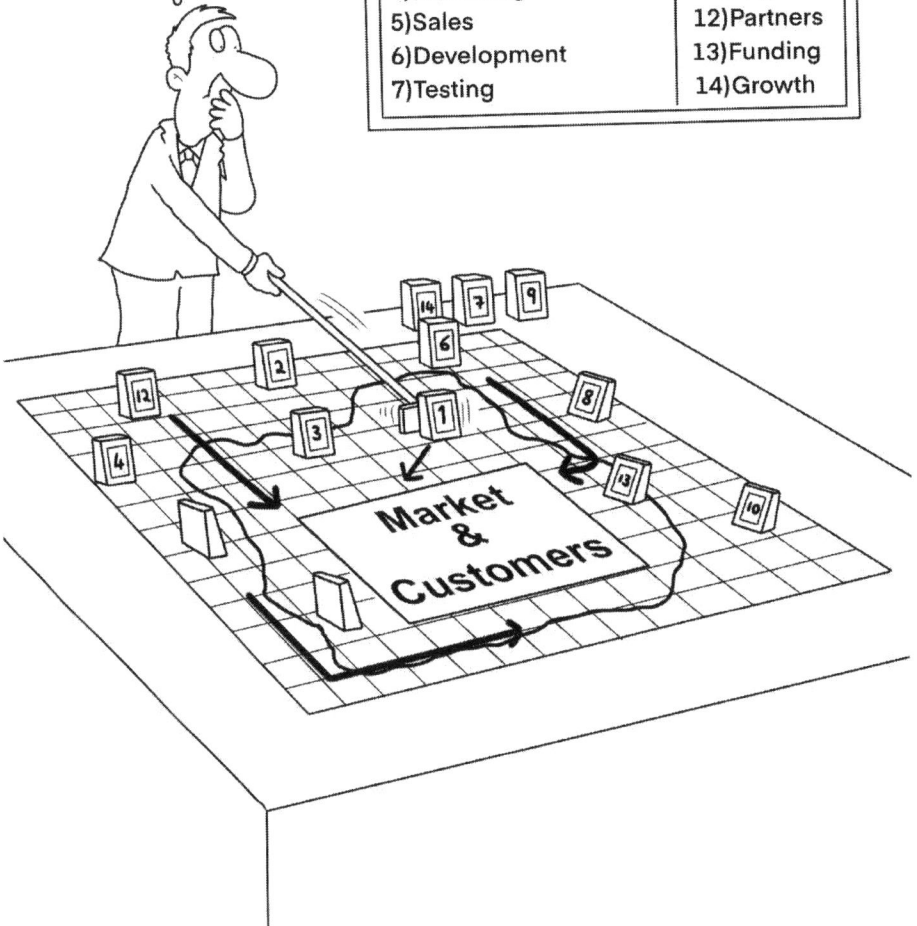

Running the Business

Generally, people who start software companies come from a technical background or a sales background. This means that there are lots of areas of the business which are a bit of a dark art and not fully understood.

Hopefully, by the time I've finished my trawl through the various aspects of running the business there will be fewer places you fear to tread. As the CEO of a start-up or early phase software company, you'll need to understand all aspects of the business and not be afraid to have an opinion on the approach in any one of them. Indeed, for the first year or so you may well be the person responsible for running most parts of the business with the exception of one or two speciality areas.

In my start-ups, I've been hands-on in all areas of the business apart from software development. However, with respect to software development, I know enough to be dangerous! That, I'd suggest, is the exact position in which you need to be when it comes to all those bits of the business you are not directly running. And, as the business grows, and specialists take over, you retain enough knowledge to be dangerous and keep them on their toes.

I hope my thoughts and recommendations will help you achieve that.

Strategy, Vision and Mission

I start with the premise that strategy, vision and mission statements are overrated, especially for start-ups and small companies. In fact, I think The Dilbert Principle[23] hits the nail on the head in describing a mission statement as "a long awkward sentence that demonstrates management's inability to think clearly". If you feel the need to demonstrate your inability to think clearly by all means craft a vision and or mission statement but please don't spend hours fine tuning them. They are not going to give you competitive advantage or even change what you do.

I know the theory that it's important to have such statement to communicate your objectives and raison d'être to the world. The reality is that no plan survives the first encounter with the enemy. It's not always clear who or what the enemy is, only that there will be one!

---

[23] A book by Scott Adams, creator of the comic strip Dilbert.

What I'm trying to say is that, in the dynamic business environment in which start-ups operate, your strategy must be a flexible notion subject to rapid change if market conditions dictate. When you are struggling through the hard yards you have to go with the flow, and it's not always clear where you will end up.

During this time you will need guiding principles. If one of them is that you want to develop a software product then it's a good idea to have a clear guiding principle of being a software products company and avoid undertaking work which isn't going to further that objective.

Make it an informal mission or vision statement if you must but there is little point in spending hours creating a deep and meaningful statement and plastering it all over your website as next month that may all change and next year it may all change again.

Probably the most ridiculous strategy I've come across was a start-up whose stated strategy was to become a unicorn! That isn't a strategy, it's an aspiration! In the early days, if you want a simple strategy statement then you could do worse than adopt the one we had at CDC: Survival, profit, fun.

Obviously this was an internal philosophy and not disseminated to clients or investors! It did however give everyone a clear understanding of the steps necessary to succeed and pointed to an aspiration for the future, i.e. fun!

As the business grows you will need simple straight forward objectives and focus which can be communicated to everyone. At PleaseTech, as we grew we started interviewing candidates who wanted to know what our strategy/vision was. We kept it very simple: firstly, we want to build the best document review product in the world! Secondly, we were also clear that we were an organic growth software company and had no plans to seek venture funding.

That was all we needed. Everyone in the company knew what they had signed up for: an organic growth software products company dedicated to building the best document review product in the world. Simple really.

It goes without saying that this was not always our strategy. In the early days we did explore venture funding and, if you've read The PleaseTech Story, you'll know we tried to launch additional products from time to time. The critical thing was we weren't religious about it or constrained by a vision or a high fluted strategy. If something wasn't working out it was dropped and we refocused. The good news was that PleaseReview was working out and so we ended up putting the wood behind the arrowhead.

The key point is not to get too hung up on the whole strategy, vision, mission stuff. Grand strategic statements will give you an illusion of progress but little else. Little else, that is, unless your seeking venture funding. The VCs do like grand, ambitious statements!

If you are compiling the whole strategy, vision mission stuff for VC consumption I'd keep it fairly generic giving yourself lots of wriggle room. There is nothing the VCs like more than having something they can beat you over the head with - metaphorically of course. So, if you pin yourself down with a specific statement and then need to change tack you've given them the ammunition to have a go at you in the board room!

So, in summary, rather than concentrate on the aforementioned grand strategic statements you should focus on generating revenue (you'll find this is a constant theme) and, as you work to define your product, product positioning.

Product Positioning
It all goes back to the so-called '4Ps' (Product, Price, Promotion & Place) or, as I prefer to think of it, the product positioning and the appropriate promotion. With a limited budget getting the focus tight and right is the most important thing.

Even if you have got a generic, horizontal product that could be used in many industries and business areas, you need to focus on a key market area, succeed in that and then expand out. Trying to spread yourself too thinly will simply dilute your effort and you'll find yourself lost in the noise.

Some products are so market specific that product positioning in different markets isn't a consideration. A good example was EZ*subs*, CDC's main product. It was designed specifically to fulfil one job in pharmaceutical and biotech companies, that of regulatory publishing. Although, theoretically, EZ*subs* could be used in other markets, the business case just wasn't there. Whilst the life sciences companies were prepared to pay $250K for the solution, no other markets had the same business imperative and, despite the occasional effort, they were not worth addressing.

The converse was true at PleaseTech. Our PleaseReview product was a genuine, generic, horizontal product which could be used in many industries and business areas, all of which had a similar (great, of course) ROI. Due to my background, selling to the regulatory departments in life sciences was the obvious initial target and it gave us our first foothold.

For several years all proactive marketing and promotion was aimed at the life sciences market. We did sell into other markets but that was reactive. We responded to enquiries but didn't seek them out. However, as the business grew we started expanding into other markets.

As we soon discovered, different markets have different degrees of sophistication and therefore require different messaging. The key lesson is not to assume that, just because it's a generic product solving the same problem in different markets, the same message, marketing materials and or terminology will hit the target. It won't.

For example, the term 'document review' has very different connotations in the legal market from most other markets. Unless you are familiar with the litigation process, you'll no doubt believe that document review is the process of commenting and marking-up draft documents to provide feedback to the author. That was certainly my understanding! However, I soon discovered that, in the legal market, the term 'document review' has an entirely different meaning. It's about going through the documents associated with a case (typically, a litigation case) and deciding whether they are relevant. A completely different process requiring different tools and approaches. Nothing to do with document review as we understood it and certainly in no way applicable to our document review product.

It's the old story of the devil being in the detail and perfectly illustrates why you need to know your markets and the terminology therein! Assumption is bad, knowledge is good!

Markets can, of course, be sliced in multiple ways. As we will discuss, one of the keys to success is the ecosystem in which you invest. At PleaseTech, because we were immersed in the document production process, we had partner relationships with a number of the major document management suppliers. Initially, we partnered with those with a presence in our focus market of Life Sciences. This naturally led to opportunities in other markets. Let me give you an example.

One of our partnerships was the OpenText Corporation. As a result of that partnership we were able to attend the OpenText user conference. At one of the conferences we met a chap who got excited about what we could do and how he could apply that to his specialism, that of the review of major bids. He worked for a defence manufacturer and they regularly bid for large government defence contracts. Such large and highly detailed bid documents had a correspondingly comprehensive document review process. No one wants to put out a bid response full of errors!

We ended up selling him a load of licenses. But, equally as importantly, it opened up a whole new market. Through this contact we discovered something called the APMP (the Association of Proposal Management Professionals) which was a whole association of people with exactly the same focus and problem. Who knew? The APMP had, of course, various conferences and via attending these we side stepped into a whole new market opportunity.

Exactly the same technology. A different business process and terminology.

So if you look back, you'll see that we started out in regulatory in the life sciences market (a niche in a vertical market). By attending the OpenText conference, were effectively addressing a niche horizontal market (that of OpenText users who spanned multiple industries and verticals) and consequently found ourselves in a horizontal niche – that of the review of major bids. That horizontal niche proved an excellent way to gain a foothold in some very large companies.

It is possible that a desk-based market research study could have identified the review of major bids as a potential market and that addressing it via the APMP was the way to go, but I doubt it!

We were able to identify the new market opportunity for two key reasons:

1. We were out there talking to people. We were in the game presenting our wares and having conversations and had an open mind.

2. We were having conversations and not making pitches. As I previously said: Every conversation, and you really need to think of it as a conversation not as a pitch, is an opportunity for market research.

So the key to successful product positioning is not only getting the focus tight and right, it's also addressing the right audience with the right terminology. However, it goes further than that. Remember my equation: Pain = pain solution = revenue = business success?

The only problem with the equation is that not all pain is equal! Not all pain makes businesses spend money on solutions. The pain needs to be in the right area of the business – usually the right area of the business for you is a business critical (frequently revenue generating) area for the client. Going back to life sciences, the regulatory departments are at the forefront of the business as no product license means no drugs to sell. Likewise, in the major contractors the bid process is critical. No winning bids means no business. I'm sure you get the picture.

So the key is to focus on a niche and to keep your eyes and ears and, most importantly, mind open to other opportunities as they present themselves. Ending up with several niches, each potentially with their own terminology and messaging, is not a bad place to be. This allows you to concentrate your limited marketing fire-power into several clearly defined areas rather than adopt a broad scattergun approach where, as previously mentioned, you'll get lost in the noise.

Product Management

If you run a software products company, product management is one of the most critical functions in your business and should report directly to you, not to sales or the CTO. Don't for a minute think that product management is an academic role - it's a hands-on role at the forefront of the business. Get it wrong and you'll struggle.

It's a well-known fact that the best technical product often doesn't win. It's not about technology; it's about the complete solution and the way it is sold. As I mention in The CDC Story, although EZ*subs* was generally considered a technically superior product, we often lost the deal because the competition were better at speaking the customers language (i.e. the opposition had a better understanding of the business problem and presented it in a way which resonated with clients).

So, product management is more than just defining the functionality moving forward. It requires an innate understanding of the business problem the product is trying to solve, how your product solves it in real life for real end users, and what functionality is required to keep it competitive going forward, or to address new markets.

There are multiple other factors that come into play.

You're not operating in a vacuum. You'll be using a development environment such as .NET or an equivalent, databases and a target platform such as Windows, Linux or whatever. You'll incorporate libraries (both open source and commercial) and perhaps sub-license some specialist technology. These products/platforms are themselves under continual development, development which is completely outside of your control. They will have their own bugs which you may need to work around.

Additionally, you'll have bugs or features in your own product which may need to be rectified. I say 'may' because some bugs never get fixed! Ultimately this is a product management call. Product management sets development priorities.

To a certain extent the complexity does depend if you are at the bleeding edge of the technology with which you are working or you are using domain knowledge to differentiate yourself. Both my companies have been breaking new technological ground. Although we gained good domain knowledge, success was based on technically advanced products which created market entry barriers.

For example, with PleaseReview, I am aware of at least a couple of other companies who tried unsuccessfully to create a PleaseReview competitor. They failed because what we were doing wasn't technically easy. As I've always explained to my staff: if it was easy everyone would do it.

Such advanced development is an art as much as a science. Even if you have the brightest people in the world (and that's always something to aim for) it's not predictable. Sometimes the coding gods smile benignly on you and it all works out in the timescales anticipated. Many times the coding gods are not so benevolent! Things don't work, you can't get the functionality stable or the new code has unintended and unforeseen consequences affecting other areas of the product, and so on. Timescales slip and sometimes you have to just give up and accept that that particular piece of functionality is beyond current technology.

So the development of an enterprise product is a juggling act. You have to juggle all the above with your finite development resources. The decisions taken can mean the difference between success and failure. This means that, by definition, those decisions are important and need to be taken by those in authority with an understanding of the consequences for the business.

Initially, product management may not be a full-time job. However, as a release draws near, you will be making daily decisions trying to optimise your development and test time to squeeze as much as you can into the release whilst keeping the quality high.

As the company grows you'll need to communicate within the business to manage expectations and ensure that people (typically, but not always, salespeople) aren't making promises to clients based on misunderstandings. In fact, it's generally not a good idea to let salespeople mention the new release at all unless it's mandatory to close the deal. Selling what you have released is by far the best approach!

So, my advice to you is to be intimately involved in product management. If you are a techie ensure that you have a senior non-techie user-focused person in the team; someone who you respect and who is sure enough of their position to argue with you. In my experience, even the best techies don't or can't see things from an end-user perspective and struggle to get beyond the code efficiency side of the equation. They simply can't understand that something so simple/stupid/archaic could be a sensible requirement.

If you come from the sales side be sure to have a technically competent person standing by to reign you in; someone who really understands the implications of requested enhancements. Nearly all of the biggest howlers I've seen are when a sales focused person promises the earth to win an order. Trust me, some orders are not worth winning.

You need to achieve a balance of the disciplines. Ultimately, if one or the other discipline holds the whip hand, the product will either become too techie or may be a jumble of features which have won orders. If you don't want to lead product management, your job is to make sure that you are on top of it and understand what is going on, giving the product manager the appropriate authority. I repeat, product management should report to you, not to sales or the CTO.

Cloud, Private Cloud and On-premise

The whole on-premise vs cloud position is changing rapidly. Does this mean my experience and advice in this area is irrelevant? I think not! In PleaseTech we started off offering on-premise software licenses, then we offered the ability to host the license for them and finally graduated to offering both on-premise and pure cloud options.

Let's define 'on-premise' vs 'cloud'. You have a picture in your mind – check? Ok, so now for my trick question: when is a cloud not a cloud? Answer: when it's private cloud! Cutting through the semantics, as far as I am concerned, any environment that you as the vendor do not control (i.e. you do not control the interdependencies and rely on others to set the variables) is 'not cloud' and is hereinafter called 'on-premise'.

I'm sure you will have a view on where the market is and where it's going and the approach to take. You may take the easy approach and develop a native multi-user cloud application, but, before you do that, work out whether you can afford to rule out all those enterprises not prepared to trust their valuable data to you. In my view there will always be a decent market for on-premise software. Some core intellectual property or other confidential information is just simply too valuable to trust to a potentially leaky third party, i.e. you.

It is a lot harder to make on-premise software than it is for a cloud environment you control. There are any number of interdependencies that can go wrong and conflict. You need to be clear on your required infrastructure and try and reduce reliance on specific releases of third party software. I came across several enterprise products that were heavily restricted in the version numbers of the underlying products. One of our successes was ensuring that we were fairly open in this respect and only relied on standard features[24].

We certainly found that if a third party (whether client or consultant) was providing installation services they very rarely RTFM. I'd say that well over 90% of the installation issues we had were because (i) someone made an assumption and didn't read the manual before cracking on, or (ii) the target environment was incomplete or incorrectly configured.

The answer, when selling to on-premise clients, is to try and control the installation if you can. Easier said than done. Even if you are doing the installation and have provided comprehensive checklists of the stuff you need available, 50% of the time it won't be. No easy answer I'm afraid. One option is to add to the price list a re-installation fee for any re-installation attempts after the first failure or to increase the installation cost offering a discount (credit) if everything does go right first time. These are all fairly complex to administer so I'd suggest you just take the rough with the smooth.

If you've chosen the native multi-user cloud application you won't have these issues, but you will have isolated yourselves from a segment of the market in which there will be less competition.

Release Cycles

Whichever approach you adopt you'll need to formalise release cycles. If you disagree with me because you've brought into the continuous development and release model, I address this in the next subsection entitled: Rapid

---

[24] Although see my point on resolution times in the support section as to why you may need to restrict the version numbers of underlying products!

Release Cycles. However, whether you agree or not, you'll still need to decide what is in the next release.

After each release we'd sit down and sketch out the next. In the very early days, you are looking to release a Minimum Viable Product (MVP). As the product matures, you need to have one eye on the future and one on the present.

In PleaseTech, we'd look at the target requirements, give them a broad order of size and complexity (broadly equivalent to coding overhead) and argue why they should be in (or not). Will it make the product more reliable (i.e. reduced the support overhead)? Is it something multiple or important customers have been complaining about? Will it materially positively impact sales? Will it open a new market? Is it something which is a major hole in the current product? In short, what is the case for including this in a release? As the product matured, my aim was always to include aspects of all three of the key items in every release, namely: (i) architecture enhancements, (ii) bug fixes, and (ii) new functionality.

If you don't do this and just race for functionality, you are in danger of ending up with a functional, buggy product build on sand (i.e. old infrastructure) and, every time you duck an infrastructure upgrade, you just increase the pain when that upgrade becomes mandatory. If you don't fix bugs you are just increasing your support overhead.

Whilst on the subject of infrastructure, if selling an on-premise version of your software, bear in mind that your corporate clients are very rarely running the latest of anything! There is a lag of as much as two or three major releases in their infrastructure. So, if you require the latest release of anything (e.g. a database or .NET version) you are probably ruling out a majority of your on-premise clients. Sometimes it's a decision you have to take but, as with all decisions, ensure you understand the consequences.

Your target list for a new release will greatly exceed the development and test time available, and therefore you need to prioritise. The critical thing is to deliver regular releases. We always aimed for one major release every 18 or so months and maybe a couple of minor releases.

Never forget that every software product in the world, unless deprecated, is a work in progress. If you hold off release for the perfect release you'll never get there. When you are providing free stuff to the consumer, keeping a product in beta for years may be acceptable, but when you are selling B2B you need released, tested software.

Some businesses have a policy of never licensing version 1.x software. That's easy then, your v2.0 comes fairly quickly after your v1.0!

In PleaseTech, at a technical level (i.e. in respect of development and testing), we treated major and minor releases in exactly the same way which meant that the decision as to the label (i.e. major or minor) became a product management decision. This decision was broadly based on how long since the last major release and the degree of new functionality in the release. However, it also had contractual issues as we only supported the last two major releases.

Another key decision was to never released betas – despite numerous client requests. The hassle with betas is that they take a lot of support when released, and your clients are giving feedback on something which may well have already changed. We therefore put the resources we would have had to dedicated to a beta project into getting the main release solid!

Once you have decided the release parameters and started on that course, remember you get can't get something for nothing. Feature creep is the enemy of all developers. If you add a feature you'll have to let something else go! You can't just magic development time out of the air. In the development section I discuss the Mythical Man Month. All product managers need to understand the practical basics of development.

In terms of practicalities, my advice is to have a process for collating all feedback, good ideas, requests, thoughts, etc. into a central easily accessible location with as much detail as you can (i.e. who made the request, why the request is a good idea, background market data, etc.). You'd be surprised how much you forget when you re-visit the list after a few weeks having been concentrating elsewhere!

The tool is unimportant; the critical thing is that you have the information to hand when considering the next release. A bit of discipline in the capture stage prevents hours of hunting through email trails and completely forgetting about vital items of feedback.

Rapid Release Cycles

I am very aware that, with the new trend of rapid release cycles and cloud delivery that you may dismiss my 'old fashioned' approach and be completely focused on Agile (discussed under development) continuous development and release.

You'd be wrong to do that if you are addressing on the B2B market.

Firstly, this continuous development and release model doesn't work for the on-premise market. Customers are slow to update working environments even if they have sexy new functionality which will help them!

Secondly, even if you are offering a cloud service, it's a simple fact that the IT departments in most businesses are supporting many hundreds or thousands of users, all of differing technical abilities and comprehension. Granted that that the general level of IT sophistication may develop over time as digital natives move through the workforce, but even digital natives won't want constant changes in their working tools. Staff in modern businesses have to 'touch' multiple systems in the course of their day-to-day activity[25]. They get familiar and comfortable with the tools and haven't got the time to learn new stuff. They just want it to work!

Also, put yourself in the position of the aforementioned IT support staff who are designing training courses and internal documentation and even business processes around the software's functionality. Every time the interface changes that's a whole load of screenshots and training videos that need updating. Every time a new button/option appears on the interface that's a whole load of support calls IT will receive!

This is why corporate IT departments generally prefer phased, measured releases that are planned and they can introduce to the user base in a controlled way. I'm personally aware of one large multinational company that stopped using several cloud applications because of the frequency of updates and the resulting workload.

---

[25] A constant battle for corporate IT departments is to minimise the number of disparate systems staff have to use in the course of day-to-day jobs. You won't be helping introducing another one so that's why you need to make it easy to use and manage. This is discussed further under the Partners chapter.

If you are going the cloud route then restrict yourself to a release every six or nine months and be absolutely clear what is in the release and give advanced warning to your customer's IT department. To achieve the desired effect you should consider creating a delay of one release cycle so that you only make a release live after the client's IT departments have had a release cycle (i.e. six or nine months) to play with it. That way they've got time for preparation and no surprises. Another alternative is to be able to hide new functionality until such time the client is ready for it.

In PleaseTech, unless the client was on our entry level multi-user native cloud service, we didn't upgrade clients without their permission. Sometimes this was not easily forthcoming.

Product Naming

There is no doubt that an aptly named product is a truly beautiful thing. Sounds simple - doesn't it? It's not, and I'm not sure it's something we got right at PleaseTech.

You may be thinking: 'What? PleaseReview is a great name for a document review product'. I'd agree with you but, if I'm honest, I think at PleaseTech we were guilty of creating brand confusion. Let me explain why.

Where we/I got it wrong is that we got caught between promoting the company and the product. Not only was there confusion between whether we were pushing the 'PleaseTech' brand and or the 'PleaseReview' brand, life got even more confused when we failed to appreciate the impact of the names of other products we tried to launch.

As I explained in The PleaseTech Story, we created complete brand confusion by launching PleaseAuthor, a structured authoring product. There is a subtle difference between 'structured authoring' and 'collaborative authoring', which structured authoring aficionados understood but a vast majority of our clients didn't. We were forced to rename PleaseAuthor to PleaseCompose, and that only partially solved the problem. It was only towards the end when we'd dropped all other products and put the wood entirely behind the PleaseReview arrowhead that I didn't have to explain to people where the products fitted.

My problem was that my aspirations of having a range of 'Please' products to match the domains I'd diligently procured, didn't follow one of the first laws of business which is KISS – Keep It Simple, Stupid.

A great example of KISS, from my world, was Documentum. Documentum was both the company and product name. It was a real simple message even through the Documentum suite was complex and comprised of many subsidiary modules.

So, the first step in the process is to decide on what you want to promote. Is it the company or the product? If you are a single product company is the name of the product and the company synonymous? If not, focus on one of the two.

Market Perception

Of course, product management is not just about functionality and naming. It's also about how you position the product and the company in the market. If you have read The PleaseTech Story you'll understand that we ultimately positioned ourselves and were recognised as thought leaders in respect of document review.

One of the reasons we ended up being successful in this is because we stopped trying to widen the product base and focused all our energies on PleaseReview. I previously mentioned the brand confusion we caused with the launch of PleaseAuthor. However, I don't believe that the launch of PleaseAuthor diluted the market perception of PleaseTech as it played into the whole co-authoring and review pitch and was therefore harmless in that respect.

However, we could have drastically changed the market perception of PleaseTech with the launch of PleaseShare. This anecdote isn't in The PleaseTech Story so listen very carefully:

In the 2009 time frame, just as Dropbox was taking off, I developed a specification for a new product called PleaseShare. This was designed to be a corporate file sharing solution allowing users to share documents securely through the firewall. The idea was that it would be packaged and sold to our existing clients as a new 'module'. Instead of creating a review, users would follow exactly the same process and create a share, leveraging

PleaseReview's existing functionality giving the users an environment with which they were familiar.

Client feedback was positive and engineering was relatively simple, so what stopped us? It was looking at market perception and positioning.

At that time everyone but everyone was jumping on the file sharing bandwagon. We felt that the danger was that, if we launched PleaseShare, the market would ignore PleaseReview, we'd be lost in the noise and the perception would be that we were just another Dropbox wannabe. Sometimes it's not what you do, it's what you don't do.

Let's go back to consider thought leadership. Being a thought leader in a market is not simply about knowledge. It also means coming up with new marketing narratives and positioning forthcoming functionality appropriately.

The example I give in The PleaseTech Story, is the narrative we developed around 'Beyond Review', trying to position PleaseReview not only as a document review tool but also as a value add business process enhancement tool. Our V5.0 release included feedback functionality and metrics (developed in response to specific client requests) which, in addition to other things, could be used to help determine authoring quality.

To capture the high ground you need to position these functional enhancements with intelligence. It's one thing to say that PleaseReview now has some new functionality, it's another to talk about this being the start of the Beyond Review strategy with an emphasis on the benefits the metrics could offer in business process optimisation. As always, it's the spin you put on it which matters!

In my experience engineers and techies tend to have an inbuilt aversion to the marketing hype whilst sales and marketing types don't get the preoccupation techies have with accuracy, not over-promising and getting it right. The truth is, of course, that you have a broad audience each with different hot buttons. You need to appeal to them all and therefore need to balance the positioning somewhere in between these two. No matter which side of the coin you come from, you need to understand and appreciate the other.

Get product management and strategy right and you are pushing at an open door. Get it wrong and you end up in a whole world of pain. Whatever you do, don't ignore it!

Marketing

You've started your business and, whether or not you've got your product finalised or are starting out with a service of some description, you've got to let the world know you and your offering exist! In this age of privacy, this is easier said than done. In the old days you could simply buy a marketing list and spam everyone[26]. Those days are over.

This is where the marketing mix comes into play. Those with a technical background may think marketing is all about advertising and those with a sales background may think it's all about lead generation. It's not that simple, and it doesn't help that there is a lot of very poorly done marketing in the industry.

I've come across so-called professional marketeers, even those working in small companies, who seem to think that the job is all about spending money and that the more they spend the more successful they will be!

It doesn't help that there are any number of marketing consultants desperate to help you spend your money – mainly on their services.

You'll have got the drift by now – marketing is all about spending money! You can spend any amount on marketing but your aim must be to spend intelligently. You are not a big corporation, most of which seem to have almost unlimited marketing budgets and apparently just throw money at the problem. We've all been to trade shows where there are massive booths/stands which cost more than your year's marketing budget or even an entire year's revenue!

In a start-up and smaller company it's about being smart and spending your money wisely, concentrating on what matters. Some call it guerrilla marketing. I'm not a huge fan of that term as, whilst it's definition does emphasise low cost, it also suggests something subversive or unconventional. I would argue that PleaseTech's marketing was mostly low cost and highly effective, but it was not in any way subversive or unconventional – subversive or unconventional are not want you need to be

---

[26] In the early days of CDC we did try list purchasing but found the lists such poor quality that we didn't pursue it as a marketing initiative. I tried it again in the early days of PleaseTech and established that list quality had not improved!

when you are trying to appeal to the largest corporates in the world. The bottom line is that our marketing was just smart and highly focused.

This section has my opinions and everything I know about marketing. I hope it helps!

Market Research

By now it won't surprise you to learn I'm not a huge fan of desk-based market research. I've seen some complete crap in my time and, frankly, it's not helped by VCs who do like a market research report (paid for by you of course).

In the CDC days we had to commission and pay for a market research report to provide our investors 'comfort' to secure an investment. I can't remember which round it was but I can remember sitting in the consultant's presentation thinking 'what a load of sh*t'. But we got the investment, so it was a means to an end. Wise Chairman Bill[27] told me to think of it as a cost of raising capital but, all these years later, it still rankles.

Anyway, you're a small business with potentially a negative cash flow and can't be wasting time and money on external consultants. You need to be doing this stuff yourself.

As I mentioned, every time you have a conversation you should be in market research mode. Talking with your ex-colleagues, talking to business partners, and when you can, to potential clients. Ask open questions. Listen to the answers, ask them why. Test what one party has said against another party in the same position. When you are in start-up mode it's very easy to be so bound up in your own little world that you ignore what people are telling you or latch onto a specific view that fits your agenda.

By having as many conversations as you can, you'll build up a market picture and understanding which far exceeds anything a consultant can offer. It will help you define the direction in which your business needs to move.

As the business grows, these conversations don't become less important, they become more important. If we take the example I gave earlier of how PleaseTech sidestepped from life sciences into proposal review, you'll see

---

[27] Bill Passmore, CDC's Chairman. See the CDC story for more detail.

having conversations and keeping open mind can make beautiful things happen!

There is a role for desk-based research but it is very specific. What conferences are there in my market sector? Which are the companies operating in the sector I am targeting, etc. Specific questions which need to be answered to help you implement specific programs.

Website and Domains

Generally the first thing a business does is have a website. You'd have thought that in a technology company this would be easy – not in my experience.

In the early days it is easy. A simple, professional looking flat HTML site will suffice. There are thousands of templates available which you can pick up for a few dollars. As an example, the template for this book's website (www.softwarecompanybook.com) cost me $25. You do not need to spend money on a website designer.

I've had limited success with website designers. The good graphic designers don't know the technology and the good technologists are 'not great' at design. Anyway, these days most try and sell you a WordPress package or equivalent. A number of major hosting companies provide one-click install on WordPress and its competitors, and there are hundreds of pre-made templates from which you can choose. Some cost a few dollars, many are free. Once installed, they are relatively simple to configure and populate. Why spend the money with designers when you don't have to? Anyone who is remotely technical can set-up, configure and populate a website these days.

However, even if you decide to pay someone to set it up, the critical thing is to keep its maintenance in your control. Make sure someone in your company can make changes. If you need to go back to a designer or a subcontractor for every change it will be punishingly expensive.

As you grow you may want a more sophisticated website. This is where you may seek external assistance as you are all too busy paddling your own canoes.

A word of caution. Websites are one thing we struggled with in both my companies. Most recently, in PleaseTech, with the advent of responsive websites, we decided to re-work our non-responsive internally developed site and entrusted the project to the marketing team. They were left on their lonesome as everyone else was busy. About a year and several thousand pounds later we started again. The main problem, this first time round, was that the sub-contract 'designers' had customised the site appearance to exact lengths of text. If marketing wanted to re-write something (and they always do) then it messed up the appearance. A school kid error which, if those of us who had experience in these matters had have given oversight or support to the project, would not have been made. But we didn't, we were all too busy with a rapidly growing business!

The second time round we did make progress but I hated the site. It was a standard WordPress site (i.e. just like every other WordPress site – about a third of all websites on the internet are based on WordPress) and the carefully chosen stock images displayed were wildly inappropriate. I think we were still arguing over it when we sold the business!

You have to remember how designers think. They didn't understand what our business did but knew it was something to do with documents. So, they chucked in document related stock images all over the site. Here were we at the forefront of document technology and I was being asked to approve a website that featured images of a load of 1970s lever arch files! To say I was 'upset' is somewhat of an understatement.

Your website is your shop window and may be the only way some people critical to your success interact with your company. Think of the corporate manager who has just been asked to sign off on a purchase order for your products. What's the first thing they do? They look at the website. Does it project the correct image?

Does it give an impression of a professional company with which they feel safe doing business? Does the site explain clearly what your company does? Does it give confidence your company provides the appropriate solutions? Are there references to other clients? It goes without saying that your site needs to give such visitors warm feelings. Different people get warm feelings in different ways.

The problem with design is it is a matter of personal taste. The problem with marketeers is they like broad messages and not details. Put the two together and you have a potential disaster. If you are going to be appealing to technologists and engineers you will need to cut back on the marketing gimmicks and have detail on the site; Basic architecture information, basic supported environment information, something addressing service levels, security information, etc.[28]

I personally refuse to deal with any company which restricts itself to high level messaging on the website. I need to see some depth and substance.

So critically examine your website. Does it project the correct image? Does it tell people what you do – what you really do? If I have a business problem to which I am seeking a solution and I visit your site will I feel that you understand the problem and have a great solution – or is it all just waffle with industry buzzwords sprinkled in abundance?

A subtopic of the website is domains. As everyone who has worked with me will attest, I love domains. IMHO, it's never wrong to purchase another domain!

The way I see it is that domains are cheap to own and can confer strategic advantage. As I write this I'm in the process of setting up another business (not a software business) and already own around 30 relevant domains! We may end up only using a couple of them however a range of domains gives me the flexibility to subtly re-brand or host micro sites dealing with specific topics. It can also provide a competitive advantage in that competitors can't use them!

It does, of course, depend on what you are planning to do. For example, writing a book on how to run a software company is, at best, a marginal business and therefore I've strictly limited my investment in domains only owning the '.com' and '.co.uk' domains (www.softwarecompanybook.com).

Your website is one of your most valuable assets. Understand your target audience, bearing in mind that the people you sell to and meet are only a

---

[28] This needn't give away confidential information and can be generic as the objective is to give potential clients a feeling for the required infrastructure. If you are purely offering cloud services then the requirement is more to do with providing confidence over your hosting and security.

subset of the target audience. Think about the whole breadth of people who may touch the order process and remember that their first point of reference will be the website. They'll need more than high level waffle.

Branding

Let's get this straight from the outset – you have to earn the right to be considered a brand.

Simply writing the company's name or the product name in big letters and believing that you have a brand that will attract people is a common fallacy. Think of the brands you know in the tech business: Dell, Intel, IBM, Oracle, Microsoft, Alphabet – wait a minute – who? You know, Alphabet, the public holding company which owns Google.

Alphabet Inc is a holding company and therefore it's not trying to be the main brand itself, but it illustrates the point that even a company as big as Alphabet Inc can't simply write its name in block capitals and expect people to know who it is and what it does. And yet, at every trade show and conference, and on endless websites, you see small companies doing exactly that!

I always like playing a little game at trade shows and conferences (hereinafter 'shows'); as I look at the booth/stand, can I tell what the company does? What problem it solves? In many cases I can't and that, I would suggest, is a major problem! Make sure you are not guilty of this branding faux pas!

Look at your booth, website and literature critically. Does it prominently address the problem you solve? If I were to check them out would I know what your software does? Is your target market obvious? What business problem do you address?

By all means make sure that your company/product name and or logo is prominently displayed. But make sure that it/they are not so prominent that people looking for a solution who never heard of you will miss the fact that you address the problem and have a great solution.

Logos and Design

As previously mentioned, design is a very personal thing. I claim to have zero artistic talent and yet I know what I like. I therefore take the view that it's my company and I want to like my website/logo/other arty stuff!

As it happens I think that many graphic artists are guilty of over design and over complication of what is, ultimately, the simple presentation of information. So, in this respect I have two pieces of advice:

The first is to trust your instinct. Just because someone is a trained graphic artist or designer doesn't mean you need to bow to their 'superior' knowledge. If you think it looks fussy and over-complicated it probably is. If you don't like it, reject it!

Remember the principal aim of the website/logo/literature is not to showcase the designer's talent, it's to present the information clearly and simply to your prospects and clients. In fact, there is an argument that says that if you notice the design in any way, it's probably over designed and not achieving the objective.

The second is to go for a simple, bold logo. Let's go back to Dell, Intel, IBM, Oracle, Microsoft. I'm sure you can instantly picture these logos in your mind. They are all simple!

There is a very practical reason for this simplicity. Let's assume that you are exhibiting at a show. As part of the package, you are likely to get a space in the program and on the show's website for your logo as a 'sponsor'. As you are a small company and not a major sponsor your space will be tiny. In fact the space will be so small that the only logos which will be legible will be the simple bold logos. Try it yourself. Take your logo and shrink it down to something like 70x50 pixels (the standard size of a thumbnail logo) and see if it's legible.

There is, of course, no harm in having different logos for different uses. Something slightly more complex for more prominent locations (like your website) so long as they are obviously related. Explain this to your designer and make them earn their living!

Trade Shows and Conferences

And so we come to shows! My favourite topic and one on which I have years of experience. I first exhibited at a show in 1988 and, as noted in The CDC Story, having a stand/booth at the Documentum user conference in 1996 was CDC's breakthrough moment. I can therefore be forgiven for holding exhibiting in close affection and it's been the mainstay of my companies' USA centric marketing programmes ever since.

The genre covers a wide spectrum. The largest I've done is Oracle OpenWorld (~60,000 attendees from 145 countries with ~500 exhibiting companies), and the smallest is probably a specialist European DIA[29] conference with less than 50 attendees where, bizarrely, the vendors probably outnumbered the paying delegates! There are, of course, considerable differences between such shows, not least of which is country location. However, there are many similarities. I've tried to break down coverage into logical subsections.

When is a Conference a Trade Show?

I think of a trade show as predominantly an exhibition space which may be accompanied by some educational sessions. The principal reason delegates attend a trade show is for the exhibition and to seek out new products and or vendors and find out what is happening in the industry.

The converse is true of a conference. Most (but certainly not all) conferences have a limited exhibition space but the principal reason delegates attend is for educational purposes. For most delegates the conference sessions are paramount as session attendance usually earns credits for the continuance of professional qualifications.

A subset of the conference genre is user conferences which are organised by specific vendors for their users, and the focus is on education around the vendor's software product(s). Typically there are a limited number of the vendor's partners sponsoring the conference (i.e. helping to defray costs) and exhibiting.

Trade shows tend to be bigger and less focused. Conferences can be highly focused on specialist industry professions or skills. Many medium sized

---

[29] DIA = Drugs Information Association which is the biggest (?) members association in the life sciences industry.

shows are hybrids. An example of a hybrid from my world is the DIA annual meeting which has around 6,000 attendees and approximately 450 exhibiting companies. In addition to the large show floor full of the 450+ booths, there is a comprehensive program of educational sessions attendance at which earns which continuing education credits.

User conferences can, of course, also be very large. The aforementioned is Oracle OpenWorld goes way beyond a user conference, although it can't be defined as a trade show as it is organised by Oracle for Oracle and attendees have some connection with Oracle.

The good news is that the basic principles are the same and I'll highlight differences as I cover the topic.

Why Exhibit?
The primary reason for attending such events is, of course, to meet the delegates and promote your products. Staying in luxury hotels in warm climates on expenses when it's winter in the UK is just a side benefit![30]

As the company grows, the reasons for doing shows change. In the early days it's all about leads. Every business card is a new business opportunity. As you become established visitors to the booth include existing clients and prospects with whom you are already engaged. Having such clients and prospects visit the booth is generally a very good thing. You get the chance for a more relaxed encounter and to meet others in the company.

This is why it's a fallacy that the success of a show is based solely on the number of new leads you generate. It is impossible to measure a show's real effectiveness. Remember there are lots of people involved in a purchase decision. If, at the show, you meet and are able to influence a couple of those involved in the process, how do you measure that? Take the following situation: a senior manager from a prospect needed to sign off a purchase order but was stalling for unknown reasons. As luck would have it, she was

---

[30] The fact is that many shows are in luxury resorts in warm climates when it's winter in the northern hemisphere. Why? Well the conferences need to attract delegates. No delegates means no vendors and no vendors or delegates means a financial disaster. Most delegates work for large corporations and usually have the budget to go to a single conference of their choosing per year. Organisers therefore hold the conferences in attractive locations people want to visit. Las Vegas is popular, as is Miami, San Diego, etc. In Europe Barcelona is a firm favourite.

attending a conference at which we were exhibiting. We were able to meet her, understand and address her concerns and she signed off the PO. How do you measure that?

Over the years, I've had numerous conversations with key individuals whilst at the booth. They either deliberately looked us up or happen to have wandered past. I've invited them to sit down (a luxury in the big trade shows style events) and have a chat. Again, I reiterate that this is not a pitch, it's a conversation. Quite frankly, I'd have flown across the Atlantic simply to have an hour's meeting with some of the people who have wandered past the booth and sat down.

Once you get to be a regular and you are embedded in your market, attending the conferences is not only good for business, it is mandatory if you want to be in the loop and find out what is happening to whom and how, i.e. good old fashioned gossip. It is advantageous to know who is winning, who isn't and the general word on the street. It's also a great opportunity to make new industry contacts and put faces to names you've come across.

And, since we are on the subject of industry contacts, shows attract others in your industry and therefore it's also a good time to meet partners and potential partners to discuss cooperation. There is plenty of time whilst the delegates are all in sessions or, of course, post-session meetings at the conference hotel bar!

You are not only there to exhibit and gossip. It is worth attending some sessions yourself. Most exhibit packages come with one full delegate pass (i.e. you can attend the sessions) and many are worth sitting in on. This is where you learn of new industry trends and what people will be spending budgets on. I clearly remember exhibiting at one pharmaceutical conference and going to sit in a session simply because one of my clients was giving the presentation. Lucky I did. From the title I hadn't thought that the subject would be pertinent to PleaseReview. I was absolutely wrong. The client was outlining a regulatory requirement coming down the track and I immediately saw how PleaseReview could help with the issues he was outlining. I discussed my thoughts with the client and with a couple of other clients attending and, by the time I'd returned to the office, had decided to add the necessary functionality into the forthcoming release.

It should be noted that such an approach ties neatly into the subject of thought leadership we discussed earlier. When we subsequently explained to other clients why we were adding the functionality it was, in many cases, it was the first they heard of the forthcoming legislation and so we reinforced our position as a trusted vendor.

It's further worth noting that this is another reason why, if you are not doing product management yourself, you need to ensure that someone with authority is. The product manager must not only be expected to attend such conferences but also to have the authority to introduce new concepts as a result – if necessary fast-tracking functionality into a new release.

As we grew and different people went to shows, we did formalise the post-show feedback process with a simple form on number of new leads, number of chats with existing prospects and customers, number of demos, etc. This helped us get a feel for shows, but the intuitive feeling of the booth staff as to whether the show had been worthwhile was our main guide.

Payback isn't always short term; there were several times at PleaseTech when we were contacted apparently out of the blue by a new prospect only to find that they'd seen us at a show a couple of years earlier. So, in summary, I'd reiterate that it's very easy and way too simplistic to judge a show purely on the new leads received.

Whether to Attend a Specific Show
The first thing you are interested in when you consider a show is the number and type of delegates. Are their job titles those of interest? When it comes to numbers make sure you understand the break down between real paying delegates (aka 'real people') and vendors. Organisers tend to talk of 'attendees' which is all registered attendees including booth personnel.

The next consideration is how long you get to spend with the real people. If it's a small conference you can assume that most of them will be in the sessions and therefore only wandering around at the breaks. Bear in mind that sessions frequently overrun and this can mean ½ hour breaks are only 10 minutes or so, just enough time to visit the toilet and grab a coffee – not enough time to chat to vendors. To be fair, most decent conference organisers understand this and arrange the timetable so that there is plenty of face time for vendors. The key point is to understand the conference dynamics and timetable.

You'll want to consider the layout. Examine the proximity of the sessions and the booths. In this respect, the worst conference I attended was at a large modern resort style conference centre in the Washington DC area. The conference centre is huge. The booths were about a 10 minute walk and two floors away from the sessions. To say that there was not a lot of traffic is an understatement! If you spot this in advance, organisers may try and convince you that delegates will still visit because 'that's where the coffee is'. Not in my experience. At more than one conference I've attended, when the coffee (and therefore booths) were too far away from the sessions, the delegates complained and the coffee was moved closer. Needless to say the booths weren't!

Finally, it's always worth asking about the percentage of new exhibitors vs returning exhibitors. Some conferences are so poorly organised that a lot of vendors do them once and never return. If there is a high percentage of new vendors and a low percentage of those returning, be afraid. Be very afraid!

When considering exhibiting at a new conference it's healthy to have a degree of paranoia. The poorer organisers simply want your money and generally adopt the attitude that they are providing the delegates, and you are the second class citizens who should be grateful for the strictly limited real people face time they deign to give you – despite the fact that you are paying handsomely for the experience!

While we are at it, let's address the common fallacy that it's worth attending a show as a delegate to scope out whether it's worth exhibiting next year. IMHO it's a costly error because you simply can't know whether it's worth exhibiting by attending as a delegate. I've heard all the arguments and, no, you are not going to get around and talk to all the delegates by networking alone – unless it's a very small conference. And, in any case, by the time you've added in travel, hotels, food, etc. the incremental cost of exhibiting is normally not a considerable amount more.

For such new conferences, it's always worth asking for a new vendor discount! Something along the lines 'we'd like to come and scope it out but it's a bit marginal for us, can you do something to help our budget?'. The good conferences normally fill up pretty quickly so, if they do offer you a discount refer you to my previous statement on paranoia!

When researching which conferences to attend don't forget to look at what other vendors in your target market are doing. Their show attendance is usually helpfully published on their website. If they are partners, or at least not competitive with you, give them a call and ask them about the show. You can learn a surprising amount that way.

Also, ask prospects and clients which shows they attend and why. Remember, once you have a client, they have a vested interest in making sure your business is successful. If it's not they could be left up the creek without the proverbial paddle. So, they are a resource whose brains you can pick!

I have always preferred the smaller specialist conferences rather than the large trade shows. The audience is more targeted and you can hone your message appropriately. However, both have their place.

One top tip is that the larger conferences do not necessarily attract the most senior delegates. In PleaseTech we found that regional one-day conferences frequently had a very high quality of delegate. The reason being that senior people in mission critical jobs frequently don't feel they can leave the office for three or four days to attend a conference. They are happy to slip out of the office for a day to a local event. So, whilst it may seem uneconomical to fly to a regional one day conference, if you get to meet the right people, it's potentially very worthwhile and, don't forget, you can always tie the trip into a visit to nearby clients or prospects.

The Difference Between the UK, Europe and America
It's critical to exhibiting success to understand that there are fundamental differences between exhibiting in the USA, Europe and the UK. At a practical level the differences may be minimal but culturally they are huge.

Shows in the USA tend to be bigger than European or UK shows and less expensive. Bigger means more delegates, and less expensive means your £/delegate investment is a lot more healthy.

For example, a specialist annual conference we used to attend in the USA had a steady circa 750 delegates. The equivalent in Europe was less than 100. The cost of exhibiting at the European conference was about the same in GBP as the US conference was in USD. In other words, if it was $5,000 for a booth in the USA it was £5,000 for the smaller European equivalent.

Expenses in Europe (hotels, etc.) also tend to be higher. The only saving is on airfares, and that is minimal!

However, forgetting the size and cost, the culture of delegates is the main issue in Europe and the UK.

Delegate attitude in the USA is very conducive to exhibitors. Thankfully, most delegates consider walking the floor and talking to the vendors as part of the experience. This means that shows the USA are much more successful.

Culturally, the Europeans see it very differently. It's much more us and them. Vendors are considered a lower species. There is also the language barrier although, for international companies, this is minimal. Having said that, possibly the worst place to do shows is in the UK. We may speak the same language but the inherent British mistrust of anything to do with sales or selling is the barrier. There appears to be an attitude that booth personnel are all there to fleece them and they fear that by actually stopping to talk to a vendor, they may, through some invisible process of osmosis, be scammed into entering into a lifetime commitment to something they don't want and can't cancel!

It follows that many American companies get burnt trying to enter Europe by attending exhibitions. I was chatting to one partner at a US conference when they mentioned that they were going to do the European equivalent conference. I warned them against this, explained we wouldn't be there and explained the different cultures. They were committed both emotionally and financially and went ahead. The next year I heard how it was possibly the worst conference they'd ever attended. So, if you run an American company and want to get into Europe, think twice about using shows as your entry route.

The good news is that, in certain industries, mainly those that have a centre of gravity in the USA (which include life sciences), many US conferences have quite a healthy number of European delegates. The even better news is the European delegates, once out of Europe, seem to adopt the American culture and do visit booths and chat to vendors!

Suffice it to say we did most of our exhibiting in the USA. If someone proposed a European conference they would have to spend a lot of time justifying the investment. We did do some but I think it was mainly because I'd forget over time how unproductive previous European ones were and assumed that my memory must be playing tricks. Generally, whenever I relented and we did a European show, I regretted it

Planning

Having decided to attend a show, the most important decision you will make is the booth location. Most conferences operate a strict seniority scheme and previous exhibitors get first choice. Then it's usually in the order of commitment i.e. the earlier you sign up the higher you'll be in the booth selection stakes. It follows that the worst thing you can do is dither in your decision making and sign up at the last minute.

Logistics is the main difference when it comes to trade shows versus conferences. Frequently conferences have what are called 'table tops' rather than full booths. Table tops are so called because you get a table and a couple of chairs in a room which usually also has the catering. In many of these the actual location of the table top you get makes little difference.

In larger shows booth location really does make a difference. Almost all larger shows have what I call the frozen wastelands where delegates seldom tread. You really don't want to end up there.

When selecting your booth make sure you understand the layout. Where is the main entrance? Are there multiple entrances? Delegate flow (known as 'traffic') is the most important aspect of the selection. Corner booths typically command a premium which I reckon is generally worth paying.

You'll want to understand where the refreshments are located and how this will affect traffic. Where are your partners and competitors? You'll want to be close to your partners if possible. Are you selecting a small booth in-between a couple of very large booths? If so, will you be lost in the noise? In short, choosing your booth location is very important.

When considering budgets there are many hidden costs associated with a booth at a show. For the trade show style events, the price of the booth space is literally the cost of the space. It does not include tables, chairs, carpet, electricity, internet, and so on. Make sure you understand exactly what is included in the package and how much the additional items are.

Everything is hideously expensive because you are a captive. For example, it's cheaper to go out and purchase a monitor and leave it behind rather than rent one from the conference organisers – except that you can't do that because you'll be charged for its disposal! Yes, if you leave too much waste behind that is another charging opportunity. Carpet isn't included (unless it's a table top show which are generally held in carpeted foyers/rooms) but its mandatory to have some and the rent for a bit of 10' x 8' carpet is outrageous. Make sure you pre-order because if you have to order onsite the cost is considerably higher!

In most cases, internet provision is thousands of dollars. The venue may offer free wifi but it will almost certainly be pitifully slow as everyone will be using it. We never had a demo which relied on internet availability. I've seen naïve vendors relying on the free wifi only to find it at a crawl. Or they reckon they can use a 4G dongle only to find there is no mobile reception in the room. Unless you are paying top dollar for a guaranteed reliable provision, assume that there is no internet available.

From a practical perspective, make sure you have all the necessities of booth life: A stapler, duct tape (most venues won't allow you to run wire under the carpet so you have to stick it down), extension leads, spare bulbs, scissors, box cutter, etc.

Finally, don't forget that most event organisers require the vendor to have third party liability insurance and require proof of this prior to the exhibition. If you don't have it you'll have to take out theirs which, as you may have already guessed, is not inexpensive! It's generally sensible to get such cover as part of your companies' 3rd party liability insurance – which of course you should have!

Booth Kit
You will probably be familiar with the type of stands there are in shows. The pop-up banner stands are the most well-known but trade show banners and booth kit is a whole industry in its own right. To have a successful show you need to think through the logistics.

Having kit delivered to the venue is usually very expensive. The term to look for is 'handling charges'. There are some exceptions (typically smaller conferences at standard hotels) but, for anywhere which is an exhibition centre and larger conference hotels, assume the worst. Therefore you need to consider the portability of kit. In the early days of PleaseTech, I got a golf flight bag and used that to transport the booth kit. I'd fly over to the USA complete with my 'golfing gear'. In those days, such kit was usually carried free. Times have changed but it may still be cost effective in the early days.

As the company grew we hired a wonderful person in the USA with a garage to manage the booth kit. She would store it in her garage and then ship it out for each show. We had several booths depending on the format and show size. We very rarely had it delivered to the conference venue due to the aforementioned costs. It was delivered to the hotel in which we were staying, to the local UPS office[31] or some other location which didn't charge a massive handling fee. We then had the problem of carting it to the venue ourselves, typically by taxi. However, we also found that if delivered to the local UPS office they would normally deliver it to the venue and occasionally collect it post-show for a nominal sum and a gratuity. Large conference venues don't like you turning up with booth kit and walking in the front door. However, there is little they can do to stop it but if they see you with it in a taxi they may direct you to shipping and, guess what, that will be a long delay and a large cost! You may have to get dropped off around the corner.

Whilst on the subject of shipping, don't make the mistake that, just because Canadians and Americans sound the same to Europeans they live in the same country. There is the small matter of a customs border between America and Canada. This does cause all sorts of complications when it comes to shipping booth kit to Canadian shows. Paperwork is required and additional costs incurred!

A major consideration is portability. How many staff will be at the show? What are their physical capabilities? Generally, they can manage one wheeled case each. Will the cases fit in a standard taxi or hire car? Normally we had one case with the booth and lights, etc. and one with a monitor and other stuff. With one wheeled case each you can normally just walk into the venue without trouble. Anything else and, well ... you'll soon learn.

If you go beyond the standard pop-up type banners and booths, make sure you use kit which is easy to erect and requires minimum tools. Venues in the USA are heavily unionised and don't allow you to construct booths onsite,

---

[31] Not all such offices are equal. Some, typically concessions in a hotel, do have handling charges.

especially if that involves power tools. There is a general rule of thumb that if it takes more than one person an hour to erect with anything other than a screwdriver or hex key, you need the very expensive unionised venue labour. I've not had it myself (and, to be fair, usually find the professional booth erectors friendly and helpful – perhaps it's the accent), but I know of one person who had a union rep monitoring their booth building activity and timing them to ensure that they didn't exceed the one hour maximum! I assume he'd managed to upset the venue staff in some way!

The balance is between having a decent booth which presents you professionally and cost/portability. You can spend a fortune on booth kit and shows and have the best booth in the world but that, in itself, won't make your shows successful. So be sensible.

I always tried to look at our booth with a dispassionate eye and compared it to other booths. Having said that, there are always new ideas in booth kit land and it's always worth wandering around other booths looking at their kit and thinking about whether it works for them and, if so, whether it would work for you.

Booth Personnel
Other than booth location the most important aspect of the show is the people you send, the booth personnel.

Many people think this is the preserve of the sales team. That is not the way I see it.

In the early days, when the company is, shall we say, 'compact', there won't be much choice as to who goes. If you come from the techie side of the business you'll probably leave this to your sales counterpart. Conversely, if you come from the sales side, you'll be on point.

Whoever attends, the key to success is making sure that you do not just see a show as a lead generating and qualification opportunity. Your booth personnel need to have brought into this as well – especially if they are in sales. I've seen two main problems with putting salespeople on the booth.

Firstly, it's one of mindset. It follows on from my previously stated assertion that that the success of a show is not based solely on the number of new leads you get. I've seen so many booths where the salesperson is qualifying the delegate on the booth and, if not a short term prospect, loses interest, gives them a brochure and moves them politely on. Who can blame them? Their job is sales and are typically under pressure to meet their quarterly target.

Secondly, pure play salespeople tend not to have the broader knowledge which is frequently necessary to answer questions on the booth. Sometimes prospects hunt in packs and have both business and technical staff wandering around. Other times the prospect is a business analyst who understands both sides of the coin. Salespeople will take the details and tell them that a techie will be in touch to answer their questions but this is a far from satisfactory approach.

As the business grows, to my mind, the ideal people to have on a booth are those from product management and business development[32]. You need people who are comfortable talking with others and have a wide understanding of the market, product and technology. They need to be able to <u>listen</u> to prospects and clients, understand their needs and nuances and provide honest feedback to the company accordingly.

However, having said that, it's frequently beneficial for all staff to get booth experience, for example, clients like meeting support staff who deal with them on a regular basis. Development staff and other techies also learn a lot. They are always amazed at how untechnical some of the end users they meet on the booth are! And, in the future when you are arguing over whether a feature is 'too stupid' to include, you can remind them of their initiation into the world of the end user whom they met at the booth.

Booth duty can also be used as a perk. In PleaseTech, the senior UK technical staff had the opportunity to do a show a year if they so wished. A few days off the day job, staying at a nice hotel with the company paying for food and refreshments, frequently in a location where the sun was shining. What was not to like?

I had two simple rules regarding booth duty:

---

[32] I explain the difference, as I see it, between sales and business development under the sales section below.

Firstly, whoever was on the booth had to want to do it and understand its value. Let me assure you that there is nothing worse than having someone on a booth who doesn't want to be there.

I've seen many examples and one stands out. We were at a user conference in the UK and the pre-sales techie on the display pod next to us didn't want to be there and clearly thought the whole thing was a complete waste of this valuable time. He spent the whole time hunched over his PC doing 'proper work'.

I watched as a delegate who clearly thought she should do her duty and 'do the rounds' walked up and asked brightly: 'What do you do'? Our man looked up briefly from his laptop with a look of sheer exasperation on his face and said: 'Do you have [insert deeply technical term here]?. The lady replied in the negative. 'In that case it's of no interest to you' he said and went back to his laptop.

She beat a hasty retreat and, I strongly suspect, never approached a booth again in her career. The idiot not only did his company a great disservice, he did all vendors worldwide a great disservice. If only she walked up to our booth! So, please, don't put people who don't want to be there on the booth.

Secondly, if anyone asked for time off in lieu it was granted with the strict proviso that they wouldn't be attending any shows at any time in the future. The problem is, of course, you are generally asking booth personnel to trash a weekend for travel and booth set-up purposes. However, my view was that the company was providing them with a decent hotel, food and refreshments in a great location at no cost. If they were going to get prickly over the lost weekend then the answer was simple, don't go and leave it to someone else! Therefore it was a perk to attend shows not a chore! Of course, in reality, no one did ever ask for time off in lieu, they knew my views and were happy to get the experience and or dose of vitamin D.

One final thought on this is dress code. This is important as it ties into the image you want to project of the company. I've always been a fan of a corporate uniform of 'conference wear' i.e. company shirt with logo (either collared or polo) and black trousers or skirt. I'm not a fan of suits on the booth. To me it screams 'sales'. In my experience delegates are more open if they don't feel they are being sold to and conference wear suggests a more laid back, approachable, non-sales culture.

Remember that the booth and specifically the booth personnel may be the first impression someone gets of your business. Make sure it's a good one!

At the Show
Show materials are a subject on which there is endless debate. In general I think people have far too much literature on their booths. We all know what happens. The delegates go around collecting the literature, and then either leave it in their hotel room as it won't fit in their carry on or, if it does find its way back to their office, drop it under their desk until they rediscover it several months later and chuck it then!

Having said that, we did try the zero paper approach but found that, even in this digital day and age, people do like a bit of paper to take away! So we compromised and had a couple of basic one page A6 flyers and postcards (see later). This made sure that people had something to take away but it had the advantage of being inexpensive. If you stick with more traditionally sized literature make sure you understand that, if exhibiting in the USA, it's US letter size and not A4.

You'll see lots of booths at the conferences with business card draws ('drawings' in American) for expensive electronic toys. Huge posters announcing 'win the latest [insert new cool gadget] here'. As far as I was concerned they were simply throwing away money. You really don't need to spend hundreds of dollars on a raffle prize! Really you don't. Just think outside the box.

In the early days we used to purchase a Harrods teddy bear (~£20) at duty free on the way out and raffle that. It always attracted a lot of attention because it was something different. Most people loved them. We then graduated to chocolate! Everyone, especially Americans, loves British chocolate. An 850g Cadbury Dairy Milk bar looks good on the booth and is a talking point. People assume it's a prop and are surprised/delighted when you explain that it is the bar of chocolate they could win. I used to call it hand luggage size (carry on size in American). Each bar is about £10 and it is permissible to take chocolate into the USA – you just need to declare it.

Other low cost items we've used when we needed a greater incentive (see the bit on research questionnaires below) are noise cancelling headphones. You can get a half-decent set for around £50. You really don't need a major brand name at £150+. If you advertise 'win noise cancelling headphones', are people really going to say I don't want to win those because aren't Bose or Beats or whatever?

The point is that most delegates will drop their card or enter any draw on any booth regardless of what they will win so long as it's not something stupid like ½ hour free consultancy! However, given that, it follows that you shouldn't think that such 'card drops' provide leads. They are strictly limited in that they provide a database and an audience for emails - that's it. In fact, many of the most senior people refuse to enter such draws as they don't want the follow-up and, in the USA, federal employees are forbidden from accepting any such prizes so won't enter. Where the drawings have their value is in giving you something to 'open with' as people walk past your booth.

"Hello, would you like to win this teddy bear/huge bar of chocolate" is a conversation opener and you can go on to talk about other things. Being proactive always brings the best results. Tying it back into the booth personnel discussion above, staff who just sit on the booth and wait to be spoken to are not maximising the opportunity and your results will be poorer for that.

The reality is that naive booth personnel from other vendors will enter your draw. Clearly you don't want to be giving your prizes away to them and therefore you obviously remove their names before carrying out the draw. Generally I suggest you remove anyone who isn't a direct client or prospect so, sorry, no 'consultants' or other hangers-on[33]. The next question is: is the draw fair or do you just select the card which you most want to win? Well that's up to you. Fixing the draw is not unheard of but my approach has always been to have a real draw but with the ancillary cards removed!

However, there if there is a special client or prospect you'd like to arrange to win, my suggested approach, which has people winning a relatively low cost item, does mean that you can have more than one winner. People always

---

[33] We always covered this in the (very) small print associated with the draw notice. We also noted that we reserved the right to contact all participants with a follow-up.

like to win and, if for the cost of an extra bar of chocolate or teddy bear, you get to open a door, well … what's not to like?

Standing out at shows is always difficult, especially in a big show where delegates walk up and down seemingly endless rows of booths. We stood out because of our cartoon program, which I've covered in a separate section. We were the only booth showing cartoons. You see delegates walking past the long line of booths glancing at them. At ours, they'd see the cartoons and stop to watch them. They then may pick-up the cartoon postcards. At that point you have an opportunity to chat.

For the larger shows we occasionally employed a 'booth host/hostess' to assist on the booth. The main attraction of these individuals is that they provide another pair of relatively cheap and safe hands at busy shows. I'd stress that these individuals were not so-called 'booth babes' in skimpy clothing but professional booth staff who understand the dynamics of a trade show and are available to hire by the day or part thereof. In the early days, we also hired a hosting professional to help out with the admin of a user group meeting held in the USA.

Our experience with these hosting professionals was very good. We found them to be very professional and good at picking up on the basic elevator message. You specify dress code and obviously provide them with any corporate shirts required. You book them and pay through an agency so there is no cash transaction on the booth unless they've done a cracking job and you feel a gratuity is in order. If they did a decent job we'd slip them an extra $50 or so, which was always much appreciated.

We found it worked best when we had a specific task for them. In the next section I explain the research questionnaires we did on the booth and tasking them with getting delegates to complete said questionnaires worked well. They know how to talk to delegates and engage them and can be quite persuasive. So, in the appropriate circumstances, I'd have no hesitation in recommending them.

There is no single formula to have a successful show. Ultimately, how you stand out at a large show and what you do to maximise your benefit from the show will depend on your industry and what you do. In the next section I discuss some of the things we tried.

Maximising Value from the Show

As previously noted, we took the 'thought leadership' approach to our marketing and, to reinforce this, we undertook our own research which generated content for our website, webinars, and so on. A show is a great place to conduct such research.

To maximise our return on the larger shows we always tried to have a research questionnaire on the booth. The aim of this was to get a statistically significant number of replies which was a useful input to our understanding of the market and allowed us to publicise anonymised summary research results.

Practically, we tried several ways of capturing the information. You either have a person with a clipboard asking the questions and noting down answers or use iPads (in suitably secure stands) with a basic questionnaire. We found that some of the most valuable information was the free text responses which were not captured with an iPad as those responding hardly wrote anything whereas people responding verbally provided useful information. The important thing to do was to keep the questionnaires short and simple. People got bored with lengthy questions and questionnaires.

The other observation I'd make on this is that people had no incentive to answers these questionnaires unless you were proactive. As mentioned above, having a dedicated hosting professional who job it was to get responses helped, as did using it as a means to enter the drawing. However, in such cases the drawing needed to be for something significant and that's when we offered the noise cancelling headphones!

What we found did not work was appealing to the delegates' charitable instincts! At one large, generic document-centric conference we were doing for the first time, we arranged a 'document review practices' survey. It seemed like an ideal opportunity to survey the broad range of people representing the many industries whom we were assured would be attending. To encourage people to participate we advertised that, for every survey completed, we would be donating $5 to the American Red Cross. The target was to raise $1,000 (200 replies) for the charity. This would raise money for a worthy cause and give us a statistically meaningful result.

Despite pre-show publicity and the booth team pushing the survey, over three days less than 20 people could find the couple of minutes required to complete the survey. I'm told that the view was 'if it isn't a draw for an iPad, I can't be bothered'. A sad reflection of the times in which we live[34].

Presentations

One of the best ways to maximise the value of a show is to be able to give a presentation. Some sponsorship packages offer presentations as part of the package. Be warned, these sponsored presentations are nowhere near as valuable as a proper slot in the main conference educational program.

However, to have a presentation accepted for the conference educational sessions it needs to have merit. Typically, such presentations must be strictly non-promotional and mentioning your own product is considered promotion. You therefore need to have a specialism you can talk about which doesn't involve your product.

At PleaseTech, we came up with a solution to this conundrum. Even as a recognised thought leader in the area of collaborative document review and co-authoring, we were unable to pass the promotional litmus test as no presentation on the subject could avoid mentioning PleaseReview. So independent consultants could talk on the subject but not us!

The solution was, what I consider to be, a marketing stroke of genius: The Microsoft Word Masterclass.

As luck would have it, one of the technical challenges we kept facing was that clients were able to really mess up Word documents when authoring them and therefore we wanted to educate our clients on how to use Word correctly. Combine this with the amount of Word expertise we had as a company and, hey presto, the Word Masterclasses were born. These Masterclasses enabled us to present at conferences and had the added benefit of educating our client base, they also made for great, well attended webinars. They were extremely well received[35] and further established us as an authoritative source.

---

[34]This was a poor show for us and we did not return. Maybe the charity angle would have worked elsewhere.

[35] I would personally give some of these Masterclasses. We all followed a script and, while I know a fair amount about Word, I wouldn't consider myself an expert so occasionally couldn't answer detailed questions. Most conferences have feedback forms the results of which they share with the presenter. I got one which marked

There is another way; case studies are always highly sought after and stand a very high chance of being accepted – if they are client-led. So, for a case study to be accepted, you will need to have the client present with you and, obviously, the case study will need to pass the client's internal authorisation processes - always a challenge.

Putting together a case study presentation can rapidly get complex. For example, who is paying for the client's flights, board and lodging? If it's you, is that a reasonable use of your limited marketing budget? It rapidly becomes a logistical nightmare and can acquire an overhead way beyond all benefit.

Meeting Real End Users

As we are on the subject of maximising value at the show, as the company develops a client base, a key part of the value is meeting your existing end users and chatting with them.

You will have formal contacts in your clients, typically an IT and a business representative, however it's normally really hard to talk with the people who use your software in their day-to-day jobs. Although these may number in their hundreds and even thousands, they concentrate on their day jobs and access to them is virtually impossible! These real end users are the ones who truly know what works and what does not work, what is good and what is bad.

Yes, you'll get the bug reports but it's the softer nuances which these real end users can provide. They frequently also have great product enhancement ideas. Ideas which will help them in their day-to-day use of your product and which, no matter how good your product management, you'd not consider. It's these little distinctions which can make the difference in a sale by showing you understand the target's working environment and have answers.

You need to attract them to your booth as some may think that, as they already use your software, they are wasting your time. At PleaseTech we

---

me down for not being a Word expert as I couldn't answer a particularly obscure question. However, in the free text comments the gentleman had written 'I learnt a lot'. Sometimes you despair. BTW: when I couldn't answer the question I used to open it to the audience. There was usually someone who could answer.

were in the lucky position of having end users approach us and tell us how much they loved PleaseReview. Obviously, this was gratifying but, as critical feedback is more valuable, I'd always ask 'what is it you'd like to see improved?' Or, 'what are the top five things that really annoy you about the software?'

This goes directly back to booth personnel. Make sure you have the people who will engage with, listen to, and report back on their conversations with your real end users.

Entertainment

You can't mention shows without discussing entertainment. The reality is that the evening activities are frequently just as valuable as anything that happens during the day's programme of booth chats, presentations and whatever. Some of the parties and associated antics are legendary.

As a vendor you have to think of it from the delegate's perspective. Once a year they are away from home, staying in a luxury hotel and on expenses. Some have such busy home lives they are simply grateful to have some 'me time' and disappear to their rooms. Many, however, want to party! The key restriction on this desire is that their expenses will be limited (or they may even be on a per diem) and this is where vendor entertainment steps in.

This doesn't necessarily mean that you need to dip into your pocket. At most shows the delegates are likely to have multiple options. As a small company it may be best not to compete and simply join in at events thrown by others, it's a lot cheaper.

The larger conferences may well have their own party night, and on other nights, there are likely to be several large parties thrown by the major vendors. Obtaining entry tickets is usually as simple as registering on a website or at the booth. Some get a bit sniffy about giving other vendors (who aren't their partners) tickets but most accept it as part of the deal. What they want is their party to be bigger and better than the competition, so typically all are welcome. These parties tend to go on well into the night.

In the CDC days, the Documentum conferences were known for their parties and it would not be uncommon for booth personnel (me very much leading from the front) to be out drinking with clients until the early hours and then back on the booth at 8:00am. Sleeping was what the flight home was for!

Not all vendors get it right; there is a memorable incident from a conference in Paris in the CDC days, when a vendor had organised a River Seine dinner cruise in a Bateaux Mouche type vessel. I remember being on the cruise and having a pleasant time. It was only the next day it transpired that one of the vendor hosts had inadvertently boarded the wrong boat which was full of tourists! Having had a bit of a 'pre-lash' he didn't spot this and was quite happily wandering around chatting to people, handing out his business cards and thanking everyone for joining his party. Apparently it didn't occur to him that he didn't recognise anyone until the boat docked and he saw the people he did recognise all getting off the boat we'd been on!

At the smaller shows, you'll typically find one or two vendors hosting a meal or drinks. Again, as a small company it's difficult to compete especially in the early days when you don't know anyone. As you develop relationships with partners and become known on the circuit, cooperating with others either formally or informally is generally a good strategy. For example, I'd often be invited to a dinner hosted by one of our informal partner companies and I'd make a point of ensuring that I more than covered my expense by buying a pre-dinner round of drinks or similar. These rounds can be expensive ($300+ would not be uncommon) but it saves your host the expense and makes it more likely you'll be invited back.

The key point is that, no matter how you are feeling, evening entertainment is very much part of the package. You may be on your third show in as many weeks and would dearly love an early night, but it's the one opportunity your clients and prospects have to have fun and so you need to be up for it.

Don't do the Extras

There are endless opportunities to spend money at shows. Would you like a padded, softer carpet? Literature in the conference backpack/bag? Hotel drops?[36] And so on …

The only one to consider is the preshow mailer. It generally depends on how this is conducted as it varies from conference to conference and in a constant state of flux due to the increasingly tough privacy laws - so anything I write will be automatically out of date. Just make sure you

---

[36] Hotel drops are where you can have your literature inserted in a plastic bag hung on the door of delegates who are staying at the official conference hotels using the official conference code.

understand what you are getting and how much it will cost. We rarely participated.

A challenging option is the automatic badge readers offered. Generally, for an extra $300 - $500 or so, you get one of those machines which automatically scans the code on the badge and, post show, delivers you all the scanned badges in a nicely formatted spreadsheet.

Even when the company got larger, we didn't use these machines unless they came as part of the booth package. Call me old fashioned, but I like a good wodge of business cards or lead forms in my back pocket. You'd be surprised how horribly inaccurate the delegate data in the system can be. Wrong email addresses, wrong names, people who've changed jobs since they registered, and so on. Occasionally, someone can't attend and a colleague uses their badge. So think twice. If it's worth getting their name surely you can have one of their business cards or complete a short lead sheet to ensure you get the correct details and, if it's secured in your back pocket, there will be no chance of technical issues depriving you of the leads. A further point is that the automatic badge readers tend to have poor facilities for making notes regarding your conversations, so you'll need a bit of paper anyway!

Another unnecessary cost is so-called marketing freebies. You know the stuff; pens, keyrings, gadgets and other branded goods typically given away from booths at the shows. Don't get me wrong, I've commissioned a few in my time but my strong advice is not to waste too much money on these frivolous knick-knacks! Before the previously mentioned teddy bears and chocolate, we had things like branded torches, USB car adaptors (when they were novel), etc. Basically the idea was you got a gift if you sat through a 15 minute demo on our booth. Did it work? No it didn't! Mainly because other booths with much larger budgets were giving away the same stuff or better with zero commitment other than contact details. The good news is that this prompted us to think outside the box and go with the teddy bears and chocolate which were not only considerably cheaper but also acted as a differentiator.

Don't forget this free stuff isn't free to you and there is little point in buying the cheapest as giving away, for example, a branded pen which doesn't work or leaks in the recipient's pocket isn't going to leave a good impression.

Therefore you need to purchase something half decent. As an example, let's consider pens and do the maths. 1,000 half decent 'give away' pens, with artwork and set-up, won't give you much change from £750. Then you have to ship them to the venue and then you have to ship them back or, as many people do, just chuck any left away. Ask yourself: is it worth £750 to be able to give away cheap pens from your booth? What have you gained from that money?

As I look around my home office I see quite a few pens, most of them picked up from booths. Some of them are quite nice and probably cost a couple of pounds each. Looking at the five immediately to hand, I only recognise the name of one company and that was picked up from my accountants! I'll repeat the question: What do you gain?

Having said that we did have marketing freebies on our booth! We settled on microfibre screen wipes. Colour printed one side with a cartoon and message with basic printing on the other side, these cost about 30 pence each and did a great job on iPad and phone screens and well as being suitable for spectacles. Cheap to ship (you could chuck a few hundred in the booth kit and not notice) and useful and different!

As for more expensive items, don't get me started! In my CDC days, I clearly remember a coffee room chat with a sales guy who had just returned from an important USA conference.

Me: How did it go?

Him: Really great, we got rid of all the golf caps[37] and a load of other stuff.

Not the answer I was looking for. Any idiot can give away free stuff. Maybe you have so much VC money you don't care. If you are bootstrapping you will care.

My point is that such extras can easily double the cost of the booth and you really need to consider whether it's money well spent. I found it generally wasn't. Think of it a bit like a budget airline flight. There are multiple cost options that can more than double the cost of the airfare but the smart people just turn up with hand luggage within the permitted parameters and

---

[37] I still have a couple of the CDC golf caps in regular use. They were good quality!

take their randomly allocated seat for the 2 hours necessary. They are the ones who get best value.

Other Thoughts on Shows

I'm going to give you two other thoughts on shows.

Firstly, make copious notes as soon as possible after you've spoken with someone. At the time you may think you'll never forget the conversation with [insert name] who is a red hot prospect. You will. After three solid days of talking to people and burning the candle at both ends, you will be mentally exhausted and will have difficulty in recalling what day it is let alone who you spoke with on day one. The other top tip is to make sure you can read your notes.

Finally, security; depending on the size of conference and the type of show, security can be an issue. If it isn't nailed down there is a good chance it will vanish. The smaller professional conferences are not the issue here, it's the large trade shows. Be especially alert if it's a closed conference which has an 'open to the public' slot. During that slot hide your valuables and be sparing with any promotional freebies you have out. I've seen people walking around with wheeled shopping bags scooping pens, pads and really anything promotional into them. It's not unknown for mobile phones and iPads to go missing in the general melee.

Other Marketing

I make no apologies for having spent so long on shows. As mentioned earlier, they were the mainstay of our proactive marketing program, especially in the USA which accounted for 75% - 80% of our revenue. However, there is a lot more to marketing which this section covers.

Advertising – i.e. Online Advertising

So let's ignore print advertising. Not only is it so yesterday, it's also a waste of money. I can't remember the last time any of my companies spent money on print adverts. I suspect it was in the '90s!

These days it is, of course, all about online advertising. One of my themes is thinking internationally and that's what the internet provides – global reach. I have to admit that I'm not an expert in this area and I'm straying slightly outside my comfort zone. The online advertising we did was strictly limited because it can get very expensive as each click incurs a cost[38]. For what it's worth here is my experience.

Search advertising: In the western world this means Google. At PleaseTech we advertised with both Google and Bing but it was Google which generated a vast majority of the clicks and thus the expense.

If you don't understand how Google Ads work there are plenty of websites dedicated to explaining it and optimising the bids and placement has become a specialist subject. In brief, you bid on key words and the amount you bid compared to others, together with a quality measure, determines your placement on the search results page. Every time someone clicks on the ad you get billed.

To do basic search advertising you don't need to employ a specialist and my advice would be to have a crack at it yourself for two to three months and then, if you've got the cash, invite a specialist to have a crack for a further two to three months. That way you can compare results and work out whether it's worth paying the specialist.

There are certain things to watch out for. The first of these is common words which mean different things in different industries. I previously explained that the term 'document review' means a very different thing in the legal industry when compared to other industries. At PleaseTech this meant that we were bidding against specialist legal vendors and some of the clicks we got (for which we had paid handsomely) were not relevant. In this case it was all about trying to ensure that the strictly limited advertisement wording excluded non-target market (i.e. the legal people) but appeal to everyone else.

If you are in a particularly specialist niche then maybe the words you are bidding on are not that popular and therefore you'll have a low cost experience! If not, you'll be bidding against others and cost can escalate. Exact costs will depend on the extent and range of your bidding. As a benchmark, our annual expenditure with Google was probably about the equivalent of attending three shows, possibly more.

---

[38] At the time of writing e-scooter start-up Unicorn, has just closed down saying, 'Unfortunately, the cost of the ads were just too expensive to build a sustainable business'. Source: https://tinyurl.com/s3t23ab

The second thing to watch out for is Google's AdSense. This is where Google ads appear on other people's websites (usually based on content relevancy) and there is a revenue share with the host site. There is nothing wrong with AdSense per se; in fact like a lot of the Google stuff, it's a brilliant conception. The problem is that it can lead to some very high costs due to the fact that your ads are reaching many more people and you'll get many more clicks.

We experimented with AdSense at PleaseTech in the early days[39]. When the firstly monthly bill came in our participation was rapidly terminated. My recollection is that we'd spent four to five times our normal monthly spend. I expended some considerable effort trying to work out whether we'd been the victims of click fraud and concluded that we hadn't. It was simply that, because the advert was much more widely spread, we'd had a huge number of additional clicks which we were able to reconcile with website stats. We'd had no noticeable increase in website leads so I concluded that the quality of an AdSense click was below that of a web search click.

It makes sense if you think about it. The web search click is as the result of a deliberate search. The AdSense click is the result of someone reading a vaguely relevant blog/website/whatever and thinking 'oh, that looks interesting. What's it all about?'. The point you have to consider is whether this casual interest is worth the additional expenditure.

We did experiment with other sites; LinkedIn is one example. You can target specific job titles and industries.

The key point is that the old marketing adage of 'I know half my advertising expenditure is wasted, I just don't know which half' is no longer relevant. With bounce rates, website stats, and so on you can work out what works and what doesn't. So experimentation is the order of the day. Try it, measure it and work out whether it's worth it.

A related but separate topic is search engine optimisation (SEO). There are some basic things you can do to ensure that the search engines (i.e. Google) like what they see on your website. There is plenty of information out there on the basic rules and you should follow them.

---

[39] So my information is 10+ years out of date in a fast moving area!

I'd strongly recommend that you ignore companies that offer to get you on the first page in the Google organic search results. The search results and algorithms are changing all the time and any such ranking won't last long. Likewise, run a mile from anyone offering to submit your domain to multiple search engines. All you do is increase your spam.

Yes, it's worth submitting your url to Google and the other decent search engines. Again, there is plenty of information out there on how to do that yourself.

In summary, it's worth spending your time, effort and (if you have any available) money on getting the basics right but there are no short cuts – no matter what people tell you.

Social Media

I have to admit to being a cynic when it comes to social media for B2B businesses. I can see the point from a B2C perspective but, if you are in B2B, ask yourself whether your target audience really does read your tweets, Facebook posts, etc.?

In B2B land I believe that there is a danger that getting too involved in social media simply provides non-value add work for marketing! They are busily retweeting each other's tweets and generating a froth which has little relevancy in the acquisition of customers.

I have no problem with basic use of Twitter and Facebook as another communications mechanism and I'd certainly advocate having a presence on both and any others which come to the fore. But the key point is that your Facebook and Twitter accounts are just another channel through which you address the market. By all means retweet partners tweets if they reciprocate (especially if they are large mainstream companies), but don't think for a minute that it's a mainstream marketing activity.

I've never used paid promotion on social media but that doesn't stop me from having an opinion! It all goes back to your target audience. Ask yourself whether a B2B target audience will really be influenced by paid social media campaigns. On a related subject, I have used advertorial which is covered briefly in the next section.

One argument for social media is that it improves your SEO. Despite Google claiming that they don't use social media for SEO, it's not hard to find articles that claim the opposite. Funnily enough all the articles seem to be by companies promoting social media!

The one exception to this cynicism is LinkedIn which I consider to be more of a business networking tool than social media. I mention LinkedIn throughout this book and have had a presence on it since its early days.

I cover the LinkedIn Sales Navigator in the sales section so let's consider the basics. The first thing you need to do is have a presence and a company page. Once the basics are in place, you need to ensure that all your staff are singing from the same hymn sheet. Issue some standard copy describing the company and ensure that everyone uses that in their description. You will need a social media policy which I address under Recruitment and Employment.

From a marketing perspective, by all means post news items and updates and encourage staff to share them but you'll probably get lost in the noise. My home page has so many updates that I view a very small random percentage of them. I say 'random' because it depends on what is current when I log-on. So, in that respect, it's simply another communications mechanism which I strongly recommend you keep professional, interesting and relevant.

There is some benefit to be had in joining groups relevant to your market and target customer base, and replying to posts to which you can add value. This doesn't mean inane responses or likes – it means providing a thoughtful, useful reply which is pertinent to the subject. This can help build the company's reputation as a knowledgeable professional organisation.

I guess the message is, as with all marketing, think carefully about what you are doing, why you are doing it and don't just jump on the bandwagon because everyone else is doing it.

Publicity (News Items and Press Releases, etc.)

We can't consider marketing without addressing the thorny question of press releases and news items.

Firstly, what is the difference? As I understand it, a news item is something you publish on your own website and will mention in your mailings but you do not proactively disseminate to the 'press'. A press release is something you actively try to get published on other websites pertinent to your prospect base and which provide 'authoritative' sources.

The difference is not semantic. There are advantages to having news items published on independent websites, especially authoritative ones, and on other media. Yes, a prospect may read it and have an interest but, almost more importantly, is the good it will do to your Google search rankings.

However press releases are not free unless you individually submit them one by one. If you search for something like 'press release website' you will get a ton of information on the costs and reach associated with the various options. Some of the names will probably be familiar to you. There is also some interesting reading around tests done to find which are the most effective options.

The important question you have to ask yourself is not 'what am I trying to achieve?' because that is obvious. You are trying to achieve widespread 'free' publicity, mentions in things like Google News, valuable links back to your site from authoritative sources, and so on. The question to ask is 'how likely is it that my press release will be used by an authoritative source?'

Those sites which publish whatever is thrown at them are unlikely to be considered authoritative and therefore are unlikely to be much use! However, the authoritative news sites/bloggers/etc. are inundated with hundreds if not thousands of press releases on a daily basis and, quite frankly, they don't care about your company.

What they do care about is hot topics or major names. So, if you've conducted some interesting market research on a current hot topic and have a newsworthy result it may be worth knocking out a press release and even paying for dissemination. Likewise, if you've just sold a contract to a household or major industry name and have had permission from them for a news item, it's something to consider. Otherwise you are just wasting your time and money!

This leads naturally to a key point; that of being able to publish a news item such as a contract win. Typically, clients will insist on a no publicity clause in the contract. There are good reasons for this. Quoted companies are heavily regulated and press releases may have an effect on their share price.

Therefore, it's usually a long and torturous process to get any publicity approved. The same applies to case studies.

Your best bets for this type of publicity are public bodies, industry associations and smaller companies. In other words, any company or organisation which isn't listed. You can see the issue here. To make it worth your while to pay for a press release you need the big names. They are the least likely to give you permission to use their name.

This shouldn't stop you asking (under the sales chapter I discuss this as a negotiating tactic), because any permission you get is valuable for your own site and client list but, those that are more likely to give permission, are likely to have much less value in the context of a proactive press release.

I'll add two further things:

1. If you are approaching a big company for permission, I'd avoid the use of the term 'press release'. Instead talk about a 'news item for your website'. Press releases immediately raise warning flags whilst a news item for your website seems relatively innocuous. Of course, if you get permission for a news item, get it approved and then publish it on your website, it's in the public domain and, once it's in the public domain, it may well be worth publicising it further!

2. I'm aware of companies who publish the names of all their clients on their website on the basis it's easier to plead for forgiveness than seek permission. I'd strongly recommend against this approach. Firstly, if the client is on the ball they may spot this and dump you in hot water but, secondly and most importantly, it will probably come out in due diligence (which we address in the chapter on exiting) and your acquirer may well demand a retention to cover any future legal costs associated with your flagrant disregard of the confidentiality clause in the client contracts. You have been warned!

Of course, client quotes and case studies are some of the best content you can get. If you are able to get a client agree to a news item and or case study, make sure you do all the hard work. The client is busy with their day job and they really aren't interested in your news item or case study. So make sure that they do the minimum amount of work possible. Therefore, if it's a news item you should have the facts and be able to write it and send for approval. If it's a case study make sure you know as much as possible about the reason they purchased before the telephone interview. It's so much easier to ask the client to confirm your understanding (correcting it where necessary) than to start with a blank sheet of paper.

By the way, you will write the client's own quotes. You are literally putting words in their mouth and, assuming you are not stupid and keep it sensible, they are more than likely to sign off your prose, perhaps with minor adjustments to feel they've had input.

This means that your news items and case studies can, and should, contain your key messages. In The PleaseTech Story I mention that a news item quoted Citrix Online's Director of IT, as saying: 'The addition of PleaseReview is a good fit, enabling us to have a truly collaborative, formal document review process with comprehensive reporting.'. It's no surprise that this was exactly the marketing message we were promoting because, obviously, we had written the release and the quote and presented it to the client for approval. Yes it was a news item and it was on the news page but, once it had been posted, it was in the public domain and we had the quote (and others of a similar nature) plastered all over the site and our presentations!

Advertorial
Times are tough in the trade press. This whole internet thing has caused their business model to implode and they are having to redefine themselves online. Many are succeeding in this redefinition. The good news is that trade press websites are likely to be considered authoritative sources and therefore getting something published on such a site is generally worth doing.

This is where advertorial comes in. I'm not talking about the obvious paid for 'articles' clearly written by a marketing department masquerading as journalist prose with the 'sponsored copy' by-line. Leave that to the large companies with more budget than sense! I'm talking about more subtle ways of generating coverage.

For example, we paid an independent expert (who happened to be the editor of a small specialist trade journal) a consultancy fee to undertake an independent review of PleaseReview. The idea was to get authoritative, independent copy for our website. That review (which was genuinely independent – we were only able to review the copy for technical inaccuracies) naturally ended up in the publication. Is that advertorial? Great question. Who cares? The resulting article was not considered sponsored copy so was authoritative and, to be fair, was a genuinely independent review by an industry expert!

Clearly, these days there is a blurring between trade press websites and authoritative blogs written by independent consultants. Asking such independent consultants to undertake independent reviews tends to be a very cost-effective way to generate copy and placement on authoritative sources. Just make sure that in the contract you retain a royalty free license to use the content in your marketing material, on your website, etc. In others words they are writing copy for your use and dissemination. If that copy happens to end up on their website as well (it generally does) then that's a bonus.

Once you have established a relationship with such a consultant (or maybe several consultants as your budget grows as you grow), it then becomes easier to engage them for major product releases. You ask them to provide a further review for your great new release. The key to a successful process is to reassure the consultant that it is a truly independent review so that their integrity is not compromised (they are well aware of their authoritative source status and want to maintain it), and that, if this project goes well, there would be further similar projects for them. There is nothing like the incentive of another consultancy assignment to help the first project go smoothly!

Webinars

No marketing plan is complete without a comprehensive webinar programme. At PleaseTech we had a variety of webinars including, as previously mentioned, those around the Word Master Classes.

As I see it, webinars split into two types: those designed to attract new prospects (marketing webinars) and those designed to help existing clients use the software and spread the use of the software within said clients (support webinars). These support webinars should be firmly restricted to clients and, whilst not strictly part of marketing, a comprehensive support webinar programme can be promoted and used as part of the sales process to show how well you support your clients as soon as they have signed up.

Marketing webinars should not be confused with sales demonstrations which are part of sales activity. Marketing webinars are designed to impart useful information to the audience, ideally to generate leads, although having further engagement with existing clients and prospects is never a bad thing.

At PleaseTech, in addition to the Masterclasses, we did webinars on the results of the research we undertook[40] and, frankly, anything that we thought would attract an audience. Obviously these sessions were recorded and some were made available via the website (with a registration requirement) or our YouTube channel. For the research we usually created an animated video to present the results.

Obviously you need to promote your webinars although simply having a programme has some benefit when prospects hit your website. You are clearly an active company with plenty to say!

The key thing to note, especially with marketing webinars, is that very few of the people who sign up actually attend – no matter how many reminders you send them. Something will always come up at the last minute, or they simply won't bother. If you have 50 people signed up and five log-on, you are doing well. This, in itself, doesn't matter. If you use the correct webinar software, the attendees can't see how few people there are on the call and you can simply crack on as if you had multitudes of eager participants. To this end it's a good idea to have pre-planned a few questions so, during the Q&A at the end, there isn't an embarrassing silence. You then have an excuse to go back to the people who registered but didn't log-on and engage with them.

One trick we were experimenting with in the latter days, was to offer our clients a private Word Masterclass webinar. The idea was that they would circulate the information inside their company and that way you'd broaden your contact base within the organisation. Clearly, to be able to propose this you need to have developed a webinar which is of value and not just a promotional piece.

---

[40] This included our own research at the shows and research commissioned from analysts. The analyst game is addressed below.

From a practical perspective, webinars are a very cost effective marketing tools which have the added advantage of creating website content. Webinar software is not overly expensive and provides an increasingly sophisticated platform through which to deliver the webinar and control the process (including the Q&A). A lot can go wrong in a webinar so make sure you practice and, in the event you are doing one of those complicated ones with multiple presenters, ensure everyone is involved in the practice!

As a final thought on this topic, bear in mind that clients will be receiving multiple webinar invitations every day so, to attract interest, yours must be highly pertinent and well targeted. No one has time to listen to a marketing spiel and, if they sign-up for a pertinent, interesting topic and all you give them is marketing spiel, they won't forgive you!

User Groups and Conferences

I've included user groups and conferences here under marketing simply because, whilst they are part of post sales custom care, marketing tends to get the responsibility of running them. So let's start with some definitions:

User Group: a formal structure whereby users of your software meet (typically virtually these days) to share experiences and provide feedback as to their priorities for development, suggestions for enhancements, etc. Typically one or two users from each client are nominated by the client to represent their interests.

Customer Advisory Board (CAB – sometimes called a Council): a formal structure which is typically a subset of the user group, and typically comprises larger, strategic customer representatives who meet with you (electronically or otherwise) on a regular basis to provide their advice and guidance in respect of industry trends, development priorities and so on. They also have a role in defining the agenda at user conferences.

User conference: a physical meeting whereby users travel to a conference to talk about, and be educated about your software. They expect to meet other users, have informative detailed sessions on the finer points of the software presented by your technical staff (not salespeople), have in-depth discussions with your management team and receive 'inside track' information about your direction and strategy. They also expect to drink a lot and have fun at your expense!

In the early days you can safely ignore all of the above because you are too small to have sufficient numbers to make it all work. Whilst it's always a good idea to consult your best customers as to their thoughts, any contacts you have will be informal one-to-one sessions. As part of your marketing strategy you'll attend partner's conferences and get a good idea how the successful ones are organised.

At some stage, as you grow, a number of customers will start asking about a user group and, specifically, user group meetings. Your sales and marketing teams will think this is a good idea and you'll be under pressure to agree to an expensive folly. I say 'expensive folly' because user conferences are not cheap to organise and run, and are, I believe, of dubious value to the smaller company.

Don't get me wrong I'm all for user group meetings. Specifically, I'm all for attending such conferences when they are run by other vendors. To organise your own you need critical mass and it's unlikely that you will have it. The reality is that it's really difficult to get people to come along to user conferences.

We tried several approaches. We tried bolting a user group meeting onto a popular industry conference on the basis that people were attending the industry conference anyway and would be happy to turn up a day early. They weren't[41].

We tried having a conference in a location where there were several existing customers in a small area (specifically, Cambridge, MA). By this stage we were fairly large and you'd have thought it would be a cake walk. It wasn't. At one point about a month out it was looking so poorly attended (despite an extensive promotional campaign around it) we were on the verge of cancelling it. After an extensive telesales campaign, it went ahead but numbers were the basic minimum to save face.

So my advice is that you'll find the idea of a user group meeting is considerably more attractive to clients than the reality of one.

---

[41] An obvious downside of this approach is that it excludes those not in that specific industry.

In PleaseTech we operated a virtual user group using a private group on LinkedIn. This was good marketing and sales material (prospective clients like the idea of a user group) but poorly supported. You are probably beginning to see a pattern here.

I'm not sure why we weren't able to get user groups and user meetings off the ground. Perhaps it was because the software just worked, was solid and did most of what people wanted so there wasn't that much to complain about. Perhaps we weren't a sufficiently strategic vendor. Perhaps people thought our parties wouldn't make the grade. Who knows? I just know we put a lot of effort into trying to get something going and failed.

One thing we did not try was a CAB. This was because I could see more downsides than upsides. I've never really understood why you'd form one. Of course, we had a group of major strategic clients with whom we were in regular communication. However, my problem with CABs is that, if you formalise a feedback and development priority setting forum, you are handing over at least some of your development priorities to the CAB because you are almost duty bound to support and implement their decisions. Clients have their own priorities and these are not necessarily the same as yours.

When you think about it, there isn't much CABs can tell you which you don't know already if you are doing your job correctly. Some will argue that it makes your larger, strategic customers feel more important and thus increases loyalty. I'd counter that by suggesting that you getting on an aeroplane and visiting your larger, strategic customers personally is more likely to make them feel important especially if it's not tied into an ongoing sales situation.

I'll summarise by reiterating that these formal user interaction structures are more complicated than you'd think. Stay clear of them apart from an electronic user group, which is good marketing.

Industry Analysts

Anyone involved in the IT business is familiar with the analyst firms: Gartner, Forrester Research, IDC to name but a few of the bigger ones. The first question to consider is: who is their target market? Is it you or your clients? The answer is, of course, that analyst firms want to have their cake and eat it by advising both sides of the supply chain.

They want to sell their research to clients and offer to help them with their buying decisions. You can be forgiven for thinking that in some companies the old saying 'no one ever got fired for buying IBM' has been replaced by Gartner's Magic Quadrants[42]. As such, at an enterprise level, they can have an influence on who gets invited to tender.

From a vendor perspective, the analysts want to sell you access to their market research to help you with your targeting, positioning, messaging and general market trends. They want to make you feel that you know nothing and that they know everything and that, if only you opened your wallet to them, the secrets to success would be revealed!

So, how important are they?

The answer depends on your size, the software you sell and on your target market. If you have taken my advice and targeted a niche then you can safely ignore analysts until you start to grow and get a reputation. If you have got a grand vision for an enterprise system which you believe will be a fundamental step change for a sector, you'll probably want to engage with the analysts sooner rather than later to try and make sure that they understand the completeness of your vision and your ability to execute!

Target markets/companies matter because the larger the company the more likely it is that they will be signed up with and listen to an analyst company. However, there is a counter argument that says that the most innovative adopters (i.e. those companies which are the most likely to try something new and therefore be interested in your software) aren't interested in analyst perspectives as they are too mainstream. In other words, those companies which seek the reassurance of an analyst endorsement are too conservative to try anything new anyway, and therefore aren't a good target for you.

The other thing to remember is that analysts tend to have a broad brush approach and focus on enterprise systems. The IT business is infinitely

---

[42] Gartner's Magic Quadrants are a standard Gartner presentation methodology which uses a square divided into four quadrants to competitively position firms ranked by 'completeness of vision' and 'ability to execute'. Everyone wants to be in the top right quadrant!

complex and, if you are operating in a specialist niche you'll be flying under the analyst's radar so they don't matter.

Unfortunately you may well be flying under the radar from a research perspective but you may not be flying under the radar from their sales perspective. The first thing an analyst company wants to do is sign you up as a client. With the bigger companies this costs a lot of money (think of it costing the equivalent of a mid-ranking headcount per year), and they can be quite aggressive with a professional sales force not used to taking no for an answer. Hang tough.

Officially, you'd be paying for access to the firm's research, and, depending on the package to which you subscribe, you may be able to commission research and talk to individual analysts to understand the market, and so on. You are not paying to be featured in an analyst's reports. The firms make a big play of the fact that their reports are unbiased and honest.

However, the salesperson may hint that once you are a client you will have greater access to the individual analysts so the analysts will understand your offering in more detail and therefore it's much more likely that you'll be featured in their reports[43]. There can be no doubt that, if an individual analyst has never heard of you, you can't feature in their analysis and reports. Likewise it follows that the more contact you have with an individual analyst, the better they will understand your product and positioning and therefore the higher the likelihood that you will feature in their analysis and reports. So why not just sign up? Answer: because generally it's not worth it, you'd be better off spending the money on increasing your headcount!

So, I'm sure the next question on your mind is: how do analysts know about and write about companies who aren't clients?

The answer is an analyst briefing. All vendors have an ability to apply to brief an analyst. You'll need to do the research and work out which analyst it is you want to brief (just check their website), and then email or fill in a form

---

[43] Despite persistent rumours that Gartner operates a 'pay-to-play' system and regularly being sued by aggrieved vendors, Gartner has consistent won such challenges. Most recently against Netscout Systems Inc. as reported by The Register here: https://tinyurl.com/tc7u55m

as required. Take care with your request and include the buzzwords the analyst you are targeting follows. Mention the names of real clients, ideally household or industry names. If you are lucky you'll then get a half hour telephone briefing. In that half hour you'll need to put forward a convincing pitch as to why your company/product matters and why they should pay attention!

Be very aware that the purpose is not for you to ask questions of the individual analyst – for that you have to pay. The analyst is in listening mode and may, but doesn't always, ask questions. It can be a bit like talking to a blank wall.

The key to a successful analyst briefing is to tell them something they don't know. These people make their living by appearing more knowledgeable than everyone else on a market sector/technology/whatever. If you can add to their knowledge, the briefing will go well, you'll begin to build up a relationship with the analyst and your next application will be accepted.

I mentioned in The PleaseTech Story that we managed to create a virtuous circle with our knowledge of document review practices. The more we emerged as a thought leader, the more people with tricky document review problems contacted us. This meant that we got to understand a wide range of the document review challenges inherent in major blue chip companies. The more we understood of these tricky review processes, the more authoritative we sounded, and the more discussions over such tricky problems came our way!

In our analyst briefings, we were explaining to the analysts the document review challenges in the real world. This was valuable information for them and ultimately led to us being deemed a 'Cool Vendor in Social Software and Collaboration' by Gartner in 2013.

So, with your vendor briefing, you'll want to set the scene with respect to your company, product and positioning, but the critical part of the presentation is why it matters. To address this, use real world examples of business problems your customers face and explain how your software helped solve them. There is nothing so convincing as real world examples!

Be aware that, as soon as you have requested an analyst briefing, if you weren't on the sales team's radar previously, you will be thereafter. Be prepared for a call. It becomes a bit of a game. They want you as a client and you want to brief their analysts. Therefore, my strategy was never to reject the sales team outright but to suggest that you see value in their offering and hint that maybe next year you'll have the budget to do something.

Does being a sales prospect for the firm mean you are more likely to succeed in your request for an analyst briefing? The analyst firms would claim not. I'm not sure I believe them. Think about it, if you were the salesperson trying to close the deal wouldn't you be damn sure to convince the analyst to take the briefing?

The game continues. Whilst we didn't sign up as a Gartner (or any other big firm) client, eventually we did commission research from a smaller boutique firm. This was not only much cheaper but it also meant that we were able to publish research from an independent analyst firm. The analysts read each other's research and, once you are on the analyst's radar, you are more likely to be featured in other firms' analysis and reports.

By the way: if you are working with a smaller boutique firm, you can change your tune in response to the larger firm's sales calls. I used to give them hope along the lines of 'we are dipping our toe in the water with a small firm which is a lot cheaper but we recognised this is limited. If it works out then I see no reason why we wouldn't want to upgrade next year'.

So my advice is:

1. Whilst you are small and establishing yourself, ignore the analysts completely.

2. Once you have a head of steam, have established a client base and have a proven solution to a clear business problem, start an analyst briefing programme. You don't need a specialist to do this - you can do it in-house.

3. Be wary of being pigeon-holed in a particular category. Analysts have a broad brush approach and want to lump similar vendors together in sectors[44]. If applicable, be sure to emphasise that you are

---

[44] See the bit about why we never launched PleaseShare in Market Perception above.

a point solution to a critical business problem and you are not trying to compete with the leaders in a particular sector.

4. Steel yourself for the salesperson's calls and always leave them with hope you'll eventually be a client.

5. Try and establish a relationship with the individual analyst. Follow them on Twitter, like and share their LinkedIn posts, send them the results of research you've undertaken with a personal note, etc. Generally, analysts want to be loved but, more importantly, they want to be thought of as market gurus. Stroke their ego.

6. Ultimately, as you get bigger, make a decision as to whether you want to spend money on research and, if so, search out the smaller boutique firms. These are frequently run by analysts previously employed by the big guns and are usually very cost effective.

In my brief research for this section I came across the Institute of Industry Analyst Relations (IIAR). They have a best practice paper on their website entitled 'Who are industry analysts and what do they do?'[45] which is well worth a read if you are new to the topic. In terms of understanding the game from an analysts' perspective I can recommend, from the same organisation, the article by Alan Pelz-Sharpe, 'Dealing with AR'[46] – where AR stands for 'analyst relations'. It's a bit old (2008) but is surprisingly blunt and nothing has changed.

Before we leave the analysts section, it's worth mentioning a different 'analyst' approach which I've come across. These companies undertake research on a market sector and may invite you to participate or, at least, confirm the facts about your company they've gathered in their research. They then publish a massive report and try and sell you a copy. Their business model is predicated on the fact that you want to check what they've said about you. They may also try and sell you re-publishing rights,

---

[45] The article is here: https://tinyurl.com/s2a3fkx
[46] The article is here: http://tinyurl.com/y6bclbjy. I pitched to Alan several times during the PleaseTech days! When I told him (via LinkedIn) I was going to reference this article in this book he re-read it and concluded that he must have been having a bad day when he wrote it!

and so on. These reports weren't cheap (several thousand pounds comes to mind) and we rapidly learnt to ignore them.

There is a lot of cynicism about industry analysts and it's not hard to find articles criticising them and their business methods. Alan Pelz-Sharpe alludes to this in his above referenced article, when he writes "I know that most analysts make their money by selling 'independent' analysis to the very people they claim to be 'independent' of". The simple fact is that, like everyone selling marketing services, analysts are ultimately trying to part you from your money by promising to give you marketing insights that will make you successful. Like them or loathe them, they can be useful if you know how to play the game.

PleaseTech's Cartoon Programme

Penultimately, I'm going to mention PleaseTech's cartoon programme. I cover it because I believe that this was one of the most effective marketing programmes we did, and whilst I'm not suggesting something similar will work for everyone, having a unique differentiator which immediately stands out is a key component of a marketing strategy.

As you can probably tell, I've always been a great fan of cartoons. One of the first things I do on a daily basis is check out a couple of cartoon sites for my daily fix of Dilbert and Alex[47]. In fact, in my experience, there are very few people who don't like cartoons!

At PleaseTech, one of the challenges we faced with PleaseReview was explaining what it did and why it mattered! So in 2009 we took a page of the website which had a lot of verbiage (relating to the current inefficient way people reviewed documents) and converted it into cartoon strips[48]. The idea was that people are much more likely to read the cartoons (which got the message across in a simple humorous way) than a long page of tedious text. The feedback was so positive we created some more cartoons and then some more ...

---

[47] Alex by Peattie & Taylor is here: https://www.alexcartoon.com. I assume everyone reading this book is familiar with Dilbert!

[48] We simply searched for an independent cartoonist and ended up working with Mark Wood who illustrated this book and can be found via markwoodcartoonist.co.uk

In fact, we soon heard from prospects that they were downloading the cartoons and using them in in-house presentations to explain what was wrong with their document review processes[49]! They clearly got our message across very effectively.

We ended up using the cartoons as a key part of our marketing. We created infographics, we created movies (i.e. animated them) which we had on the website and playing at the booth. I've already mentioned how at large shows, you'd see delegates walking past the long line of booths glancing at them but stopping at ours to watch the cartoon.

I have to admit there was one sticky moment on the booth when a client questioned why the hapless 'star' of our cartoons was called 'Norm'. I was a bit confused by the question until I noticed his name badge which proudly stated that his name was, you guessed correctly, 'Norman'! I just blamed the cartoonist!

We developed cartoon postcards and had these on the booth as literature. People would take them to give to their colleagues as they related to the challenges explored. We involved our clients by asking them to come up with document review practices from their experience which we could 'cartoonise'. For those we accepted their reward was a personalised cartoon.

We had a whole separate cartoon website where we regularly uploaded cartoons about current world events imagining how they would be different if there had been a better document review process in place[50]!

It may sound like that all we did was think of cartoons! Maybe that's not so far from the truth. It is fair to say that I always looked at the news wondering how we could get a document review cartoon out of the events being described. However, the fact remains that this approach was extremely cost effective (each cartoon was not expensive) and provided a clear differentiator. We stood apart from the standard 'corporate output' and, I

---

[49] See the PleaseTech website via the WayBackMachine here: https://tinyurl.com/y3zfpj9o
[50] Some of these are currently available to view on Mark's website: https://tinyurl.com/yykohx6d

like to think, gave prospects a warm feeling about the company. Afterall, a sense of humour is one of the keys factors in likability!

Other Marketing Miscellany

Finally, we come to the end of marketing. I've aimed to cover the main topics of a marketing programme. This section covers off some additional thoughts on marketing related stuff that doesn't merit a section on its own or fit in anywhere else!

Building up a marketing list of suspects and prospects to whom you want to send regular mailshots is, of course, a good thing to do and has been the traditional mainstay of marketing campaigns. In the UK (and Europe) the GDPR legislation has made this a lot more complex[51]. The rules are fairly simple and there are GDPR compliant mailing systems around to help you.

We'd sold PleaseTech before (the nightmare that is) GDPR made its appearance and therefore I have no direct experience of it. I'm therefore restricting my mailing list advice to a simple: don't harass people. Use the list sparingly and think through why you are emailing them. I'm sure you hate getting spam just as much as anyone.

As always, put yourself in the recipient's shoes. Pretend you are the client. What would you like to receive and how often would you like to receive it? There is no surer way of teeing someone off than frequently sending them a load of irrelevant tosh. You need to ensure that your sparing communications are relevant, succinct and interesting!

Continuing the theme of relevant, succinct and interesting, a key requirement is to get decent content for your website. You may recall I mentioned under the website section that I was 'somewhat adverse' to websites which just contain high level marketing waffle. I maintain my stance but would suggest that content doesn't all have to be plain old boring text.

At PleaseTech we created a wide range of infographics, animated videos and so on. The availability and cost of the tools to make such content have never

---

[51] This is not the place to address the requirements of GDPR and there is plenty of information available on the web some of which actually gives good advice! As with all such things it's best to get your advice from an independent source rather than a consultant or organisation with a vested interest.

been better so there is no excuse to have your website populated solely with text however elegantly it may be written. A couple of late nights with VideoScribe or similar and you can have decent dynamic content.

Having an informal personal blog worked well for us at PleaseTech. It was mainly my mouthpiece to clients and prospects. My approach was to write the sort of stuff I'd say to a client if I dropped into see them. How we were doing, what my thoughts on the latest market developments were, why our latest release was delayed, etc. Clearly there is a balance as it's in the public domain and you don't want to be too candid! But something genuine which isn't the standard marketing drivel can enhance the perception of your business and get pertinent information across. It gives you a chance to put your spin on events. For example, we delayed the release because we weren't happy with the quality and we'd rather delay a release than release a poor quality product. No client is going to argue with that approach!

I address working with partners under the Partners section. Don't forget that partners can be a good source of market information, intelligence and content. Joint webinars in which you and the partner promote the webinar to your own lists helps get your name to people who may not have you on their radar. Partners may have white papers you can reference and so on. This ingratiates you with the partner and helps you, all good.

Marketing controls the message and the polished veneer you represent to the outside world. It brings to mind the old analogy of the swan gliding gracefully over the surface but paddling like hell underneath it. Your messaging should always be positive and reassuring, no matter how hard you are pedalling. The key thing is to make sure that neither you nor your staff believe your own bullshit!

A Final Word on Marketing

Marketing is not rocket science. Perhaps the most obvious reason it isn't rocket science is that there is no magic marketing formula you can use to get your spaceship launched. Each company will need a different marketing mix and marketing approach.

In my opinion too many companies simply throw money at the problem without thinking through their approach and what will work. Why are they doing stuff? Is it because they have thought about it or simply that they have seen other apparently successful companies doing it? The cynic in me says many marketing people do things simply because that is what they know how to do and have always done.

I'd reiterate that in a start-up and smaller company it's about being smart and spending your money wisely. An intelligent, focused marketing campaign requires thought and is not beyond the intelligence of your average CEO and, if you are not doing it yourself, at the very least you need to be able to ask the difficult questions.

Sales

It's a simple fact that B2B software needs to be sold, and eventually this will mean recruiting and employing salespeople. If you come from a techie background the procurement and management of these alien beings probably fills you with dread!

There is no doubt that sales has a bad rap among techies and this, as far as I can tell, is true on both sides of the Atlantic. Fear not! Not all salespeople deserve the reputation of being dishonest and unethical. The best ones are knowledgeable, have a high degree of personal integrity and represent the company professionally, and thereby gain customer respect and trust.

To provide some background, while I've sold an awful lot of software in my time, I've never plied my trade as a targeted salesman. When I entered the software business I did so as a marketing manager and then moved into business development – a role I think is under-appreciated and which I address below. I have employed salespeople in both the UK and the USA. On the whole the recruitment process has been successful but it's difficult to get it right and, as with all recruitment and personnel matters, painful and expensive when you get it wrong. There is no identikit. As with all aspects of your business, the people you need to employ and skillsets required will be different as the business matures and grows.

If you come from the sales side you are probably fairly confident in this respect and will be tempted to skip this chapter. If you do decide to skip, the key takeaway for you is that the type of salesperson you need for a start-up is very different from the type of salesperson you need for a mature product. So, if you've come from a largish company, don't assume that the process you know will be suitable for your new life in start-up land!

Early Days

There is no point in having a sales team and full sales process if your product is immature and you are still working out what will sell and why. You need the right tool (in this case person or people) for the right job.

In the early days of the business your product will be evolving rapidly. If you are moving from a service or other start-up revenue earning approach into developing and offering your own product, you need to understand that selling your own product is a completely different mindset. You call the shots, set the price and you need to make decisions as to future direction and functionality. In short, you have to make decisions as to what you sell.

The problem is that in the early days formal product management will be pretty much non-existent. Therefore, if you put a 'traditional' salesperson into the role it will be their natural inclination to sell whatever is easiest - to take the path of least resistance. Salespeople sell things. It's how they validate their existence and earn their money. Before you think how marvellous that is and what a stupid point I'm making, think through the implications.

The main implication is that important factors like product strategy, technical architecture, etc. will be secondary to making the sale. Allowing a salesperson a free reign is the path to madness or, at least as previously mentioned, a product comprised of a jumble of features that have won orders. So, in the event that you have a successful sales team selling your current bread and butter, it would be a mistake to think you can simply transition them to sort out your new product until it is mature.

You really don't want to get into the culture whereby the salesperson sells what they can and it's the techie's problem to deliver! You want to establish a high quality, stable product that can be rolled out to multiple customers. This needs an innate understanding of what will work, what won't work, whether a feature is achievable, whether it's generic or client specific, etc. Think of the early days of product sales as a constant feedback loop. You need to define exactly what you are selling and how to sell it prior to letting a sales team have a crack.

This is why I strongly suggest you start off by being hands on, selling your own product and really understanding the market and customer motivation. If you are a techie and sales truly isn't your thing then you need to ensure your customer facing person is capable of acting intelligently when discussing options with a potential customer and providing the appropriate feedback. You aren't looking for a 'pure play' targeted salesperson, but for a business development person with a background in a similar position. Or perhaps, for someone with experience of selling systems integration services where the salesperson needs to have a decent technical understanding and needs to work out what is mandatory. Don't be tempted by the confident product salesperson who has sold the large enterprise systems and has hit huge targets in a large company. They'll flounder without the associated support team. Self-sufficiency is what it's all about. You need someone who is multi-skilled.

The main point is that in the early days a decent technical understanding is almost mandatory because when your salesperson is having a discussion with the customer, it is absolutely necessary to know what is possible and what isn't possible. Yes there are some times when it will be necessary to check back with the real techies, but having that basic knowledge will facilitate the process and rapidly establish whether you and the prospect are wasting each other's time!

Selling isn't Hard
There are whole books and websites dedicated to sales techniques, processes and so on. It's not my intention to precis those. Read them by all means, but I can't help feeling that they take the 'science' of sales to the extreme. At the base level sales is a pretty simple process if you get the fundamentals right.

Willing Buyers
A good start is a willing buyer and a willing seller. You are the willing seller and it's so much easier to sell to a willing buyer or, in other words, a company that can benefit from your solution! You can use all the sales techniques in the world but if you don't have a willing buyer you are making a rod for your own back. The very nature of software means that there will be a long term relationship between the vendor and the client and it's as well to start that relationship by selling the customer something which will work for them.

There are, of course, checks and balances within client companies and the purchase decision is rarely one for a single individual. There will be several people who need convincing that your product is a worthwhile investment – another good reason to only attempt to make sales to appropriate prospects. Identifying the purchase decision makers and influencers, and overcoming their objections is key to success. Many sales techniques simply formalise this identification into a structured process.

My approach to identifying this information was simply to ask the prospect to explain the decision making process. If the prospect isn't willing to share this information you have to ask yourself why. What are they hiding? Is there a real opportunity or are they simply wasting your time? In the early days of product maturity, it's not unknown for prospects to spend time picking your brain and then be convinced by an incumbent supplier that they can deliver an equivalent. So you need to check that they are a willing buyer and, I believe, transparency is very much part of that process. If they aren't prepared to put you in front of their colleagues fairly quickly question why that may be!

Just because they are a willing buyer doesn't mean there aren't going to be objections or concerns. Teasing out these concerns is more art than science. It all goes back to the conversation you should be having with your prospect and, once again, asking outright is frequently the best strategy. Sometimes the objection or concern is within your control and you can address it. Sometimes it's entirely outside of your control and you need to consider whether to spend more time with the prospect or focus your energies elsewhere.

In fact, there is an argument that, in a sales process, it's almost as valuable to get a firm 'no' as it is a 'yes'. If you are ultimately going not going to close the deal, the earlier you find that out that you are flogging a dead horse the better. You can stop wasting your time and move onto greener pastures.

Be realistic in your objectives. Very rarely does a client purchase a huge corporate license of an unproven product from a small unknown vendor. Therefore you are much more likely to sell a small pilot proof of concept project which, if you and the client get it right, will lead to a rollout.

In fact, at PleaseTech as we matured we refused to accept orders from client's who hadn't undertaken an evaluation. Our reasoning was quite simple: There is nothing so onerous as an unhappy client. So our sales position was very simply in that the client had to undertake an evaluation and be happy that the product met their requirements before we would accept their order[52]. This atypical stance (many vendors offer only very controlled evaluations or no evaluations at all) took prospects by surprise

---

[52] The only exception to this rule was when the client had previously used PleaseReview at a previous company and were introducing it into their new company. This gave us the confidence they knew what they were doing.

especially as we doubled down on this by demanding that the evaluation team undertake a free training session prior to the evaluation commencing.

It certainly sorted the wheat from the chaff. If the prospect can't commit to undertaking a free evaluation of the software they profess to being interested in purchasing, how committed are they and how much of your time will they waste not committing? In demanding the evaluation we were showing confidence in our product. In undertaking an evaluation the prospect is investing in the process and taking ownership. This was a good thing as, if the evaluation went well, they'd effectively made the decision to buy

Our approach also meant that the process was low risk for the client. We were effectively selling a free evaluation. What's not to like?

In summary, sell to someone who genuinely needs your software and work hard to make it low risk for them.

Identifying Willing Buyers (i.e. Qualification)

You've got some enquiries and you've got to work out whether they are real prospects or just have a passing interest (suspects). A real prospect is a prospective client who not only has a genuine need for your solution but is prepared to do the work and commit the time to further investigate it.

Sorting out those actually likely to buy and therefore worth spending your time and effort on, compared to those who are interested but are ultimately not going to move forward, is called qualification. There is an old sales mantra: qualify, qualify, qualify. However, the mistake classically trained salespeople make in the early days of a business is over qualification. It's easy to rule out everyone and have nothing left in the sales pipeline. Granted, you only want real prospects in the sales pipeline but, when you first start a business, every lead is hard won and therefore valuable. Treat them with respect and nurture them.

The first stage in the qualification process is to understand where the lead came from. If someone has visited your website and completed a 'contact us' form or sent an email, I'd argue that that is a pretty strong lead. Someone has taken the time to find your website, presumably read it and then think that it's worth contacting you.

Leads from a show are somewhat different. Unless you (or the booth personnel at the time) were able to determine a need in the booth conversation, you'll need to qualify. Don't make the mistake of sending a generic marketing email as a follow-up (unless the contacts are from card drops), as the prospect will have received many of those in the days after the event. What is required is a nice personal email[53] reminding them of who you are and what you do[54] and any follow-up actions agreed on the booth. The general test is to include a call to action i.e. ask them something which requires a response. This will be your first gauge of interest.

Remember that your prospect is a busy person and if they don't respond then that doesn't necessarily mean that they are not interested. It may just mean that the day job is getting in the way[55]. For example, when we were selling to the proposals market, we rapidly learnt that when there was a major bid underway everything else was ignored. Patience was a virtue as eventually the bid would be submitted and people would come up for air again!

Therefore a gentle reminder after a couple of weeks is the approach I'd recommend. In PleaseTech, if they hadn't got back to us after several reminders, we used to send them what I called a 'Dear John' email. It said that despite several follow-ups they hadn't got back to us and that therefore we assume that the requirement was no longer on their immediate radar and we would no longer proactively follow-up but that they knew where we were if their interest reactivated. You'd be surprised how many people then replied confirming that they remained interested but that they were too busy to do anything right away.

---

[53] I say 'email' but you can of course try calling them. It's my experience that it is very hard to get hold of busy people by phone and leaving a voice mail is, I believe, counterproductive. Personally, I hate receiving voice mails which say something like: 'Hi this is Fred, I was trying to get hold of you but will call again'. Better to send an email saying that you tried to call, got voice mail but didn't leave one. I believe that the prospect will be grateful you didn't clutter up their voice mail system.

[54] This is really important as delegates will have spoken with multiple vendors and won't remember each one individually.

[55] If they've been at a conference for a few days they'll have some catching up to do!

This, of course, leads to another challenge – that of working out whether they'd ever be sufficiently free to engage with you. But at least there was a response! Sometimes it was the catalyst that got the whole process moving.

Classic qualification methodology uses something called 'BANT' which stands for Budget, Authority, Needs, and Timeline. Whilst these are ultimately all important aspects of a deal, it is thankfully being recognised that BANT isn't necessarily suitable for the modern day era! I generally ignored the budget aspect until towards the end of the process. Just because there isn't an allocated budget shouldn't mean qualifying the prospect out. I think it's more a question of affordability. So long as the prospect knows the order of magnitude of the costs, one can safely assume that they won't be wasting their time with you if they didn't think they could swing the budget. Typically large corporates will have the budget slack to be able to run unscheduled pilots and make non-budgeted purchases via their contingency.

Clearly, it depends on how much you are charging. If it's enterprise scale systems with prices to match, you have to take a long term view. Sometimes the purpose of sales activity is simply to get into the budget for next year! However, we advertised on our website and in the initial sales presentation the broad cost per user so the prospect was in no doubt as to the monetary investment. There is no point in trying to hide the costs as, if the client can't afford it and gets a shock later on in the process, you've wasted your time.

The most important thing from my perspective was 'need'. I go back to my pain equation. Were they suffering sufficient pain to make it likely that they were a good prospect? There is no big secret to qualification. Basically learn as much about the prospect as possible, ask some pertinent questions and take a judgement as to whether they are worth pursuing.

When you are doing this yourself you can make judgement calls. As the business grows you will be a more formal sales qualification process but bear in mind that some of the prospects need months and even years of nurturing. It is unlikely your targeted salespeople will have the patience for this nurturing as they have targets to achieve. This is why you need a means of passing such prospects to a business development function which has longer term, more strategic considerations and targets.

Sales Process

In the early days the sales process may be a bit chaotic. So long as you go through the basic steps you will prevail. What are the basic steps? For a software product they are generally: demo, evaluation, purchase.

In PleaseTech we developed a sales process which we explained to the prospect up front so there were no surprises. At each stage we were looking for increasing commitment from the prospect. From a lead and an initial conversation (whether by email or telephone) we aimed to gain a commitment to a remote demo. Occasionally we would have someone want a demo for themselves prior to committing to promote it to a wider internal audience. I was always happy to do this as they were protecting their reputation and didn't want to waste their colleagues' time. It actually reassured me that I was dealing with someone sensible. We were in principle happy to provide as many remote demos as necessary to get to the next stage which was the aforementioned evaluation.

A successful evaluation almost always led to a purchase! Sometimes, we'd get to the evaluation stage and the client wouldn't actually do the evaluation and the evaluation system sat there idle. This could be for many reasons. Generally it meant that their pain was not sufficiently overwhelming to interfere with the day job. That's life. Not every prospect will turn into a client.

What we didn't do was say to the prospect 'this is our process'. We'd say something like 'what we find works well for most clients is …' leaving it open to change if the prospect objected. Typically they were happy to go with the flow. Whether the above process works for you or not, as you grow, it's important to develop the basis of a repeatable process.

In most sales processes, it is necessary to find and support an internal champion. Someone in the prospective client company who is going to push the product internally. Frequently this is the individual who visited the booth or made the initial enquiry. They make the internal running and arrange the demos, led the evaluations, etc. However, it's not unknown for that person to delegate moving the project forward to a colleague if they are max'd out. The secret to handling this is to maintain your relationship with both parties but not to bombard the original contact with emails or copy them in on everything. Keep in touch, perhaps give them a progress report on significant milestones, and if you are making no headway, you have kept open the opportunity to go back to them.

A sales process is about engaging with the prospect and gaining more and more commitment at each stage, generally you can tell how you are doing through communication. If the prospect is responding to you, asking questions and is engaged it's going well. If communication stops (unless there is a specific reason such as the aforementioned focus on a proposal or similar) be afraid, be very afraid.

Sales Demos

A critical part of the software sales cycle is the presentation and demo. A poor presentation and demo can kill the opportunity stone dead. Think about it from the client's perspective, not only have they convinced a bunch of their colleagues that it would be worth their while understanding your product, they've gone to a lot of effort to make available a number of very busy people at the same point in the space time continuum. That in itself is quite a commitment. If you turn up and bore the pants off them with a 'death by a thousand bullet points' presentation and a demo which they don't understand, not only have you lost them, you've probably made an enemy of the internal champion who pushed your case. Generally there is no way back.

The presentation and demo needs to be succinct, pertinent and understandable. You'd be surprised how many boring presentations and incomprehensible demos your average corporate executive sits through in a year. Dare to be different. Have an engaging presentation, use graphics (even cartoons!), present information in an interesting way. Develop a demo which tells a story and speaks to their business process. One of the best compliments I've ever had was in the early days of PleaseTech when, after a remote demo, an anonymous voice at the end of the phone line was heard to say 'that's the first demo I've understood this year'!

Involve the prospect. Is there a particular aspect of the business process they want to be covered in more depth? In our case, we'd regularly invite clients to send us one of their own documents which we'd use as the review document in the demo.

The reality is that, in this day and age, a vast majority of such presentations and demos are remote. On the rare occasion I've attended a client site I generally found that a majority of the people were dialled in! Presenting whilst being physically on a client site is usually a nightmare. In no particular order you'll find that the projector is old and can't cope with your graphics resolution, you can't connect to the internet to join the remote meeting the attendees not in the conference room are on, etc. I know what you're thinking! Why didn't he check this stuff in advance! I'm always did but, believe me, don't rely on what you are told. Have a standby plan.

I've had several occasions where I'd checked that I would be able use the company's guest internet only to find that it wasn't available in the allocated conference room or it was down that day. My standby plan for this was to hotspot my phone and use that. Surely that would work? In one company the conference room was underground and therefore there was no mobile signal. Be prepared for everything that can go wrong to go wrong. In case you're wondering, in the underground bunker I used the prospect's laptop to log-onto our online demo system!

There are, of course, many remote presentation products available these days but be sure to check that your choice is permitted through the corporate firewall. Set up a test before you embarrass yourself and your prospect in front of everyone invited. There is nothing worse than having a room full of people eager to see your demo and find that there is no way to project your screen as their corporate systems are blocking the tool you use. The bigger the company the more of a danger this is. If in doubt test beforehand. One option is to have the client set-up the remote meeting using their own software as they know that works. In this case you need to check that you can access it and be made a presenter – not always the case!

There is an art to managing and presenting remote presentations. The first thing you need to work out is whether their screen is keeping up with your screen. Corporate firewalls can be somewhat inefficient and introduce a significant lag. I always used to say: 'What you should be seeing on your screen now is ...'

The second thing you need to understand is that you have no control over what the 'attendees' are doing. Are they all avidly fixated on your presentation or are they ordering their groceries or clearing their in-box? You simply don't know. They may be listening to you but not necessarily paying attention to the screen. I refer you to my previous point about making the presentation interesting and the demo relevant! It's also worth adjusting your patter to ensure that you repeat verbally any important points on your slides or in the demo. That way those concentrating on their in-boxes will pick-up the important bits.

You then get the 'constant interrupters'. Always jumping in with a question or trying to jump ahead. Sometimes you can tell that these people are irritating their colleagues just as much as they are irritating you. Let's not forget the late comers who have missed the first 20 minutes, don't understand what they are seeing, are confused and are fairly voluble about that.

My approach was always to be 'assertive'. You have to command the airways. This is your hour – don't waste it by being too polite.

To deal with the interrupters, I'd explain that we'd be covering a lot in the demo and therefore, unless there was a pressing question about what was on the screen at that time, perhaps they'd be kind enough to hold questions to the end. To deal with the latecomers, I'd normally suggest that they dropped out, allowed the rest to crack on and offer to arrange a one to one presentation at a more convenient time.

As a general point, always leave enough time for questions and a discussion. Establish upfront how long you have. We always asked for an hour and a half. Frequently all we got was an hour! Bear in mind that you never start at the correct time. The meeting start time is frequently the time that the client gets access to the conference room they've booked or when they start to try and dial-in. It is not the time that the presentation starts. Also bear in mind that you can't necessarily overrun as your client may be kicked out of a conference room at the end of the booking. Many will have back to back meetings. So, for an hour's slot, expect to get around 50 minutes of real time if you are lucky. Your presentation should therefore be a maximum of around 15 minutes, the demo should be around 20 - 25 minutes maximum leaving 10 - 15 minutes for a Q&A and discussion. This final part of the session is generally very valuable for you as you get feedback and can broadly judge how it was received. Do not over run and miss it!

There are some, let's call them 'old fashion', salespeople who insist on a face-to-face presentation because that way you get to see the body language and gauge interest from that. I'm sorry to tell them that business has moved on. I've sold hundreds of thousands of dollars of software remotely never having physically been within several thousand miles of the client.

Proposals

Before clients commit they need to know what they are purchasing for how much and on what terms. This is called a proposal. A proposal doesn't have to be a large document. For a software product, a letter proposal (i.e. a letter covering these points) is perfectly adequate. At PleaseTech even the largest deals (and towards the end we are talking hundreds of thousands of dollars) were based on a letter proposal.

Never include 'copy and paste' boilerplate in your proposal document whether it's a letter proposal or a more formal proposal document[56]. Always bear in mind that this document is going to be viewed by busy people who have a day job. They are not going to look kindly on reams of boilerplate from which they need to distil the facts. KISS – Keep it simple. Give a bit of background, the facts, the cost, the terms and that's all you need.

Set out the background (a couple of paragraphs), the license/service they are purchasing (i.e. how many users, of which level, etc. and any associated limitations), the support, the payment terms, reference the license and that is all you need. The license agreement itself was a separate document. In my view the proposal isn't a sales document as such but a factual statement of what they will purchase on what terms.[57]

There is a key sales mantra which is 'when you've sold stop selling'. So, when the client has indicated they are minded to buy, you move into implementation mode, i.e. get the proposal in place or re-validate it, ensure it reflects what was agreed (no surprises) and, if you have read the runes correctly, all they need is a document against which they can raise a Purchase Order (PO). Is it really that simple? Yes!

---

[56] Please, please do not base your proposal on a freely available template. Please. OK, if you must, use the headings but DO NOT use boilerplate text.
[57] Until the PO is received, technically everything is a sales document.

Occasionally, you'll be invited to respond to an RFI or an RFP[58]. We very rarely had these in PleaseTech because we didn't have a direct competitor but they are more common if you are one of several vendors competing in the same space. Responding to RFIs or RFPs is not exactly intellectually challenging, just arduous. You have to go through and answer the questions. The key is to answer in a way which minimises non-compliance, especially in mandatory requirements. If that means you offer to meet that particular requirement by building it (perhaps as a cost option) then, as far as I am concerned, you say you are compliant with the appropriate caveat in the notes![59]

Remember, someone is going to go through the proposals and immediately weed out the most non-compliant responses and only bother to read a subset. The real question is, 'is it worth your responding at all'?

There is a strong argument that says that if you weren't aware of the project before the RFI or RFP arrives then it's a stitch up and the client is just going through their internal processes prior to awarding the contract to the vendor who helped shape the requirements. This will be confirmed if you glance through the requirements and spot some mandatories which you can't do and you know your competitors can!

So, if an RFI or RFP of which you were not previously aware does land in your inbox be wary. It may have been shaped by a competitor who has the inside track and you are just making up the numbers. Many clients need three separate quotes to comply with their internal purchasing process.[60] You will want to talk to the client in some detail prior to spending any time responding. If the client isn't prepared to invest the time talking with you are you prepared to invest the time responding to their request?

At this point, it's worth noting that the difference between an RFI and RFP can be blurred. Sometimes a prospect issues a genuine RFI which is a formal

---

[58] An RFI (Request for Information) typically becomes before an RFP (Request for Proposal).

[59] It's important to include the caveats as occasionally the RFP and your answers are referenced in the formal contract. The caveat is your get out of jail clause.

[60] This actually caused us quite a lot of grief. When you are selling a unique product which no one else offers, the client can't obtain three separate quotes. Most of the time the purchasing process can be circumvented but, occasionally, to get around this, we'd have to ask a couple of friendly partner companies to provide a quote.

request to learn more about your products, company and the costs associated with your solution prior to deciding a shortlist for an RFP. For some of the larger companies an RFI is mandatory before an RFP, which is mandatory before a PO.

The main point with RFPs is that you shouldn't automatically respond. You will still want to talk to the prospect in some detail before committing the necessary time and effort. What are they looking for? What are their selection criteria? Are you ruled out because you are too small? Do they have an established vendor? Knowledge is power. If you do respond take heed of my note above that you need to do it in a way which minimises non-compliance.

Some more observations on proposals:

1. Always have an expiry date on your proposals such as 'this proposal is valid for 30 days', or whatever. I've been caught previously. After we'd raised our prices (see pricing), a client's purchasing department demanded to place a PO against a six month old proposal because it hadn't expired.

2. Always have someone check proposals for spelling, grammar and numbers. As you grow and multiple people generate proposals (i.e. the sales team) this becomes especially important. In PleaseTech no proposal could leave the building unless it had been checked by the 'spelling and grammar police' and accounts had checked the numbers. The spelling and grammar are purely about professionalism. The numbers are crucial as it's really hard to claw it back if you've managed to mess up the numbers and offer an unintended discount.

3. No matter how complicated your proposals, always make the purchase order amount very clear. Purchasing people are not on your side and if it's not absolutely obvious how much the purchase order should be for they'll conspire to get it wrong. They never get in wrong in your favour.

4. Presentation of figures is important. Once again it's important to remember that people who are not intimately acquainted with the deal and your software are going to review and potentially approve

the order. Even if we were selling a perpetual on-premise license we made sure that the 'cost per user' was prominent. For example, if a license costs $250,000 for 3,000 users it is only $83 per user. I'd suggest that whoever is approving the PO should have the $83 per user figure front and centre rather than the $250,000.

5.   Always include a rider that explains that VAT and or Sales Tax is not included. Also that the proposal is subject to your software license terms and conditions.

In summary, unless there is a more formal RFP process involved, your selling should have been concluded by the time you submit your proposal - which should simply be a document against which an order can be pleased. Keep it simple, factual and accurate.

Closing the Deal
There are whole books written around closing techniques. You're welcome to read them but I suspect you'll find them more appropriate for selling to individuals than to businesses[61]. If you have a unique product and have set the expectations correctly at the start of the process and the process is correct, the logical conclusion is a PO. So the whole sales process is designed to be a closing technique leading irresistibly towards the final order.

Having said that you could have the best sales process in the world but if the product doesn't meet the need, have a good ROI or solve real pain, you aren't going to get an order no matter how refined your closing techniques![62] Let's assume that you do solve real pain, what are the key aspects of closing the deal?

The first thing to make sure the prospects understand is that you are working with them because you want to sell them a license. This is a professional transaction the purpose of which is to ascertain whether your product is suitable for their needs and, if so, you'd like an order please! Ask

---

[61] There is a game I like to play much to the annoyance of my wife. When someone is trying to sell us something I like to count and identify the closing techniques used and then, after the meeting, give my wife a run down of them.

[62] If you read the PleaseTech story you'll read understand that our first XML publishing offering failed to sell despite getting great feedback. It didn't solve pain and didn't offer an ROI so no one brought it. It wasn't because I forgot how to sell overnight!

your prospect what their timescales are and the steps they need to go through to get an order approved.

A common mistake made by inexperienced salespeople is not to ask for the order! The client has undertaken a successful evaluation and you submitted a proposal for the agreed user numbers, it's time to ask for the PO. Don't be shy.

Just because the prospect wants to purchase doesn't necessarily mean you will get the order immediately. The prospect will need to initiate the purchasing process, the output of which should be a PO - the larger the company the more hurdles there are and the longer it will take. This process can lead to a period of paralysis in which not a lot appears to be happening as the order has got stuck/become lost/whatever in the purchasing/legal/IT/whatever department in the client company.

It's difficult to accelerate purchasing paralysis. You can try, but the bottom line is that companies have a process through which they go to issue a PO, and once the purchase order process is initiated it's not all over – it's just beginning! You need to keep on top of this process but it will be outside of your hands and probably outside of your champion's hands. I've seen many clients frustrated by their own purchasing procedures! You can do little but gently prod, respond promptly to their correspondence, and wait it out.

Occasionally, you'll get a purchasing department wanting to justify their existence by beating your price down. This is covered under the pricing and discounting section below but, spoiler alert, don't do it. Very rarely does a purchasing department have the power to prevent a PO if they don't get a discount - unless you are selling standardised widgets. When you are selling unique, highly functional business software they are trying it on. In order to encourage you not to skip the pricing and discounting section despite the spoiler, in it I tell a little story about this and how I dealt with it at PleaseTech.

Salespeople talk about 'compelling events' and try and manufacture deadlines to compel the client to place an order in their desired timelines. Most of this is a waste of time. Ultimately, I believe that almost every deal has its own symmetry and will come in 'when it's ready'. There is little point in trying to 'rush' sales through an organisation. Once it's in progress it's in progress – it will pop out of the process eventually. Sometimes sooner than expected, sometimes later than expected. Clearly you need to monitor progress and chivvy it along but do not be tempted to try and rush it through to meet some artificial deadline. You'll rarely succeed and expend a lot of energy which would be best used elsewhere.

Having said that, time of year is important. If you are selling to large companies at the end of their financial year and therefore their budget year[63], you have a compelling event. It's the biggest compelling event that there is. Throughout my business career, no matter how hard I've fought against it, Q4 and Q1 have always been the big sales quarters. Q4 because companies are trying to spend their budgets which are allocated on a 'use it or lose it' basis and Q1 because new budgets have been allocated and people can spend the money, or because it's spill over from the previous year.

It's important to position yourself for the end of budget year spend. Remember that companies will have an 'invoice receipt' cut off which is typically in the middle of December. So be prepared to work very hard in Q4[64]. One year we got a call from a client which went along the following lines: We have some surplus budget and have allocated $800,000 to PleaseReview. Can I please have a quote today and we will need the invoice at the same time! Our response? No problem at all, sir!

It's also worth noting that I've also experienced the downside of this spending frenzy. We were expecting an order in Q4 and, despite client promises, nothing was happening. I eventually got to the bottom of the problem. The client was having to spend so much money in Q4 that the purchasing department wasn't even going to look at deals under £500k until the following year. Unfortunately, we were not a $500k plus deal. There was no way we were going to close the deal that year and it would spill over!

Finally, a critical point in closing deals is to be an easy company with which to do business. Although software is traditionally sold in US Dollars, quote in the currency of the client[65]. You might argue that it's not your job to take the

---

[63] Typically the end of the calendar year – but not always

[64] PleaseTech always used to have its annual Christmas party in January because December was simply too busy.

[65] At PleaseTech we offered our price list as standard in US Dollars, UK pounds and Euros although we did quote in South African Rand, Australian Dollars and quite a

foreign exchange risk. Whose job is it? You can be pretty sure that all the client wants is certainty as their budget won't vary with the exchange rate.

Have a software license that is clear, fair and not onerous on the client. It makes it so much easier to negotiate and, by definition, a reduced negotiating period means a faster order. Look at the way you handle client negotiations. Are you trying to make it easy for the client? If not, why not? I've seen so many companies whose attitude is confrontational when it's in their interests to cooperate. You don't give way on important matters but there is little point in fighting over clauses that don't make a material difference.

In summary, there are two aspects to closing a deal in B2B sales. The first is getting the department initiating the purchase to raise a PO request. The second is the navigation through the purchasing process. In my experience, you can attempt to shift heaven and earth by manufacturing artificial deadline after artificial deadline to try and hasten the process but it's generally not worth the effort. Get the sales process right and the purchasing process will be initiated. Be an easy company to do business with and the purchasing process will be faster and less painful. Simple really.

Client References
At some stage in the sales process the prospective client may ask for an existing client reference[66]. My strong advice is to put this off as long as possible. Guard your client references closely and use them sparingly for they are valuable and, unfortunately, much abused!

Unless contracted (see discounts below), you need to understand that your clients are doing you a favour by acting as a reference. These are typically very busy people and there's nothing in it for them. In fact, it's something they could do without. It's not helped by some prospects who seem to think they can treat client referees as they treat the vendor. Unfortunately, on several occasions, after arranging a client reference and making the introductions, I found that my reference client had arranged and waited for

---

few other currencies. By all means build in some slack, all the client is looking for is certainty!

[66] In many industries people will be taking informal client references from their industry contacts. Therefore it generally a good idea to treat every client as a potential client reference!

a call only to be stood up by the prospect. Subsequently some weak excuse was put forward. This reflects poorly on you and makes it a lot less likely the client will agree to act as a reference again. It also means that the client reference wasn't as important as you'd perceived it to be!

So you need to qualify the real need for a client reference and delay any introductions as long as possible. The simple fact is that some clients ask for these references as a matter of course and at a fairly early stage in the sales process. If asked, simply agree to provide references at an appropriate juncture. Only make the introductions when it's clear that having a satisfactory client reference is one of the critical things stopping the purchase order.

Licensing Models

For those who believe that everything these days is priced per user per month (aka a subscription model), it may come as a bit of a shock to learn that there are other strategies! So let's examine them.

A perpetual license: This is the traditional license granted for the client to use the software in perpetuity. An upfront one-off license fee was paid and the client had use of the software forever. I still have a copy of Microsoft Office 2007 sitting on my shelf. I have a perpetual license to use it and could, if I wished, install it again.

A term license: This provides for the client to use the software for a specific term. One year, eighteen months, five years, etc. It follows that the software contains an activation key that allows it to work for a specific period.

A subscription service: This is the more modern per user per month approach to licensing the use of the service. I use the term 'service' rather than 'software' because it's not just about use of the software but it's availability (i.e. Service Level Agreement (SLA)) and so on.

It should be noted that the license models are not dependent on whether they are provisioned via on-premise or hosted. The term 'cloud service' is synonymous with a subscription service while traditionally on-premise licenses were perpetual. However, you can provide (and we did) term licenses for on-premise installation and hosted perpetual licenses. I'm not saying it's a good idea, but I am saying that sometimes you have to think outside the box.

When considering 'per user' pricing you have the option of charging per registered user or using some form of a concurrent user model. Both are equally valid and your approach will depend on the software you provide. If the software is something a very wide variety of users will use occasionally then charging per registered user may make your licensing model uneconomical for the client. If you then lower the cost per user to make it economical for the client, you may have reduced the cost per user too far to make small deals economical for you. This is where concurrency comes in.

The thing to watch in concurrency is time zones. For a truly concurrent license users in Japan and the USA can share a concurrent license as they will very rarely be online together. Therefore you need to think through the consequences of licensing schemes. In PleaseTech, we offered two licensing schemes. There was the standard registered user license scheme and an 'Active' user licensing scheme. The latter scheme was not dissimilar to a concurrent model but addressed the time zone issue!

The beauty of software is that it is infinitely flexible and you can invent and offer schemes that make sense for your user base. The trick is to keep it simple and ensure that the client has a clear definition of when a license is charged and when it isn't.

A final thought considering site or unlimited licenses. This is something we never provided. We always had limits. Let's consider the scenarios:

1. Unlimited Corporate license: an unlimited license for corporation XYZ Inc to use the software. What happens when XYZ Inc is acquired by a company twice its size? Or when XYZ Inc decides it's strategy is growth by acquisition? You could easily end up in a situation when your software is being used by double the number of people for no additional license fee and, importantly, no increase in support charges.

2. Site license: what is a site these days?

My advice would be to avoid any form of unlimited licenses. Always have a cap. Apart from the scenarios discussed above, unlimited licenses can also complicate sub-licensing of 3rd party technology. As you grow your product's functionality you are more than likely to end up sub-licensing 3rd party specialist technology, and those licensees are generally not happy about providing unlimited licenses to your clients.

Moving onto the annual maintenance and support charge; if you are providing a cloud service the subscription fee typically incorporates support and, by definition, maintenance. For perpetual licenses this charge is typically around 20% of the original license fee per year.

It's called 'maintenance and support' because it covers two separate things.

Maintenance concerns maintenance upgrades. All successful software vendors keep investing in and developing their software and, by paying the annual maintenance, the clients are buying into future releases of the software. So maintenance upgrades, which I would expect to include functional enhancements, are provided to clients under maintenance for free.

Support is the traditional access to support personnel to cover troubleshooting, usability support, etc.

When you develop a software product you need to consider your licensing strategy and have appropriate controls built into the software. If, for example, you charge per user you need to have a mechanism to control the number of users. Likewise different user types will require similar controls. If you offer term licenses you'll need a means of controlling the term and reactivating or extending said term. This stuff is expensive to change (in terms of development time) so it's something which needs to be considered in advance.

It's worth noting that not every software product is best charged by the user. Sometimes a charge per server is more appropriate or a combination of the two. In CDC, EZ*subs* was licensed per server. This was because publishing was a specialist subject and, even in the largest companies, you'd be unlikely to have more than five or six users. $50,000 per user can be a difficult sell and what happens if they decide they only wanted two users, so we sold a server license with unlimited users. It was different for our other product, PDF*aqua*. This was rolled out to multiple users and therefore charged on a per user basis with a one-off server charge which provided an base level license fee even if there weren't many users.

Some large corporates still prefer to purchase a perpetual license upfront as this initial license fee can be classed as a capital item and depreciated over time, whereas the subscription charges are considered a direct business expense.

Let's also not forget that there are several advantages to the traditional upfront license fee model for your company. The main one is that you get more money sooner and this has a very positive impact on your cash flow! One of the softer benefits is that the client may be more committed to your software. Having spent a large chuck of change on it upfront there is an imperative to get it implemented and delivering the promised ROI.

A subscription model offers a long term gain over a short term hit. The money comes in over time and doesn't give a one-off cash injection and the client's commitment will be weaker. Weaker because if they hit a couple of potholes in the implementation it's a relatively easy decision to abandon the project because the financial investment is significantly less.

The long term gain aspect is based on the premise that, at present, ARR (Annual Recurring Revenue) is more highly valued in company exit valuations because ultimately you will earn more total revenue with the subscription model. This assumes that your software is embedded in the client's business process and that they are committed for the long term.

The answer is, ideally, to offer both. This will take a bit of tinkering with the in-built license model but, if you think about it up front, the overhead won't be that high and the flexibility it will give you will be enormous. Later on in this sales chapter we talk about being an easy company to do business with. Offering the client their preferred license model just makes it easier for everyone!

Pricing

How much to charge for software? It's a difficult question. The answer is: as much as you can!

I've always been a fan of premium pricing. You can always come down in price, it's a lot harder to go up! Many clients are not as price sensitive as you may think. If they are going to invest in your product they want also want to invest in a growing successful business with a vision, not necessarily the cheapest vendor.

Keeping prices low also means that you need to sell a lot more to have a decent business. In The PleaseTech Story I explain how our public subscription service was barely paying its way. The simple lesson was that if you are going offer a low cost service you'd better make sure that it is cheap to sell and that there is high demand. It can be as just as hard to sell a £5,000 deal as a £50,000 deal.[67]

Every software product is different as is every industry. The amount you can charge will depend on whether there is competition, how business critical your product is, and whether it provides a clear ROI. However, there are some basics that are worth addressing.

Creating a price list that encourages companies to purchase more licenses rather than less is par for the course. So the higher the number of licenses a client buys the cheaper the cost per license. You also want to encourage money up front. With cloud licensing this is harder as not many companies will pre-pay future years as it is treated as an annual expense. It's also worth noting that whilst the software is sold as a per user per month cost, you really don't want to be submitting monthly invoices. Getting prepayment for a year is, I would suggest, highly desirable if not mandatory.

When you do your sums make sure you take into account your expenses with each option. For an on-premise sale you don't need to provide hosting, unlike a cloud model where you'll have significant infrastructure overheads. Therefore, in a like for like solution comparison (i.e. for the same number of users), you should charging a lot more for a cloud solution than for an on-premise license.

In PleaseTech we started with on-premise perpetual licenses and then went onto offer term and cloud options. The calculation we did to calculate the term license was to work out what we'd earn (including support) over approximately a three year period for an on-premise license and then divide that by the term and add a bit. So, broadly, if the client used the software for over three years they'd save by paying upfront compared with an annual term license fee. The smarter clients spotted this and wanted not only their

---

[67] One mistake many people make is to target the SME market and find that they are having go through an entire sales process for a £5,000 deal (because to the SME it's a significant sum). At that point the sums don't add up. £50,000 to a major corporate is nothing.

cake but to eat it as well and asked to convert the license to perpetual after three years, in effect, getting zero percent financing. Nope, it doesn't work like that!

For cloud pricing we took the term license as a base and added the costs associated with hosting (and don't forget to include all the security costs, pen testing, personnel overheads, etc.) and a healthy margin. That was then sold on a per user per month basis payable annually. It gets complex when clients add users during the year. The secret is to ensure that everyone on the same license renews their term simultaneously, otherwise it can get into an awful mess[68].

The problem with price lists is that they can rapidly become extremely complex. At one point in PleaseTech we offered two different license schemes, three different user levels in each scheme, the standard tiered pricing (i.e. the more users purchased the lower the cost), various optional software modules, and the options of perpetual and term on-premise licenses with a separate cloud alternative!

The other problem you'll find is that some salespeople are not very good at maths! To help our team cut through the complexity and keep everything consistent, we developed a (protected) spreadsheet which automatically incorporated these multi user discounts, etc. You simply selected your preferred licensing option, typed in the number of each type of user, selected which options were required and the spreadsheet delivered the license cost. It's an overhead to maintain such a spreadsheet but it cuts down on errors and ensures everyone is quoting on the same basis.

Some additional points on pricing.

1. Incorporate some stuff you don't mind giving away on your price list. Despite my rant about discounting (see below), I fully accept the need to make the prospect feel that they managed to negotiate a great deal. So rather than discount the licenses we had things like configuration workshops, remote training sessions and other such services which we could either discount or provide on a

---

[68] Sales don't like this because they want to charge the client for the new users for a full year. I sympathise with this desire but you need to find a way of managing it administratively otherwise the awful mess is a given.

complimentary basis. The way we saw it was we could, within reason, chuck in more or less anything which didn't have direct costs associated with it. Anything to avoid discounting the software itself[69] [70].

2. Consider what is appropriate for different markets. Having separate price lists for separate markets becomes complicated. However, there are some markets which impose high overheads and you need to work out how to recoup these costs. For example, there are inspection overheads (such as audit questionnaires and inspection visits) which apply to the pharmaceutical market that don't apply to other markets. We handled this by having such audit questionnaires and inspection visits as price list items. Did pharmaceutical clients like it? No, they did not. They went to great effort to point out that other vendors provided these things for free! We stuck to our guns and explained that this was an overhead of doing business with them and therefore we either charged them more for their licenses and hide the cost or charged everyone across all industries the same amount and charged for the extras[71].

3. As you grow and the software becomes more functional, there is no reason why you shouldn't raise your prices. We did. We issued a new price list every year and there was only one way it went! Towards the end we also managed to pull off the trick of building in an automatic increase in the annual support contract. It was fixed for the first three years and thereafter went up with an official inflation measure[72]. If you are charging on a subscription basis you'll

---

[69] You will need to account internally for this using an equality of discount approach as discussed in the accounting chapter.

[70] Discounting the software means that your annual support charge is also discounted.

[71] We had some standard boilerplate text which set out our reasoning and most accepted that our approach was rational. It had the added bonus of some clients deciding that auditing us was not a priority after all!

[72] When we presented the increased invoice for year 4, clients generally complained like hell - mainly because they hadn't budgeted for it. So we simply brought goodwill by waiving the increase for the year but asking them to increase their budget for the following year!

need to build in the flexibility to increase the subscription prices in your contract[73].

4.   One means of getting more cash from existing clients is creating optional complementary modules that offer functionality over and above the base and are therefore not included in the maintenance release. Some clients will want the extra functionality and will pay for it. This approach also allows you to have a cheaper base entry level product and a premium offering. However, the trick is to avoid ending up with endless optional modules. The way we handled this was that after about three years or so, some of the more generic module functionality was incorporated into the base product keeping the number of options to an acceptable level.

5.   Carrying on from the above point, at one point we found our pricing model getting too complex and had to simplify it. We consolidated a couple of user types and so on. The problem with making such changes to a price list is how do you handle existing clients? What happens when the client's module is no longer a cost option? When the raft of user types they have are consolidated? So, constant change of the price list is to be avoided. It can create a massive administrative overhead and confused clients. Neither of which are a good thing.

Pricing software is complex. You want to maximise revenue but minimise complexity. It's a difficult juggling act. Understanding how your clients want to purchase and building in flexibility is a good start. Thereafter, it's broadly what you can get away with. Who is to say what software is worth? It's worth what you can sell it for!

Pricing and Delivering Services
Many software companies provide a wide range of implementation and associated services. These are sold alongside the software licenses and can add considerable value to the overall sale.

---

[73] We found the costs associated providing a cloud service rapidly escalated. Not only was there the cost of the underlying infrastructure, there were all the additional security overheads and business continuity overheads, etc.

In neither of my companies did we sell any significant level services. To sell such services you need to build up a professional services team and keep them occupied. There is a general rule of thumb that utilisation needs to be 70% or higher to make a profitable software services business. In the early days you probably aren't going to get consistent business, and therefore can't justify dedicated consultants. As the business grows, if you decide to go down the professional services route there will be a constant juggling act around the number of consultants you have, against the need to keep them occupied, against the need not to hold up deals (and therefore delay revenue) waiting for said busy consultants.

There are practical issues as well. If you are selling globally do your services have to be delivered physically onsite? If so, you have a problem. For example, visiting the USA to do business such as selling, attending conferences, visiting client sites for account management, etc. can be done on a standard ESTA – assuming you and or your staff qualify for one. If you need to ship a consultant over there to undertake paid work (i.e. implement a system as part of a paid consultancy project) that is a different ball game as the ESTA does not cover 'the performance of skilled or unskilled labor'. There is allegedly an exception for the performance of professional services on behalf of a foreign firm, although at the time of writing it seems that this exception is under review and not all immigration officers may be aware of it.

The point is that shipping consultants around the world to undertake paid professional services is not only complex but also an expensive business for both you and the client. The costs can kill a deal. Many services can be delivered remotely these days and therefore it's the way forward.

Our approach to delivering what few services we offered, was to package them rather than charge a day rate – although we did include a suitably high day rate on the price list to ensure that (i) the packages look like a good deal and (ii) clients were discouraged from purchasing consultancy services. It also makes it simpler for a sales team to understand. Not every quote is a custom quote.

My objective was to sell software licenses and minimise service provision. This was simply because, having worked for a professional services company early in my career, I understood the dynamics of such a business and didn't want to take on the overhead, either financial or managerial. Therefore, as a company, we worked hard on making the software straight forward to install and configure. We provided comprehensive documentation, including things like configuration questionnaires, free online training and so on. It's worth noting that this approach doesn't necessarily endear you to potential professional service partners which is something we discuss under the Partners chapter.

You can't sell a complex, enterprise software without some level of associated services but you have to be careful that the tail doesn't wag the dog. By focusing on being a pure play software vendor we weren't distracted and were able to put all our efforts behind enhancing the software as a product.

So, especially in the early days, ask yourself whether you really need a professional services capability. Can people not double up? For example, we had product management not only developing online training movies but also delivering the online training in real time when a client had purchased the same. Remote installation was undertaken by support staff. This helped them understand the type of problems clients may encounter which may result in a support ticket.

Did our approach leave 'money on the table'? Absolutely. We could have sold a lot more services but with that opportunity would have come the overheads of running a professional services organisation. You need to be mindful that jumping on the services bandwagon comes at a price.

Discounting
With pricing comes discounting strategies. I think that the software industry has a problem. The problem is that at the first opportunity the price book flies out of the window and they discount. Discounts of 50%, 60% or more are not uncommon. Why have a price book if you fold at the first hurdle?

My approach has always been different (I suspect that, if you've read this far, you've already worked that out). A price list is there for a reason. If you aren't going to stick to it, why bother? Just make it up as you go along!

I've always resisted discounting. You are (hopefully) selling a highly functional software product which will give the client a great ROI (otherwise why would they purchase it) at a fair price (otherwise the ROI wouldn't be there). In short, you are a professional representing a professional high quality company, why act like some market trader in the Far East?

Sure, in the early years there will be some give and take as you build a client base but always, always, get something back if you discount. Despite my protestations above, I have discounted but always for a reason and never anywhere near that level. The first client in a new industry springs to mind, another is a particularly strategic client whose name on our client list would command instant admiration and respect. And there's the rub – 'whose name on our client list'. There is little point having that name as a client if you can't tell other people.

Let me introduce the 'promotional discount'. Your client wants a discount because they have a limited budget or a particularly insistent purchasing department or whatever. Fine. You want the ability to (i) add their name to your client list, (ii) have a news item on your website, (iii) use them as a case study after six months[74], and (iv) use them as a reference client. Job done.

If the client really can't agree a promotional discount and you still need to discount to secure the order, use something else. An order before a date, quicker payment, or anything to create a quid pro quo. But don't bluff. I had a point of principle which I made sure that the prospective client knew in advance and knew that I stuck to it. If I offered such a deal and the prospect didn't deliver their side of the bargain (i.e. an order by a certain date or whatever), they never got a deal that sweet again. Even if it cost me the order – it never did!

This book is not the place to go into depth on negotiation techniques. However, if your software is priced sensibly and it meets the client's needs and they want to buy it, have faith in yourself and your product. Don't assume you need to discount to win a deal. Inexperienced salespeople are always too quick to offer a discount with no counter balance. If you are going to discount make the client ask for it and work for it.

Another trick typical of purchasing departments is to request a discount on the promise of a future rollout. Do not fall for this one unless the rollout is contracted (i.e. in a legally binding contract with no wriggle room). You can

---

[74] You will have to cede copy approval but that approval should not be unreasonably withheld.

build future discounted rollouts into a client specific pricing structure which is part of the contract but only comes into play when they spend the money and roll out. You know it makes sense.

Purchasing departments aren't stupid. They understand the pressure on salespeople to meet their quarterly targets and use that to try and leverage discounts. One of the advantages of being a private company is that, unless you are VC backed, quarters have no meaning. Cash flow is where it's at, and if you have a reasonable cash balance you are beholden to no-one other than yourself.

I regularly had purchasing departments offering to expedite the process of placing their order to ensure it arrived before the end of the month/quarter/year if we gave them a discount. I always thanked them profusely for their kind and generous offer and, regardless of the real situation, told them that it was fine, we had already met our monthly/quarterly/yearly target and, actually, they'd be doing me a favour to bounce it into the next period.

It can be moderately amusing playing the game, but playing from a position of strength is always better. Regardless of your position the key is to never let exude anything but confidence. If you do, for example, have cash flow issues and are desperate for the order, don't let on. They will pounce on any hint of weakness and, if they cotton on you are concerned about your cash flow, they may well withhold the order in case you go bust. Remember, they play this game every day.

Finally, in the last section, I promised you a story about a purchasing department.

We had been engaged with the prospect (a very large company) for months. We'd jumped through more hoops than you can imagine. We'd haggled, agreed prices for rollouts, negotiated the software license and so on. It had all been passed to purchasing to raise the order. We waited. Nothing. I chased and got a response along the lines of the fact that they couldn't possibly place the PO at the prices we'd negotiated and we'd have to reduce the prices by (I think it was) 5% and then they'd be able to place the PO.

Something snapped. I forwarded the purchasing department's email to everyone we'd ever had a discussion with in the client company and explained in words of one syllable that I considered this completely unprofessional, I thought we'd built a good working relationship and couldn't understand why they were trying to destroy this, and we'd jumped through every hoop they'd put our way, we'd given all we could and wouldn't do the deal for a penny less. Furthermore, we had a planned price rise in the next quarter and if the order wasn't placed they'd have to pay the new price!

It's probably worth mentioning that at the time there were around ten of us and while we had gained some traction the client would be a serious feather in our cap and the deal would make the year! There was a long silence and we got the order ten days later. Have confidence in your product and your ROI. If you don't why should the prospect?

Recruiting a Sales Team

There will come a point when you can't personally sell everything and run the business and so, as the business grows and in order to grow the business, you'll need to recruit a sales team. This is an area fraught with challenges. How to find the individuals who will represent the company professionally and whom you can trust?

There are a lot of considerations, not least of which is cost. Sales teams are notoriously expensive. They are expensive to run, expensive to get wrong and not inexpensive if you get it right!

In this section I go through a number of the decisions trying to highlight the their advantages and disadvantages before explaining what we did at PleaseTech and how that worked extremely well.

Sales vs Business Development

Before we go any further it's worth differentiating between different types of salespeople. Specifically, I want to address the difference between 'targeted salespeople' and 'business development people'. In my opinion, they are very different types of people, have different renumeration strategies and should be deployed at different stages and in different areas of your business.

Differentiation is not helped by the fact that a lot of companies use these jobs titles interchangeably. Sometimes targeted salespeople are given the title of business development as it feels less aggressive and more consultancy led. So I'm going to ignore the titles and focus on the role and the remuneration which is the real acid test.

Let's start with the easiest. Targeted salespeople are the classic 'quota carrying salespeople' whose job it is to sell your products, hit their sales target and generate revenue. Their OTE (On Target Earnings) is typically comprised 50% base salary and 50% sales commission. They should be actively discouraged from selling anything that isn't on the price list.

To have effective targeted salespeople and a targeted sales team, you need to have a defined product, a clear market target, a clear ROI and have developed an effective, repeatable sales process with a mature price list. You don't want your targeted sales team making stuff up. You want clearly defined targets, bounds and limits. Then you can let them loose!

Business development is an altogether softer concept. It's a lot harder to measure. Typically, renumeration is much more certain and less success based. OTE is typically lower than top salespeople and is comprised 80% base salary and 20% commission with the commission not necessarily being based on a personal sales target. It may be partially associated with the company's quarterly revenue or some other similar company performance measure. So, a base salary with commission split between personal sales involvement[75] and company performance would not be unreasonable.

I see business development as being more strategic and longer term. Business development people should have an ability to sell but also to consider the broader aspects and implications for the business. They are not focused on a quarterly target and they may well have to make stuff up! In short, if you are struggling to define a product, don't have a clear target market or an effective, repeatable sales process, and still need sales support, you should be looking to recruit a business development person, not a targeted salesperson.

---

[75] Note the difference between the term 'involvement' and 'target'. If a business development person is involved in a particularly strategic sale you may need to pay commission to both the salesperson and the business development person. Another option is to tie business development commission exclusively to new business although this has downsides as, frequently, the initial order is a 'starter for ten'.

I should say not everyone agrees with me. The internet has a very wide range of opinions and definitions. Some suggest that business development is solely associated with finding new markets for your product. Some suggest that if business development people have any sales role, they are salespeople. Still others define business development as lead generation! I'm happy with my definitions.

I think what most people agree is that business development comes before sales - preparing the ground for the sales assault. Sales is a clear repeatable process. Business development is not. The other thing I'd say is that business development teams tend to be much smaller teams, frequently comprising a single person. If you start trying to build a business development team because you don't have a clear repeatable sales process then stop and think. You are in danger of having too many irons in too many fires. As the business matures you must identify a clear target niche and have a clear repeatable process in that niche to establish a clear base from which to expand.

By the way, this doesn't mean that once you have a targeted sales team you need to fire your business development people as they have outgrown their usefulness or try and fit a square peg in a round hole by forcing them into a targeted sales role. Once a particular market sector is suitably defined and handed over to the targeted sales team, you simply refocus them and get them to identify and prepare the ground in a new market segment. Business development people are the pathfinders.

In summary, the type of person/team you need will depend on your business's maturity. Be wary of hiring targeted salespeople prematurely. In the early days you probably need someone with more generic business development skills rather pure play sales skills.

Inside Sales vs Lead Generation
You've probably heard the term 'inside sales' and may have wondered what it means. What about lead generation? Is that the same as inside sales? In a word: no!

It doesn't help that many companies and recruiters confuse inside sales with lead generation and even use them interchangeably.

As far as I am concerned, the term 'inside sales' is simply the new name for remote selling whether it be via the telephone, internet, or other communication mechanisms. It used to be called 'telesales' although the term telesales suggests a more aggressive outbound approach. So let's define inside sales as dealing with the prospect/client remotely. As such, it's part of the job description of every salesperson in a B2B environment.

In the modern age, the first reaction to a lead is not jump into a car or onto a plane to see the prospect. It's to exchange emails and arrange a chat. Selling remotely is the new motorway bashing and one's grammar and telephone manner is more important than the sharpness of one's suit!

So, as far as I am concerned, there is no difference between inside sales and so-called 'outside' sales. If you were feeling particularly pedantic you could point out that inside salespeople never get to physically meet the client whereas outside salespeople may. That wouldn't endear you to me. Let's just not differentiate.

Lead generation is another ball game. Confusion arises because proactive outbound lead generation tends to fall under the sales management structure rather than marketing. In the old days this involved cold calling suspects hoping to turn them into prospects. Sometimes, to give it a veneer of respectability, it was called telemarketing.

Cold calling is no longer an appropriate way of contacting prospects although, except in some circumstances, it is not illegal. If you are in the UK and really want to try cold calling you need to be aware of the Telephone Preference Service and its business counterpart, the Corporate Telephone Preference Service. The USA has equivalent Do Not Call Registers.

The modern equivalent to cold calling is the LinkedIn Sales Navigator and equivalents. These tools provide market intelligence, extensive search tools and, with Sales Navigator, the ability to contact prospects directly and legally via InMail. As always there is a considerable amount of information and debate on the web regarding the efficacy and the 'do's and don'ts' of these tools. LinkedIn's professional version is not inexpensive but can be a very efficient way of identifying prospects and potentially contacting them. We used it as we grew the sales team in PleaseTech.

Sales Engineers (aka pre-Sales Techies)
Finally there is another class of salesperson to consider. This is definitely a case of 'last but by no means least' as, in many companies, the Sales

Engineers (known universally as the 'pre-sales techies') are the heart and soul of the sales effort even though they are there to win the 'technical sale'. In many companies they also do the sales demos and will deal with any and all technical aspects of the sales process.

They differ from consultants in that they work with the sales team and their time is usually free to the prospect as part of the sales process. They are not involved in the post-sales delivery process. They are remunerated with a base and sales commission but tend to align with the business development end of success based remuneration i.e. higher base percentage of OTE. They do not carry a personal sales target and their commission is normally based on a group target rather than any individual's performance.

The skill set is a combination of technical and people skills. The reality is that you wouldn't put many of your development engineers in front of a prospect for fear of what they may say. A pre-sales techie is attuned to the sales environment and, because they are seen as techies and not salespeople, frequently get inside information. This can contribute greatly to the understanding of the prospect's environment and therefore the ultimate sales success.

They can also overcome any innate suspicion of salespeople. In the words of an individual who once undertook this role: "I always saw myself as the salesperson's credibility. I could say similar things as the salesperson but I would be believed whereas the salesperson was viewed with some scepticism." I think that sums it up perfectly.

In short, I have a lot of time for them and the good ones are worth their weight in gold. Should you employ them?

The bottom line is that they are an expensive resource. Ultimately, the need for them depends to a large extent on the technical complexity of the product being sold. If your product is a highly configurable, enterprise level, on-premise solution which requires significant levels of integration with other systems, etc. then they will almost certainly be required. If you are selling a commercial off-the-shelf product with limited configurability and either a clearly defined target infrastructure or as a service, then the answer is somewhat different.

Another dependency is on the type of developers and support staff you have. In CDC we did have pre-sales techies. In PleaseTech, we were lucky in that we had developers and support staff whom we could put in front of prospects and who had a sufficiently generic skillset to be able to handle the role for the rare times we needed to deploy them. If we had grown much larger I can see that handling the technical side of sales would have eventually become a full-time job and at that point we'd have recruited.

Almost all B2B sales will require some level of technical input. The judgement you need to make is whether the level of technical input per sale or the sheer volume of sales means that you need an expensive dedicated resource to handle the workload.

It has to be said that there are some advantages to involving your developers and support staff in answering pre-sales technical queries. It educates them and doesn't insulate them from the cut and thrust of the commercial world and it can bring to the fore experience which is buried in the organisation, as in: client XYZ has that environment and it's a support nightmare! This in itself can alert you to the fact that, if you win the deal, the client may have a high support overhead.

For the extremely well-funded strategic, high-end enterprise sales companies I've seen a one-to-one relationship between salespeople and pre-sales techies. It is more typical for a pre-sales resource to be shared in a sales group. Obviously this requires careful resource allocation and prioritisation by sales management which itself is an overhead.

Sales Remuneration
We've already discussed the OTE base/commission splits for targeted salespeople and there is no point in discussing actual salaries as these are determined by the market and constantly changing. Therefore this section is more about commission schemes than anything else.

The first point to understand is that commission schemes drive behaviour. Targeted salespeople are driven by money in a way that technical and non-sales staff find hard to understand. Therefore design a commission scheme which ensures that the behaviour you want is rewarded. Likewise, if you don't understand why the salespeople are acting as they are, examine the commission scheme.

At a basic level, if you want to push product 'X' because it is high margin you may want to up the commission on product 'X' and so on. However, for the smaller single product company the key decisions are generally around accelerators. How do you want the salesperson to behave when they've hit their target for the quarter? Should they concentrate on next quarter or pull as much in as soon as possible?

If you want them to keep selling you can add an accelerator which pays them an additional percentage of the deal once they exceed their target (an accelerator). However, bear in mind the behaviour that that drives. The salesperson may well pull forward revenue from next quarter into this quarter in order to earn more on the same deal size and therefore not be in a position to make their target the following quarter.

A well-designed commission scheme will address such issues and may, for example, have a retrospective bonus percentage applying to sales once the target has been met (target bonus) rather than a simple linear progression. It may be appropriate to have a commission threshold which means no commission is paid until such time the salesperson has covered their costs i.e. base salary, employment overheads, expenses, etc.

The reverse is also true. A lack of accelerators may drive the opposite behaviour with salespeople padding the following quarter (i.e. delaying deals they could have closed this quarter) to ensure that they earn commission and meet their target.

Remember you are driving sales and thus company revenue with your commission scheme. There is an argument which says that delaying a deal just increases the possibility it will go away as circumstances change so get everything in while you can. For a small, organic growth company generally the more revenue the earlier is a good thing. However, for a VC backed company, quarterly revenue progression may be important and any over performance will rapidly be forgotten once a new quarter or year is started.

Other factors you need to consider in designing a commission scheme are the complexion of the deal i.e. the item types sold. Are there different commission percentages on software licenses, support services, professional services, etc.? These will have very different gross margins and therefore you may wish to commission them separately. How do you remunerate annual renewable software services?

As the business grows is there a higher reward for new business compared with additional licenses from existing clients or renewals? Do you only pay out commission when the client pays or do you pay the commission on order receipt or revenue recognition? Is there a clawback if the client doesn't pay?

How does the sales management scheme compare to the individual salesperson's scheme? Presumably achievement of team targets are rewarded? For example, when considering the commission scheme for a Sales VP you are recruiting to build a sales team, you need to carefully consider whether they have a personal sales target or they are remunerated against overall company revenue. Is there a new business element vs a renewable? What behaviour do you want to reward? Remember, giving the Sales VP a personal quota will probably save a bit of commission which can be a fair chunk of change on big deals.

A few more points to consider:

1. When recruiting, be aware of the potential need to offer guaranteed commission for the first couple of quarters. This is generally subject to negotiation especially if staff are being tempted away from an existing role.

2. Decide whether you are setting an earnings limit i.e. a maximum commission. What happens if the salesperson brings a million dollar deal when their target is half of that? Generally, an upper limit is disincentivising but the counter argument is that such deals typically involve a whole company effort and therefore the commission should be split with those involved or the whole company.

3. Be very clear what happens when a salesperson resigns or is fired. From a legal perspective the key issue is when the salesperson has been deemed to have 'earnt' the commission. If they have earnt it, it is due to them. Is it earnt when the sale is made (even if it's not paid out until the customer has paid), or is it earnt once the customer pays, or when the revenue is recognised? You need to clearly define the rules of the scheme (using the word 'earnt' knowing it has a legal context) and ensure that the employment contract references these rules. From the employer's perspective you'll want to ensure that (i) there is a clean break (paying someone once they've left is a real

pain administratively) and (ii) the departing salesperson gets as little as possible.

4. It's quite common for commissions schemes to change on an annual basis. So ensure that any scheme has a time limit (typically the financial year) and be prepared to alter it in line with your growing business.

As you can imagine, commission schemes can get very complex very quickly and in most cases, certainly at the early stages of the business, it best to keep them simple as there is a significant overhead to managing a complex scheme.

Whatever you do, ensure that the rules of the commission scheme are very clear, have a very clear definition of 'earnt' and are understood by the all the relevant staff, especially the salespeople involved.

Cost of Sales

Sales is important, right? Therefore the temptation is to throw money at the problem - just like marketing! There is no need to do this. Yes, as I previously mentioned, sales teams are notoriously expensive to run but it is imperative that you make them work for their money and keep the cost of sales as low as possible.

To be clear, this doesn't mean underpaying salespeople. As in all aspects of the company you want to attract the best and therefore you'll have to pay accordingly. However, a sales team will always suck as much resource as you can give it. You need to get the sales team working for the company and not the other way round.

One of the ways to keep the cost of the sales team down is to ensure that they are self-sufficient and don't need constant support. In PleaseTech, I absolutely insisted that all salespeople conduct their own demos. Every salesperson had to learn the demo and pass a demo test before they were let loose on prospects. If the salesperson didn't run their own demos we'd have had to provide another resource to support them. What would the salesperson's role be? Something like a glorified secretary arranging for others to interact with their prospect?[76]

This approach not only kept the cost of sales down, it had two additional benefits: (i) the sales team actually understood the product and it's capabilities and therefore were more likely to be able to answer customer questions without seeking help elsewhere, and (ii) they gained respect in the eyes of the customer who realised that here was a salesperson who actually understood their product – unfortunately not always the case!

In PleaseTech, when I finally relinquished responsibility for sales activity,[77] the approach we took was to get an excellent Sales VP in place with a brief (and budget) to build a team[78]. The approach he took was to employ new graduates who he could train and mentor to reflect the sales approach and professionalism he wanted to instil. There are several specialist graduate sales recruitment companies[79] in the UK and the graduates were sourced from these companies. I have to admit I was sceptical. However, I was wrong. We recruited some excellent young sales professionals and the process worked very well.

One of the key benefits was that the salaries of said graduates were lower than would be the case if they'd had a few years of experience and this made them very cost effective. To be clear, I'm not recommending this approach for everyone and it wouldn't have worked without a dedicated Sales VP who was prepared to provide the mentoring and support to deliver the benefits. But there is no doubt it has its advantages!

---

[76] This raises an interesting point. Some salespeople see themselves as a project manager, manging the company's resources to achieve the sale. There is an element of project management in the job but they really should be earning their salary by doing rather than organising.

[77] I probably clung on for too long as I've never felt comfortable employing or recruiting salespeople. I'd recruited one business development type person to support me but had stayed away from any targeted salespeople.

[78] This wasn't an instant thing. He had to do six months of the hard yards first!

[79] These companies specialise in identifying and placing graduates in sales positions. They undertake a thorough assessment to identify graduates suitable to become sales professionals and provide initial and ongoing training for the first year of the graduates employment.

In this respect it's worth noting that as the business grows so will the size of deals. When we were first selling PleaseReview I'd get excited by deals worth £10,000. By the time we sold the business I'd only be really interested if the deal size was in excess of £200,000! But the £10k - £20k deals were still around, were good 'bread and butter' and ideal for the graduates to cut their teeth on.

The cost of sales is inextricably bound up with the people you employ and the support they need. You do not want a high maintenance sales team!

Recruitment of Sales Staff

This section briefly covers the sales recruitment process itself. I do cover recruitment in more detail later on and the sales recruitment process is no different. My advice is, as with all recruitment, is to be thorough.

Think through what a salesperson has to do in their day to day activities and try and replicate this to test them. If you are not confident yourself, get a sales professional in to assist. There are any number of ex Sales Managers/VPs plying their trade as independent sales consultants. I'm not ashamed to admit that I used one of these consultants when I recruited the Sales VP in PleaseTech. It reduced my workload so I was able to keep concentrating on selling, and it provided a valuable second opinion.

Don't worry too much about the cost of this support. The consultancy fee will save you a fortune if it means you get the right person in the job and don't have to fire them after six months!

Regardless of who is involved, have extensive telephone interviews and email correspondence. How does their telephone voice come across? Is their email correspondence professional, correctly spelt and grammatically correct? Check they can put a document together? See the recruitment section for more detail.

Ask them to undertake both in person and remote presentations. How to they come across? Have they prepared? Does their presentation have typos? Do they know their subject? Have they practiced or are they winging it? Do they get flustered with difficult questions?

Some will be 'upset' at your approach. They're used to selling large corporate systems and feel that they should be judged on their record. Don't fall for this excuse. Remember they'll have had massive support systems in place to assist them. You need people who can fit into your environment, are self-sufficient and can do the hard yards. Remember who will be paying whom!

Selling to the USA and Europe

America is the largest software market in the world. Exact figures are hard to come by without subscribing to paid for research but the SelectUSA[80] website suggests more than a quarter of the $3.8 trillion global IT market is in the United States. It's a market you simply cannot ignore. However, it has always been regarded as the graveyard of British software companies so be aware of how easy it is to get sucked in to spending money.

Europe represents a different challenge and, as at the time of writing, we are in the middle of Brexit so who knows what barriers to selling to Europeans companies may be erected in the future. Europe is very different to the USA. The main difference is that it is not a single homogeneous market with a common language and business culture.

I've had all my success in the USA and certainly wouldn't profess to be an expert in selling to European companies. On this basis let's deal with the USA first.

Success in the USA

The first thing to understand about the USA is that they 'get' distance. The USA is vast and covers six time zones although for most business purposes, it's the main four (Eastern, Central, Mountain and Pacific) which matter.

Americans are very used to and comfortable with remote presentations and remote selling. In fact, elsewhere in this chapter (under 'Sales demos') I mention all the problems you can face if you turn up on site for a presentation. This means that you absolutely do not have to have a base in the USA to be successful. You can sell to the USA quite happily from the UK. Granted, you need to work late into the night, but sitting comfortably in your home office with a headset on and a glass of something red is a lot cheaper than having an office in the States.

---

[80] SelectUSA (https://tinyurl.com/y46o7dwf) is led by the U.S. Department of Commerce.

Some may tell you that America has a 'not invented here' syndrome. This is certainly not true in my experience. In fact, if anything, it's the other way around. UK companies find it hard to believe that world class software is available on their doorstep from a local British company! In fact, in my experience, if you have a British accent you have a natural advantage in selling to Americans!

There is a considerable body of literature which suggests that, as The Washington Post so eloquently puts it, Americans "associate a British accent with someone being more intelligent, more sophisticated and more competent"[81] or, as a 2016 article in Psychology Today asks: Why Do British Accents Sound Intelligent to Americans?[82]. Not surprisingly, I consider this a good thing and long may it continue!

Just because they like a British accent doesn't mean that you should have everything British! At PleaseTech our website was in American English because, after all, America was our largest market by far and therefore it's sensible to localise your promotional material for your largest market. They will hit and read the website before they get the opportunity to listen to your highly intelligent musings!

In thinking about how to start tackling the American market, I'd refer you back to the discussion under the Marketing chapter around trade shows and conferences. There is a trade show or conference for everything in the USA. Yes, everything! As an example, I was flying back to the UK from a conference in Las Vegas and got chatting with a chap sitting next to me. I guessed he was a techie and had been at a conference so asked the question. His answer wasn't quite what I was expecting but close enough!

It turns out that he had an interest in and collected high voltage insulators. These are the insulators which they use on electricity transmission pylons to support the wires! He had been at a conference dedicated to this subject[83]. Yes - every year a couple of hundred people fly in from across the world to discuss the delights of collecting high voltage insulators. Who knew? So,

---

[81] The Washington Post article 'Why do Americans think British accents are sexy?', is here: https://tinyurl.com/y3px4tw8.
[82] The article is here: https://tinyurl.com/y2n2v3bt.
[83] Subsequent research has identified The National Insulator Association (NIA) (http://www.nia.org) annual conference.

m'lud, I rest my case! The Americans have a trade show or conference for absolutely everything. It follows that you simply pick your subject, take a booth, get on an aeroplane and meet your prospective clients.

To be successful, you do need to speak a bit of American and understand the basics of American culture. Remember that Americans are 'pissed' not 'pissed off'. They get 'hammered' or 'wrecked' not 'pissed' and go to the 'rest room' not the toilet. Pants are, of course trousers and I'm absolutely not going to comment on the 'fanny pack'. I think my personal favourite is when it is announced that 'the plane will land momentarily' which, obviously to a Brit, means that it will touch down for a very short period of time!

When making small talk, there is very little commonality in sport, so make a point of having attended an (American) football game and a baseball game. That way, if the topic comes up you can chat about your experience. It's advisable to stay off politics and keep an eye on the comings and goings of the Royal family as they just love the Queen!

You also have to understand important American holidays! For example, you'll soon learn that everything shuts down for Thanksgiving and if you haven't sold it by this fourth Thursday in November, it's unlikely to happen that year. Once the Americans return from eating their turkeys there are only about three weeks until Christmas and therefore the focus is on raising purchase orders on decisions made before Thanksgiving.

It's also worth mentioning that it is increasingly common, at least for multi-national businesses, to have a Christmas shutdown. However, the Christmas/New Year period is nowhere near as important in the States as it is in the UK so expect many to be in work between Christmas and New Year.

I found a vast majority of the Americans I dealt with had an admirable sense of humour and, at the appropriate time of year, I'd always affect a misunderstanding as to why they celebrated independence day! Didn't they enjoy being Her Majesty's subjects?

A brief word on time zones: on the whole, the time zones work out very well for British companies selling to the USA. You can sort out your European and UK stuff in the morning and, in the afternoon, turn your attention to the States. It's worth noting that I've found that companies on the West coast frequently start early and finish early (making them more in line with the

East coast) which suits the British just fine! The one 'gotcha' to be aware of is the different daylight saving dates. The Americans 'spring forward' and 'fall back' at different times to the UK.

One final point about working with the States from the UK, is that most Americans will not and in most cases cannot dial internationally. Therefore have virtual American numbers using soft call forwarding options. These work well and are very cost effective.

Setting-up in the USA

If you do decide to set up in the USA and test the graveyard theory to the max, be prepared to invest heavily. It's not for the faint-hearted or the smaller underfunded company! Make sure that you have substantial reserves available. Do your research. There are a vast number local rules and nuances you'll have to understand and implement. It's not for nothing that America and Britain are considered two cultures separated by a common language[84].

It's not only the challenges presented by the different culture and jurisdiction. Consider how much you are going to have to pay people! When I last looked at salaries and the total cost of employing people in the USA compared with the UK, the UK was significantly cheaper[85].

Location is extremely important. It's a key point to understand that, unlike the UK which has a uniform employment overhead, in the USA taxes and therefore employment overheads vary from state to state and even from city to city within a state! This not only applies to employer taxes but also affects the tax employees pay. Therefore, select the wrong side of the street and your employees may be liable for city income tax (in addition to the state income tax) and you'll have to pay people more as a consequence!

Aim to set up your office near a major hub airport. As I mention in The CDC Story, if you need someone to be travelling around the USA, you need them

---

[84] Attributed to George Bernard Shaw.

[85] Don't forget to factor in overheads such as healthcare. The 2019 Milliman Medical Index notes that "the cost of healthcare for a hypothetical American family of four covered by an average employer-sponsored preferred provider organization (PPO) plan is $28,386" (source: https://tinyurl.com/yz4z98nt) while the US Bureau of Labor Statistics suggests that benefits costs account for 37.7% of total of state and local government compensation (Source: https://tinyurl.com/huwtoyz).

to be located near a major airport for both convenience and cost. If located near a regional airport the expense claims will start racking up as it will take two flights to get anywhere sensible.

You'll also have to consider whether to transfer UK personnel to the USA or staff the office entirely with newly hired Americans. Personally I don't think transferring personnel is a sensible approach for three reasons:

1. There is a major overhead in obtaining the various visas and permits. Assuming you achieve this, you'll have to address to what extent you adjust the individual's salary and provide cover for aspects such as accommodation, living expenses, healthcare, schooling costs, etc. In short, providing someone with an 'expat' lifestyle is a significant overhead and can lead to all sorts of internal pay equality issues.

2. Anyone relocating will never have their full attention on the job. They will need to sort out their living arrangements. Find an apartment, get a car, register with the local authorities, work out where to get healthcare, try and forge a social life, etc. This is aggravated if they are relocating a family as there potentially will be schools to consider and how to keep the spouse happy. In short, you will not have the undivided attention of a transferred employee and therefore do not expect them to be fully productive for a considerable period.

3. If the person being transferred is not one of the founders, there is nothing to stop them resigning and moving on once you've set them up in the States. You need to be absolutely sure of their commitment and competence before making such an investment!

Far better, in my opinion, to hire an American who doesn't have these overheads and for you to spend a bit of time on an aeroplane. In the manic days of CDC, it would not be uncommon for me to be flying back to the UK overnight Friday and being back out to the USA on Monday evening.

The Challenge of Europe
The mistake many Americans make when considering Europe is to think of it as a single market like the USA. Europe cannot be considered a single market as it is a series of individual markets each with their own language, business culture and local laws. Some of these markets can be quite small.

Whereas I'm unequivocal that you do not have to be in the USA to be successful there, I have the opposite opinion on Europe. If not actually going as far as setting up an office in each major country, to make any headway outside of the major multinationals, you at least need to have a native speaker doing your selling, be prepared to offer support in the local language and have your user interface and all your documentation translated.

I've always struggled in Europe. I think it takes a significant investment which, for a small company, doesn't always add up. The good news is that we frequently met prospective European clients at American shows - although it's worth noting that these prospects were almost exclusively major multinationals which used English as their business language.

I guess the key point about Europe is that, just because it is closer, doesn't mean it's a better opportunity!

Other Sales Miscellany

As we come to the end of the sales chapter, I'll add some additional thoughts on sales related stuff that don't merit a section on their own or fit in anywhere else!

You'll note that I haven't mentioned CRM systems. I have minimal experience of these tools. In PleaseTech we eventually implemented Mircosoft Dynamics primarily because it was free as we were a Microsoft partner. I know many large software companies use SalesForce and base their whole sales process around it. I also know that SalesForce is not inexpensive!

Given that in the early days of your company the sales process won't have been established, a process based CRM may not be something you want to rush into! In my experience, the principal requirement is to keep a contacts database and a note of when people need to be next contacted.

There are some who swear by CRM and the metrics they produce. Ask yourself this: If you have a small sales team, a dozen or so customers and a commensurate number of prospects, do you really need a CRM system's metrics to tell you what is going on? If you do, you are not doing enough sales management!

Be wary if, after you have recruited your first sales type person, they spend all their time fussing about sales infrastructure rather than interacting with clients. They can do their job without CRM. If they claim otherwise they are out of their depth and clinging onto something they know.

Unfortunately in these GDPR days, I suspect that the initial approach we adopted at PleaseTech (everything was done through Microsoft Outlook) won't wash, and a more formal system of some description will be required almost from the get-go. I can only advise you to keep it as simple and cheap as possible in the early days. You really don't want to be wrestling with a complex CRM system as that will keep you from the day job. A basic GDPR compliant solution which meets the rudimentary requirements is all you need. You can always upgrade as you grow, establish a sales force and a sales process, and start to find the metrics are a useful resource.

Even if you have a CRM system, unless everyone in the company uses it to send and receive all email, you won't get a complete picture of all correspondence to a prospect (for example, during an evaluation prospects will email the support system and receive a response from that). So, one top tip I have is to ensure that all significant email correspondence (including support emails for prospects) is blind copied (bcc) to a central email repository which is searchable! This way, if you ever want a complete picture of who has said what to whom it's very easy to put together. You need to instil the discipline in all staff early on and make sure that everyone understands the importance of the bcc and actually does it.

In the early days I used to get these emails copied to my inbox so I always had a view of what was being said to whom by whom. If I'd had a conversation with a prospect and wanted to make notes, I'd simply email to the internal email address or, if it was an internal email about a prospect, the repository would be copied. Even when we had a sales team and a CRM system, I'd use the repository to work out what was happening rather than wrestle with the CRM system. This approach (i.e. a central master information source in which you can search for all correspondence to a particular client or domain) has saved me hours of trying to piece together what was happening or had happened when it has mattered.

As your product develops and your competitors emerge you'll need to develop literature comparing your product/offering to the competition[86]. My personal view is that these are not marketing documents (although marketing can help them look pretty) or technical documents (although they will need to be technically accurate) but sales documents and should be owned and driven by sales with significant product management input/oversight. These 'commercial in confidence' documents should provide a clear comparison between your product and the competition. If there is no direct competition there are always other ways of doing something, so address those.

Another useful document to develop for sales purposes is a sample statement of requirements which can be provided to prospects so they can compare competitive offerings. You will obviously want to include several key requirements which can only be met by your product. I refer you to my previous thoughts on whether you should respond to ITTs to demonstrate the value of such documents. Anything which makes life easier for your prospect is going to be welcome and make you one of the good guys.

Finally, assuming you are selling internationally, your price list will come under pressure when selling to some developing countries. However, if you do decide to discount into these developing countries, make sure you know where your licenses are going and have a very clear legal restriction in the terms. It is not unknown for multinationals to attempt a bit of arbitrage by spotting that you are selling more cheaply in, for example, South Africa, and trying to purchase licenses via their local company for their entire corporation.

Sales Summary

There is no point in pretending that building and running a sales team isn't a challenge. Likewise, there is no point in pretending that, for your business to grow, establishing a professional, dedicated sales team and process isn't vitally important.

However, like everything else, there is no one specific secret to it and a lot of it is common sense. The key messages are that you shouldn't jump into a

---

[86] Frequently known as 'knock sheets'.

targeted sales force too early, that you need to establish a repeatable sales process and that your sales commission structure drives behaviour.

I think the critical mistake many people make is not providing the sales team with clear boundaries. The sales team needs to work for the company and not the other way around. Therefore you need to establish very clear guidelines in what they are able to sell, on what basis and to whom. Like all teams, they need clear objectives and clear management.

Development

Earlier in the book I assert that software development is way beyond hard. You should know that this was stated with feeling and based on personal experience.

Developing an advanced enterprise scalable software product is a daunting task which is as much about art as it is science. You can have all the processes and coding standards in the world but, if the coding gods aren't smiling benignly on you, your timescales slip and no matter how diligently people labour away, sometimes the desired functionality simply isn't deliverable.

Remember, the objective is not to make something work in a defined test environment, it's making it work consistently when end users are unwittingly doing everything in their power to break it. I'd stress that users are not deliberately trying to break it but the only predictable thing about end users is that no one can predict what they will do next, in what sequence or with what intention. What will they copy and try to paste? Which series of buttons will they click? How many times will they click and will they double or treble click? And so on.

If you are restricting your offering to a hosted cloud service, you are making life a lot easier for yourself. It's just the randomness at the front end you have to worry about as the backend environment is under your control. If you are supplying on-premise software you've just doubled your workload as you've got the backend configuration and interactions to worry about as well.

There are, of course, degrees of difficulty. A standardised database application with controlled inputs is at the easier end of the scale. The downside is that it will be easy for everyone and you'll be playing in a competitive market. If you want to create some clear blue water between you and everyone else and to increase the value of your IP, you'll need to be at the bleeding edge of the technology spectrum. This is the difficult end!

Regardless of which end of the spectrum you end up inhabiting, the development of an enterprise product is a juggling act. You have finite development resources and infinite demands. As we noted when discussing Product Management, the decisions taken can mean the difference between success and failure. The good news for you is that I have no intention of repeating the product management discussion here, so this section focuses purely on the development approach, process and management.

It is also worth making clear that, unlike other disciplines within a company, I have no personal experience of software development - I've never been a developer myself. However, over the years I've learnt enough to ask the difficult questions and understand whether the answers make sense. Once again, it's knowing enough to be dangerous!

If you are wondering why you can't just leave development to your CTO, the answer is that some of the CEO's and founders of the most successful software companies in the world recognise the importance of being on top of their development teams and understanding what is going on. After all development is all about building the company's crown jewels!

Mark J. Barrenechea is the Vice Chair and Chief Executive Officer of OpenText Corporation, a $3 Billion company. He is also its Chief Technology Officer.

Everyone assumes that Larry Ellison is the CEO of Oracle. Wrong! He is currently listed as Co-Founder, Executive Chairman and Chief Technology Officer. He is quoted as saying: "I have run engineering since day one at Oracle, and I still run engineering. I hold meetings every week with the database team, the middleware team, the applications team. I run engineering and I will do that until the board throws me out of there." [87]

So getting to grips with development is a good thing and well worth doing.

Development Teams
Before you start trying to comprehend development you would do yourself a favour if you acquainted yourself with the theory of the Mythical Man Month. This is a book written in 1975 by Fred Brooks who managed the development of IBM's OS/360. You can still get copies but there is a huge amount of summary information on the internet[88].

---

[87] Source: Forbes.com; Lunching with Larry; 2006: https://tinyurl.com/yeoju3zy
[88] To be clear I've not personally read the book but have been aware of the key principles it explored since the late 1980s when I first got involved with software.

The key point the book makes is that throwing resources at a software development project does not necessarily mean that it will happen faster. There are two reasons for this:

1. Some tasks are inherently sequential. The frequently quoted example is that nine women can't produce a baby in one month. However, it depends on the nature of the task, and I prefer the example of people digging a trench compared with a shaft.

   If you are digging a trench then many people can work in parallel and, broadly, the more hands on shovels the faster the trench will be dug. However, a lot of software development is inherently sequential with latter steps depending on the existence of the initial steps. In our example, this is the shaft. You can't remove the earth in parallel. You have to dig downwards and, whilst having extra bodies available to cart away the spoil will assist, no matter what the resource is available there is only so fast a shaft can be dug.

2. The law of diminishing returns mainly based around communication. As the team grows so do the lines of communication. For example, adding one person to a team of two triples the lines of communication. Brooks observed that adding resource to an overdue project didn't necessarily speed it up and he put this down to this communication explosion which starts to dominate the project.

There is a lot of research on the tendency for large teams to be less productive than small teams and it goes well beyond the communications explanation which Brooks put forward. If you are interested read up on 'Social Loafing'.

Related to this is the general understanding that in software development you are better off having a small high calibre team of developers than a large team of average developers. In software development the concept that small teams out perform large teams has become known as the 'two pizza' rule. The two pizza rule is attributed to Jeff Bezos, the Founder (and CEO/ Chairman/ President) of Amazon. Its basic principle is that if a team can't be fed by two pizzas then it is too big!

The general rule that it is better to employ a small team of brilliant developers than a large team of not so brilliant developers is certainly true in my experience and, as in all parts of the business, I would strongly endorse employing the highest calibre people you possibly can.

Development Estimates

A further point of discussion in Brooks' book and closely related to the teams discussion, is the difficulty of estimating development time. It won't surprise you to learn that this topic is also covered extensively on the internet.

Again, I have a long history of personal experience in this field. My experience doesn't however match that of the literature on the subject which generally states that software developers are guilty of over optimism and assume nothing will go wrong. I've found that my teams have tended to be overly pessimistic. I have two explanations for this.

Firstly, both my companies have operated at the 'breaking new technological ground or pushing technology to its limits' end of the easy/hard spectrum. Therefore, given the unknown nature of the task, estimates tended to be over cautious.

Secondly, I've always employed experienced software engineers. The problem is that experience teaches developers that an estimate which in reality can be nothing more than a rough order of magnitude (ROM), rapidly becomes a deadline and so subconsciously they make the appropriate adjustments. They know that there will be difficulties, change requests, diversions and so on, and are simply trying to be realistic.

The difficulty of estimating how long a software development will take shouldn't be underestimated. It is however very important that you establish an estimating modus operandi which allows the company to plan releases. Having a good CTO with an understanding of commercial reality is undoubtedly helpful in this respect but the question you have to address as the CEO is how you put pressure on your development team to keep focused.

One of the first things I learnt when I entered the workforce was Parkinson's law which is that 'work expands to fill the time available'.[89] So how do you ensure that the time available is used to maximum effect? My approach was to 'shoot for the stars in the hope of hitting the moon' and set an ambitious release date in the certain knowledge that we were going to miss it, but also in the knowledge that it would focus the minds of the developers and hopefully spur them onto great things.

I took the view that there was no point in having one deadline inside the company and telling the customers a different deadline because, if you do that, the developers know for certain that their deadline is an artificial one. So, in so far as we announced it at all (see below), we'd be somewhat vague saying something like 'we anticipate a release in the Q2 timeframe'. The point being that for most releases you are not contractually obliged to meet any deadline. It follows that you should ensure that your software license (or equivalent) doesn't commit you to any release schedule.

Occasionally, especially in the early days, you will have to commit to develop an enhancement within a specific period for an individual customer. They will almost certainly want the deadline to be contractual. This is the one time when you do need to be pessimistic in your estimating include plenty of padding. Whenever we had that situation we'd make sure that it was easily deliverable in the timeframe contracted and there would be a very clear focus on getting it delivered and out of the door. We would rarely bundle it in a general release as that was simply asking for trouble.

Generally little good comes from announcing forthcoming releases too early. Firstly, it can delay purchasing as customers wait for the new release. Secondly, it can lead the sales team to sell the future not the present, which is never a good thing. Thirdly, it sets you up for a fall as you know you will miss the deadline!

If customers ask you need to be very careful how you put the message across. More than once I've described a deadline as an 'ambitious target'. Frequently I'd privately mentioned to a client that we didn't stand a hope in

---

[89] In my case it was 'work expands to fill the <u>overtime</u> available'. The lesson from this is paying overtime to people to work longer hours doesn't result in more work being completed!

hell of hitting the ambitious target but it was there to concentrate minds internally.

The reality is that you need to keep the pressure on internally without backing yourself into a corner with the clients.

Development Management

The management of a development team is not straight forward. Top developers have their own culture and have an informal hierarchy based on peer respect rather than an organisation chart[90]. The challenge of development team management is earning their respect. The tricky thing is that the best techies are seldom great people managers or even decent communicators outside of the technical sphere.

The challenge is also reversed as the individuals who have these management skills are frequently individuals who have opted out of the technical side and are therefore not necessarily respected by those still in it. A common view is that they were unable to hack it as a real techie and have taken the soft option!

The problem is exacerbated as the company grows, especially as the start-up technical team is likely to have been working as a part of a single peer group and being managed, in so far as they are managed at all, directly by you. With growth you need to introduce more formal reporting and management controls and this is seldom welcomed. Remember that you can't just force a solution as top techies are hard to come by and the last thing you want is for them to start feeling excluded and to examine other options on job sites.

How to square the circle? The answer is 'with difficulty'. I think the solution is multi-faceted.

Firstly, the key is not to force your best technical staff into management roles for which they are ill-suited. That will end in tears all round. Break management down into technical management, project management and personnel management. You can leave technical management with the

---

[90] One 'test' all techies had to endure on day one at PleaseTech was the provision of a blank keyboard as part of their kit. This tested their mettle! It was, of course, a joke.

techies and then have the other two aspects of management undertaken by others or by yourself and gradually passed to others.

It's not uncommon for the CTO to be the technical lead, responsible for architecture, technical research, environment and direction, innovation, etc. and a separate development manager to have oversight of the development projects. The development manager may report directly to you or elsewhere in the organisation. If it keeps the developers happy, the development management role can be cast as a coordination role and not necessarily a direct management role.

Secondly, with respect to the start-up team, some degree of obfuscation will be necessary. You may introduce formal reporting lines on the organisation chart but so long as everyone knows that, in *actualité*, they are just pretty lines on a diagram, everyone will be happy. Clearly you can't push this too far and have everyone in the technical team reporting to you, but I've certainly found that a certain degree of muddying of the waters can serve to everyone's advantage.

Thirdly, don't punish techies salary wise for not being in management. Pay your top techies well and lock them in as they are beyond valuable! It's not necessary for development management to be more senior and therefore earn more! I accept that this challenges the corporate norm and it's difficult to ask someone to manage someone more senior and paid more than them. This re-emphasises the need for obfuscation. There is no reason that managers need to know their senior staff's remuneration. That aspect of the job can be kept between you and the individual team members.

You must remember what motivates out-and-out techies:

1. Peer respect;
2. Technical challenges;
3. Recognition of technical achievement;
4. Feeling that they can make a difference;
5. Working on interesting projects/technology;
6. Working on software that actually does something useful and is used!

It's difficult to overstate that last point. I remember a friend of mine who worked for one of the big consultancy integration contractors being thoroughly depressed when he turned forty because he'd worked out that not one of the projects he'd worked on in the last few years had actually been completed and delivered! Simply knowing that the software you've worked on is being used by real people in real jobs and is making a difference to them is a huge motivator!

It's really important to keep on top of development without diverting their attention from the job in hand. There are only so many hours in a day and every hour spent preparing management reports is an hour not spent on code. I came across an interesting 2005 paper which illustrates this point. A Microsoft team was able to go from 'Worst to Best in 9 months'[91] with no additional resources and no changes to how the team performed software engineering tasks like design, coding and testing. There was a 155% productivity gain in that nine month period. How? In short, by rationalising the management overheads imposed on the team especially in terms of the estimating of change requests. It was discovered that these estimates alone accounted for 40% of available capacity.

They had been caught in the classic Catch 22 situation. Management weren't happy with the unit's performance so they demanded more data. Delivering that data took time and effort and was prioritised so the actual work fell further behind! It's a natural large company management reaction to request more data. In your business, if it's important, you need to roll up your sleeves and understand the detail of the situation.

In PleaseTech when we encountered a major loss of productivity when we introduce Agile (discussed below), rather than demand more data I spent time to really understand the issues. I held workshops with the teams and had private one to one sessions with each developer and tester with the reassurance that no-one but myself would know what they had said! By adopting that approach, I was able to identify the issues, minimise the disruption and we modified our approach to reset the process. Asking for more data would not have solved anything!

Finally, don't be phased by jargon! There is a lot of it in techie land and one of the most powerful things you can do is admit you don't understand it and

[91] The referencing article by Gene Kim is here: https://tinyurl.com/yaj6rwbu and the original 2005 paper here: https://tinyurl.com/y396dltw

ask for an explanation. Any techie who has worked with me will recognise my common refrain: I am but a simple man - explain it to me real slow.

This approach coupled with the word 'why' is very powerful.

If you are told it can't be done or will take too long or whatever, ask why. Continue asking why and getting simple explanations until you are happy that you really understand the issues. I've regularly found that during such sessions the answer or another way forward presents itself. If not, at least you know you've explored the possibilities and have a good understanding of the issues.

In summary, technical staff need to be managed differently from others in the company.

I remember the CEO of an American consultancy, which was starting to develop their own products, called me to discuss whether I knew anyone I could recommend for CTO as they were having difficulty getting their fledgling development team to buy into their culture. That, I explained, was their first mistake. My advice was to allow the techies to have their own culture.

Like all people techies appreciate recognition for a job well done or an effort above and beyond the call of duty. However, they are generally a logical and somewhat cynical bunch. Not for them the rousing rah-rah speech a sales manager may give to their team. Any such emotional bunkum will be dismissed with a sarcastic grimace and a disdainful shrug of the shoulders. You need to present your arguments and have discussions based on rational data and thought.

Development Methodology

I previously mentioned that developing an advanced enterprise scalable software product is a daunting task and that it is. However, you will be approaching this task incrementally. In the first instance you are likely to have one or two people developing the basics of the product and getting the first release out of the door.

As the company and development team expands you'll need to introduce a development process (aka methodology). Methodologies are continually evolving and there is much debate on the relative merits of the approaches.

The current fad is the Agile methodology. I say 'fad' but for some it's closer to a religion and, as true believers, they believe that it can do no wrong. It can.

At this point the purists will argue that Agile isn't a methodology but a philosophy and the underlying methodology is SCRUM. I'm not a pedant and as far as I am concerned the whole thing is covered by the term 'Agile'. However, it is worth noting that, in the same way there are different ways to implement the 'traditional' Waterfall approach, there are different ways to implement Agile.

The Waterall methodology/approach/philosophy/call it what you will, is a sequential process of Analysis → Design → Code → Test → Release. Agile tries to compress those stages into a number of single smaller steps that aim to provide continuous incremental delivery. Theoretically this is a great idea although, as we will see, theory is not always practical.

For most of my career my companies used a variant of Waterfall and, in PleaseTech, we transitioned to Agile. The transition was painful and we ended up using a hybrid approach that had elements of both Agile and Waterfall which, in retrospect, was probably more closely aligned to RAD (Rapid Application Development) than anything else. As always there is a considerable amount of information available on the web. In this section I'll simply be covering my experience of both approaches as they both have their advantages and disadvantages.

Waterfall has recently had a bad press and been blamed for many failed software projects, and there is no doubt that it does have its negatives. It also has many positives. The principal benefit as far as I am concerned is the upfront requirements definition and analysis which ensures that the product is built on a solid architecture.

I see it much like building a house. You need the big picture so you can establish solid foundations. At the outset you really need to understand some fundamentals such as where supporting walls are likely to be, the probable locations of door and windows, the number of levels, the construction materials (you'll need different foundation strengths for a traditional American wooden framed house compared with a traditional British house with rendered concrete blocks), and so on. An understanding of what you are attempting to build is useful!

If the house was being built under Agile most of this stuff would be decided further down the track and you then have to start bashing holes in already built walls and retrofitting lintels to create windows, doors and other openings. Underpinning inadequate foundations would almost certainly be a constant source of work as you wouldn't know where the supporting walls were in advance or what load they would end up supporting. I'm sure you get my drift.

I base my position on the one constant theme in my life as a software company CEO, namely the 'techies lament'. It goes something like this: if only we'd known! If only we'd known in advance that we may have to do [insert functionality here], it would have been so much easier as we'd have left an API or designed it differently, or whatever.

The point is that having as much of an upfront picture as possible is essential. It gives everyone involved in the development and test of the product a clear understanding of the objectives. However, one has to be realistic. Even with a considerable amount of upfront thinking, it's simply not possible to define or architect your entire enterprise product in advance. You don't know where you will end up and where all the software equivalents of the doors and windows will be.

To go back to the house-building analogy, there will undoubtedly be future extensions and re-modelling which will be decided at a later stage. But, to support these future developments it is vital to have a solid high quality first build. To achieve this it is necessary to have some degree of upfront analysis and planning and not just launch off into a developing frenzy.

Waterfall is criticised for being too rigid and not permitting changes. I suspect that is more a feature of contractual realities (whether they be between client and contractor or via an SLA within a company) than the methodology itself. A valid criticism is that it tends to be overly documentation centric and prototyping light. I am a great fan of visualisation when it comes to the user interface (UI).

Perhaps the most significant criticism of Waterfall is that it tends to cause a panic towards the end of the cycle when everyone is working manically towards a release, which rarely goes smoothly because testing is backend loaded and there is significant rework which can change documentation which needs to be reworked, etc.

Agile attempts to establish a constant velocity of continuous incremental delivery. It's based around 'Sprints' (typically a two-week work cycle) and Stories (description of the work packet a sub-team will undertake within a Sprint). Theoretically, after each Sprint the product is ready for release as it stands. Note I said 'theoretically'! In reality, there are always functional interdependencies that require multiple Sprints to deliver and therefore it's simply not possible to have a release ready state at the end of every Sprint.

Forgetting for a moment the lack of a blueprint in Agile, my main problem with it is that every work packet is seen as a separate task that has no consequence or impact on anything else. That means that when a developer picks an approach for the particular task in hand there is no consideration of whether it is optimal for subsequent tasks. This is clearly not realistic in a complex enterprise-scale product with multiple interdependencies.

I could rant for pages on the problem with 'pure play' Agile but I'll restrict myself to a few bullets:

- It is very communications heavy with a lot of time spent in meetings to ensure everyone is on the same page. In PleaseTech we estimated that developers and testers spent 20% of their time in meetings.

- There is a requirement for constant product management or user involvement as the prototyping isn't prototyping as such, but real code being cut and being adjusted in 'real time' as feedback is given. Once agreed it is signed off and the process moves on with no scope for a wider review of usability or suitability.

- The process assumes automated integral testing is developed alongside the code. We'll discuss this more under the testing section below so I'll restrict my comments here to the observation that this is useless for existing legacy code.

- It's documentation light which can be a problem with respect to meeting quality standards and future code maintenance.

- The methodology itself does not allow for code reviews. IMHO, code reviews are a vital quality process which keep the overall codebase to a high standard with good quality, commented and documented code for future maintainability. In other words, vital if you want a high quality product on which to base your business and growth.

It's not all bad. There are positives to Agile. The approach shares knowledge and minimises silos of specialism within a team. It is potentially a lot more scalable than Waterfall and there is much closer co-operation between development and test. However, while such co-operation is a positive it is also a negative. You don't want to allow development and test to get too close (I discuss this under testing below).

As previously mentioned, in PleaseTech I took a long detailed look at Agile and how we'd initially implemented it (very much from the pure play approach) and my thoughts resulting from this experience are below:

1. A blueprint of the overall aim of the release is essential. In PleaseTech we called this a 'Product Enhancement Proposition'. It had a functional/user benefit focus and described the overall aim of the functional enhancements and the associated user experience in as much detail as we had. This ensured that all teams were working on the same understanding of the same goal. The blueprint is not as detailed as functional requirements would be in Waterfall but there needs to be a clear scope and clear functional objectives.

2. It's very easy to get suckered into the belief that every work packet is seen as a separate task. In reality it isn't. For every release you need upfront analysis to identify broadly similar functionality. This needs to go through formal technical analysis to identify sensible technical interdependent 'chunks' to be divided up into individual stories and sequenced efficiently.

3. Following on from this, prioritisation needs to take a holistic view incorporating both business priorities and technical rationalisation. In other words, simply focusing on business priorities without technical considerations is not sensible. You have to take into account technical interdependencies for productivity.

4. In detailed Story scheduling you should aim to complete features even if they run over several Sprints rather than leaving them incomplete at the end of a Sprint and then move on to another area

of the code. Once again, theoretically this shouldn't matter because in Agile every task is the same as any other task in that it is a self-contained task with no consequence or dependencies. And, once again, I'd reiterate that this isn't true.

5. Make sure that there is comprehensive cross referencing and documentation of completed stories. For future maintainability you will need to be able to go back and rapidly understand why a feature was implemented the way it was. The Agile approach values 'working software over comprehensive documentation'. The purists tend to interpret this as meaning documentation and records are bad. They aren't. They are vital.

6. Have a process of handling support queries that require development input in the middle of a Sprint. Clients are not going to be happy with you saying something like: 'I'm terribly sorry, I know this is causing an issue in a mission critical system, but I'm afraid we have just started a Sprint and we will include it in the next one when that starts in a couple of weeks – so think in terms of a four to six weeks delivery of the fix'.

Agile is really designed for starting from scratch on brand new codebases in which automated testing can be used. As I discovered, it gets much more complicated when you want to introduce Agile to an existing codebase. The methodology has no inherent answers for this and you need to ensure that the 'process tail' doesn't wag the 'reality dog'. Disregard the purists and adapt it as necessary to ensure that it works for your situation.

Development Environment and Resources

There is a huge amount of information on the web regarding what should be in the software development environment and I certainly don't feel qualified to comment on the detail. What I do feel qualified to comment upon is the aspects which affect you as a CEO.

Under the product management section I discussed the fact that you won't be building your product in a vacuum. You'll be using development tools, databases and have a target platform. You'll almost certainly be incorporating third party libraries (both open source and commercial) and, as you grow, you may have to sub-license some specialist technology. All of this needs to be managed and controlled. You need full traceability.

Without control and traceability you can't impose development standards or trace the use of third party code (which has IP implications) or, in fact, have a scalable business! You certainly will have no hope in passing due diligence when it comes to exiting or, indeed, of passing quality audits if you are working in an industry in which these are the standard.

It follows that not resourcing a proper development environment is a false economy. That doesn't mean it has to be expensive as there are plenty of open source tools around, but it does mean making sure that an appropriate environment is in place. The last thing you need is for development to be the wild west. Control, traceability, documented code and tested code all require appropriate tools, and you need to ensure that your developers have them and are using them.

Another point to understand is that developers need a lot of powerful kit. Development, especially on-premise development which may have several target environment variants is kit hungry. If you work with partners and have integrations you'll need development and test environments for those. If developers need to spend time setting these up and maintaining them you are wasting development time.

In PleaseTech, as we grew, we employed a dedicated development support engineer. His job was to take the strain when it came to maintaining, upgrading, backing up, etc. the systems the developers used day in and day out. You really don't want your highly paid specialist developers doing these mundane tasks. You want them focused on developing the product!

The two key messages are: (i) ensure that your development environment is under control and (ii) don't stint on resources (i.e. tools, kit, support and the like) as they are key to developer productivity.

Development Culture

The fact that you want your developers focused on the job in hand brings us neatly into development culture!

I mentioned earlier in this chapter that top developers have their own culture and it is necessary to accept and support that. To a certain extent the culture is set by the CTO (you want the culture to be one of technical excellence) but it is also influenced by the environment you provide.

Many companies believe that development success is achieved by providing a 'Silicon Valley' workplace with ample opportunities for distraction littered around the place. In my companies, there was absolutely no place for bean bags, table football, table tennis, etc. My objective was always to ensure that developers had everything they need to be successful so we never stinted on kit and resources but, to my mind, if they were playing table tennis, they weren't cutting code or even thinking about the code they needed to cut!

I was recently chatting with an ex-colleague who was working for a VC backed start-up which, when funding was initially obtained, was state of the art in their chosen field. Unfortunately, the VC dollar had meant that they were no longer focused and competitors had caught up and even overtaken them technically. He blamed this on the development culture. Too many developers fiddling with bits of string (he had no idea why - I'm guessing it was some wacky Agile approach), sitting in meetings all day and no one actually doing any real work!

Bear in mind that there are numerous studies that show that developers only spend between 25% and 30% of their time developing! Clearly there are management overheads on time and, as previously discussed, high meeting requirements inherent in Agile, so you really need to minimise distractions.

If I were investing in a software company I'd check out development and if the company provided any such superfluous entertainment, I would keep my money firmly in my bank account. To my mind such an approach is the very epitome of 'all the gear and no idea'. Remember I said that the general rule is that it is better to employ a small team of brilliant developers than a large team of not so brilliant developers? It's my experience that the brilliant developers aren't that interested in lounging around on bean bags!

Coding Policies and Standards
We talked about having a controlled development environment. This is not only good practice but it's also important from a IP management perspective. You need to know which third party libraries and other code you are using and where they are being used. As you grow you'll need to

develop formal coding standards and guidelines which cover the coding best practice.

From a practical perspective it's better to have an abstract code naming convention as the product name may change. In CDC we had some code still called 'Topaz' years after we ceased our brief use of that as a name and moved to EZ*Subs*. One mistake frequently made is to call code developed for a custom client development after the client. If you do this, shipping the code as part of your product will automatically break any confidentiality agreements you have.

One key policy to enforce <u>from day one</u> is no copying of code. Ensure that all developers are aware of the perils of code reuse and or copying code and the associated IP implications.

It goes without saying that developers should not be reusing code from jobs with previous employers (they shouldn't even have kept the code). Clearly it's different if they have developed the code themselves (not as an employee) and own the copyright therein. If this is the case, so long as they grant you an irrevocable, perpetual, royalty-free license (and make sure that this is a formal document signed by both parties), reuse should be OK.

Where it gets tricky is when code is copied from the internet. Not all developers understand that, just because it's in the public domain, it isn't free to copy. It may be published under an open source license (there are several variants available) which may or may not have commercial use permitted. Some license variants only permit the use of the code if the software license you attach to your derivative code has the same terms. This is clearly not going to be the case (unless you are developing open source software) as you'll be licensing your software to clients under a proprietary license.

If there is no explicitly attached license that doesn't alter anything. The person who wrote it still owns the copyright. Unfortunately a lot of developers believe that so long as it's a small snippet it is permissible to copy it under a 'fair use' provision. Equally unfortunately, it's not that simple.

It is true that there is a legal concept of 'de minimis' which, in summary, means that the matter is so small it is trivial and therefore not subject to legal consequences. However, there are no set legal rules and, if you've copied something, de minimis may or may not be a defence depending on circumstances. As I understand it, it depends on the importance of the code snippet. If the copied code is original and creative in nature and becomes a material component of the developed code then, even if it is a tiny fraction of the overall code base, it would not be considered de minimis. If the code is a standard non-material snippet which is not creative it is likely to be considered de minimis.

In short, you can see that this sort of thing can keep lawyers amused for many expensive hours. Furthermore it not just legal costs which are to be considered. At exit, the acquirer will look at whether you've behaved by the rules in creating your product. If not, they'll either back out or seek a retention.

Having a very clear explicit statement and practice with respect to the copying and reuse of code is essential from day one. If someone does have a good reason for copying the code it must go through an approval process in which the license conditions are checked, and you establish and implement any accreditation conditions.

Product Releases

We discussed releases and rapid release cycles under Product Management. From a development perspective it's important to have a clear release plan and process. You will also want to have a definition of major release, minor release and patch along with a clear (and ideally documented) process for each type of release.

There needs to be clearly defined parameters on what levels of known bugs may be included in the release. Presumably no critical or major bugs should be present. A known level of minor bugs in obscure areas of the code is usually acceptable. Cosmetic bugs are more open to discussion. If the cosmetic bug is on the first screen a user sees it should perhaps be addressed. If the cosmetic bug is somewhere on a sub menu it may be considered not material.

As you grow, it will also become necessary to develop an emergency patch process.

This next bit is so important that I'm putting it in capitals:

YOU DO NOT WANT DEVELOPERS SENDING CODE TO CLIENTS (TEST OR OTHERWISE) DIRECTLY!

All code exiting the building must go through a release process in which it is tested and signed off by the CTO or a senior designated techie – even if it is an emergency. There is nothing that decimates client confidence more that an endless stream of patches thrown over the wall which, for one reason or another, fail!

Your release process is there to ensure that you have solid, tested code – and testing is not limited to functionality. If it's on premise you'll need to undertake installation tests on target environments. You'll need to run upgrade tests and you may need upgrade scripts, etc. There will also need to be appropriate documentation (i.e. environment, installation, user, etc.)

From a management perspective, you need to recognise that no release can or will contain everything you want. You need to draw a line in the sand, stop development and get on with preparing for the release. Regardless of your methodology, a release is typically a considerable overhead and frequently a whole company effort. New user documentation (aka electronic help or otherwise) will be required. New training videos recorded. New functionality highlight tours provided and so on.

The need for release management should not be underestimated. Having a clear release process and plan with a detailed list of the accompaniments (which also need to go through their own cycle of development, review and approval) will provide for a smooth ride. The times I've witnessed releases going wrong is when they are rushed, there is no coordination or plan and everyone has a separate understanding of what is required.

If you are operating in a professional B2B environment, the only thing the clients see is the end result of the release process. A good solid, high quality release will do wonders for client perception of your company and its confidence in you. Make sure you get it right.

Offshoring, Outsourcing and Subcontracting

Let's start by making sure we understand the definitions.

Offshoring: Locating your development team (or part thereof) in a location other than your home country. The individuals are still employed by your company (well, your subsidiary) and spent 100% of their time working for you. As the developers are your employees your priorities are their priorities.

Outsourcing: Paying another company to undertake development on your behalf. It matters not where the company is located – it's still outsourcing. The individuals developing your software work for the outsourcer and their priorities are not your priorities.

Subcontracting: As far as I am concerned the difference between outsourcing and subcontracting is one of scale. Outsourcing is technically subcontracting but implies a whole function (i.e. development or support, etc.) is subcontracted.

My main experience is with offshoring and therefore this section is predominantly around how to make that successful. In the CDC days we did trying a bit of outsourcing (or was it subcontracting?) and I have regularly used subcontractors, therefore I cover the lessons learnt.

Offshoring

The main reason people seek to offshore is, of course, cost. When we sought to expand our development in PleaseTech we found we could get three developers and a serviced office in Kuala Lumpur, Malaysia for about the same cost of one developer in the UK[92]. The thought process we went through is covered in in The PleaseTech Story.

The key reason to consider offshoring as opposed to outsourcing is control. As noted above, you employ the staff directly and therefore have control over their priorities. In a software company where priorities can change in

---

[92] At the time of writing, this would no longer be the case as salaries in Malaysia have risen and the pound has fallen. However, the principle holds true.

an instant this is a good thing. An outsourcer or subcontractor will not have the same urgency to respond to your priorities and, if they do, it is likely you'll face a steep bill!

In PleaseTech we grew the Malaysian development centre from an initial two people to a team of just under 20. So, how did we make offshoring a cost effective success? Let's look at some of the issues.

Business and Legal Environment

Having English widely spoken and used as the de facto business language is a major benefit. This saves considerably on translation costs. It also means you are less reliant on specific agents whose sole interest is generally to maximise their personal income.

Having staff who understand and can communicate in English is likewise highly beneficial. In the CDC days we tried outsourcing/subcontracting to eastern Europe but, whilst the company's frontmen spoke decent English, we were unable to communicate directly with the developers themselves. This led to a lot of nuances being lost in translation. Do not underestimate the need for communication.

It helps if the legal system is broadly similar to one which you understand (for us that was the UK). Most commonwealth countries will have their legal system based on English common law. If you understand a different law (e.g. USA, French, etc.) it's easy enough to identify which basic law system the country of interest uses. Once having established the basis of law, there are two key things to consider:

1. Local ideocracies which can affect the type of entity you set-up and the manner in which you operate. For example, if you set-up the local equivalent of a limited company do you need to have local Directors and shareholders[93]? Many countries have special enterprise zones where there are different rules designed to attract foreign investment. However, these special zones may not be near a suitable labour pool (e.g. they may be best suited to manufacturing

---

[93] In the USA this would be and Incorporated company, i.e. Inc. Directors of a Limited company are the equivalent of Officers in an Incorporated company.

industries). Research and specialist local knowledge and advice is an absolute necessity.

2. Is the legal system effective and broadly neutral (i.e. not biased against foreigners)? It's all very well have a legal system but if it is not effective and will discriminate against you, you may as well not have it. For example, India's legal system is notoriously slow and judgements may take many years even though it is allegedly possible to get interim injunctions. If you are pursuing an employee for ripping off your IP can you afford an interim injunction, can you afford to enforce it and is it worth waiting for years for the final decision? Obviously a further consideration with any country is political interference in the judiciary.

What is the tax environment? Is there a tax treaty with your home country? What are the rules on transfer pricing?

At a practical level make sure you understand what a standard contract of employment looks like. How often are people paid? In some places it's every two weeks rather than monthly. What is the holiday culture and the number of public holidays? Many countries have both national and regional public holidays. For example, we discovered that Malaysia had quite a few more public holidays than the UK. What are standard job perks? Is it standard to offer health cover and similar benefits?

The key point is that you need to understand the political, business and legal environment as well as the tax and employment position before you invest. A lot of this may seem unimportant if you start small but will become pertinent as you grow. You don't want to put all that effort into growing your offshore team only to find that it becomes prohibitively expensive and eliminates most of the benefits.

First Steps

Getting started is always the tricky thing. It's all very well identifying some competent advisors and, with their help, establishing a legal entity that can employ people, a bank account and so on. The key question is: how do you get your first employees?

I know of a number of companies who have based this around a current employee 'returning home'. The employee decides for whatever reasons to return to their native country and, rather than lose their skills, the company continues to employ the returnee who becomes the 'local' who sets up the offshore office.

Another option is to transfer an employee for a while. This can be expensive and is fraught with difficulty, and is a subject I cover when discussing options regarding selling to the USA. The same basic obstacles exist whenever you transfer someone to establish a new entity.

If you don't have an expat who wants to return home, the only sensible answer is to recruit locally. To do this you need to establish how to contact and attract local staff. The world is moving on and it may be that you can do this via LinkedIn or an equivalent business networking tool. There may well be relevant technical discussions forums or groups which can be used to identify suitable candidates. However, your target countries will also have established local IT jobs portals. This is the approach we adopted. We simply identified a couple of appropriate portals and placed an advert.

The key is to recruit your manager or team leader and then allow them to lead the recruitment of any additional personnel. If, when they join, they can bring a couple of colleagues with them so much the better. Having said that, if they decamp as a group to you there is nothing stopping them decamping as a group somewhere else in the future. So, beware the 'poaching a whole team' approach. Having a diversified portfolio is never a bad thing.

It's worth noting that, in PleaseTech, we avoided titles such as 'Country Manager' and started with a 'technical team leader' which we felt was an accurate description of the role. The fact that the person would also be the senior person in the country and responsible for local management was understood but their title left no doubt as to the primary purpose their job[94]. The title also gave us flexibility as we could always appoint a manager above the team leader if it became necessary. In many cultures job titles are extremely important and people do like a nice progression on their CV so you may have to be flexible, but always leave yourself wriggle room!

---

[94] Some people feel that if they are a 'manager' they don't actually have to do anything except manage. As in: Why aren't you doing any development yourself? Because I'm a manager!

In my experience, getting someone who has lived and worked in a western environment is highly beneficial. There are any number of people who have lived and worked in western countries and have returned home for whatever reason. They have a broader perspective and have a much better understanding of your culture than you will of theirs!

Ultimately, you do have to take a risk because, remember, you are asking your candidates to take a risk! If you are reading this book with a view of taking advice you are unlikely to be a large software company. Therefore, if you look at it from your prospective local team leader's perspective, you are asking them to join a small start-up (risky enough for some) but also asking them to be the first in an experiment you are conducting in offshoring. If it doesn't go well for you you'll just shut up shop and consolidate at home. They'll be left up the creek without a paddle.

It's also worth remembering that it's not only the money that will attract people. If you are willing to offer someone a major step-up in responsibility to a managerial level which would take several years in an established company, you'll soon find yourself a few keen, ambitious youngsters willing to take a chance. Don't expect to be able to tempt someone with extensive management experience in a settled job unless you are willing to pay well over the odds and then ask if it's really what you want!

In this respect it's well worth thinking carefully about the type of individual you do want. If you recruit someone with extensive management experience from a large company they'll be used to extensive support networks. So, ultimately, you are likely to end up recruiting someone who is sufficiently entrepreneurial to take a risk in their career and can be hands on - someone like yourself in fact!

Offshore Culture

The first thing you need to accept is that the offshore office will have its own culture. There is absolutely no point in trying to force your development culture on it (with the exception of standards which I address below). By all means, set some high level guidelines but trust your local team to establish a suitable working culture that is appropriate to them.

Perhaps a harder aspect is understanding and setting your own expectations appropriately with respect to the local culture and the effect it has on their approach to life. For example, we found the Malaysians prepared to work extremely hard but not trained to think outside the box. Research seemed to be an alien concept. Implementation was their forte. In the early days we tried asking them to undertake a research project to establish the best approach to address a particular technical problem. This appeared not to compute and was understood as 'find a way to do it and do it'. At one point, we were told they wanted less uncertainty and just wanted to know what they had to do to earn their bonus. We didn't think they had any uncertainty!

As the Malaysian team grew and matured, I like to think that we met somewhere in the middle and we slowly moved them more towards our way of thinking. However, clearly you need to work around such realities and adjust accordingly. This is why I recommend getting someone who has lived and worked in a western environment as the team leader. There is less of a culture clash and more common ground.

Managing the Offshore Business

The first rule of offshore management is constant communication. In fact, at PleaseTech, the Malaysian development team was very much part of the overall development team and it certainly was not a case of 'chucking a specification over the wall' to await some developed software. There was daily communication, and integrated development environment and regular conference calls. We also had a policy of a senior person from the UK visiting Malaysia at least every quarter so we had 'eyes on' on a regular basis.

I personally visited the Malaysia office at least twice a year to, as I used to say, 'remind them who pays them'. Joking aside, I was careful not to be a seagull manager[95] and used to use my visit, inter alia, to provide a company update outlining where we were, the current vision for the future and the product plans for the next six months. All stuff which I assume that people in the UK office would know as they were around, if not party to, the discussions. It actually transpired that, as the company grew, the UK staff didn't know all that stuff and, as a result of the Malaysian sessions, we implemented equivalent UK sessions.

---

[95] Apparently this term originated from the book 'Leadership and the One Minute Manager' by Ken Blanchard which described Seagull managers as managers who 'fly in, make a lot of noise, dump on everyone, then fly out'. I've also heard it called Sparrow management.

Perhaps, the most important aspect is educating and ensuring that your offshore team understands the IP implications of ripping of software from the internet. This is covered in the 'Coding policies and standards' section above and it is imperative that this is reinforced at every opportunity. Developing countries frequently have a more 'fluid' attitude to IP protection and this permeates down into development, so it's a battle you have to fight as ultimately you'll be judged by western standards.

Financial management is another key aspect to consider. Use of external agencies such as payroll agencies to which you transfer the payroll cash directly minimises the administrative overhead of your offshore office (after all they are there to develop software) and minimises opportunities for misunderstandings. In fact, in PleaseTech, all administration except that which absolutely had to be done locally was done directly via the UK admin team. This allowed the Malaysian team to concentrate on their job rather than keeping the office running. As we grew we employed a local office manager who worked for both the UK admin team and the Malaysian team leader via the matrix management system described below.

We ended up developing a matrix management approach in which the Malaysian team reported to the Malaysian Team Lead for day-to-day personnel management issues and, where appropriate, development and the appropriate UK team for work related aspects. So, for example, the test team reported to the UK based Test Manager for work purposes and both the Test Manager and the Malaysian Team Lead if they wished to book a holiday or attend a doctor's appointment, etc.

It goes back to constant communication and making sure that the offshore team understand that you want the reality reported (as horrible as that may be) rather than a sanitised and optimistic version of the development status. An integrated development environment also helps in this respect because source code can easily be examined by the parent company team.

This may all sound more hassle than it's worth. It's not. At PleaseTech, over the 10 years we ran the Malaysian office, we developed a good working methodology and established a very high performance, relatively low cost development team. This was a significant attraction when we came to exit and our acquirer has continued to invest in the Malaysian team and, in fact, has recently announced that it is establishing one of its centres of excellence in Kuala Lumpur[96]. A great result all round.

Outsourcing and Subcontracting

I have no experience of outsourcing except as a supplier having to deal with clients whom have outsourced various parts of their IT operation. This was not a pleasant experience for us or the clients. The outsourcing companies generally grasped the opportunity to maximise their income while minimising their work.

I've read and heard so many horror stories about outsourcing I think you'd be mad to outsource any significant part of your development team. Leaving the IP issues aside for a minute, when you are operating in a dynamic environment the ability to react quickly to events is one of the main advantages of being a small software company. To react quickly you need control over priorities and I remain unconvinced that, no matter how tight the contract, you get that with a subcontractor.

I've already mentioned the CDC 'outsourcing' experience which, because the developers themselves didn't speak English and a lot of nuances were lost in translation, was unsuccessful. However, I do have a number of highly successful subcontracting experiences. These range from long term subcontracting relationships (as mentioned in The CDC Story) to one off specialist algorithms developed by contractors via sites on which freelancers bid against your specification.

The key commonality has been that we have subcontracted in highly specialist areas in which it makes sense for other experts to do the development. The key to a successful subcontracting experience is to get the contract, specifications and expectations right.

The principal reason for the contract is to protect your IP. No matter how small the sub-contractor and how insignificant the code item, ensure that there is a *signed* contract in place which, at the least, gives you a comprehensive royalty free license to use, distribute, further develop, etc. the software. The contract should also ensure that the subcontractor warrants that they have the power to grant the license and that the

---

[96] There is quite a lot of press about this. One link is here: https://tinyurl.com/y5vzrnhw

developed code is their own original work or, if it includes third party libraries understand what those libraries are and the associated license, just as you would do if your own team had written the code. Always get the source code.

This may seem like teaching your grandmother to suck eggs but it's neglecting these things which trip people up in due diligence when you are exiting.

In terms of the specification, it depends on the nature of the relationship but both parties need to understand the basics of what needs to be done for how much and in what timescale.

The obvious disadvantage to subcontracting is the lack of flexibility and control. If the subcontractor doesn't deliver on time there is little you can do. Even in long standing subcontract relationships, I've occasionally been 'frustrated' by delays to critical code outside of our control. The simple reality is that subcontractors have their own priorities and you are but one of their customers and, if they are any good, they'll be very busy.

Testing

Throughout the chapter on development I have emphasised product quality. I had first-hand experience in the CDC days of what happens when you release buggy code, and it's not pleasant. From a practical perspective, a huge amount of company resources are diverted to the non-productive effort needed to rectify the issues, pacify affected customers and repair your damaged reputation.

It's a truism in software development that 'a stitch in time saves nine'. In other words, an upfront investment in testing saves a huge amount of wasted effort further down the road. You can have the best developers in the world but you'll still need to test their output and ensure it is fit for purpose!

There is no doubt that the approach to software testing is changing as the automated testing inherent in the Agile approach gains momentum. On this subject I'd say two things: (i) automated testing is not a panacea, and (ii) it's my belief that you'll never be able to move away completely from manual testing especially where complex user interfaces are involved.

So, regardless of how Agile your process is you'll need to establish an independent test team. Their job is quite simply to try and break the software. Once they identify bugs they can be classified (as Critical, Major, Minor, Cosmetic or Feature[97]) and product management can decide what to do with them and whether they need to be fixed before the release.

Test Team Independence

The first thing is to establish is that the test team must be independent. The test team should not report into the development manager and probably not even the CTO. In PleaseTech, I always had the head of testing reporting directly to me. It sent a clear message to the whole company on how important I perceived testing to be and the fact that they were independent of development.

---

[97] It's not my job to explain what these classifications entail as there is plenty of literature on the subject.

Clearly there needs to be a high degree of co-operation between the development and test teams but the test team must have an independent mandate to approach the testing as they see fit.

The key point is that you don't want development managing the testers and specifying how and what to test. Likewise you don't want developers developing to a test script as giving them advanced sight of the test script is not going to bring out the best in anyone. Developers need to develop to the spec and testers need to be given free rein to test what they like when they like and how they like!

It follows that it's necessary for the process and developers to accept that testers are there to find faults and that is their job – whether the fault is part of a test script or not. Every fault must be formally recorded, classified and managed.

Conversely, the developers have to accept that they bear responsibility for basic checks before handing the code over to test. I was chatting with another CEO and he explained a situation where, in the name of Agile, developers refused to even do the most basic of checks before throwing the code over to the independent test team. This created a never ending cycle of acrimony and arguments between the developers and testers. He solved this, by implementing a 'pre-release' sign-off which required the developers undertake some basic tests and confirm that the software was ready for release and extensive testing.

It's not unknown for developers and testers to understand the specification differently and for testers to identify a 'bug' which the developer claims is not a bug and is behaviour in accordance with the specification. Where this happens product management need to adjudicate.

None of this changes with automated testing.

Automated Testing

I said that automated testing is not a panacea and it's important to remember that automated test harnesses are a software product in themselves. As such they need to be written, tested and maintained. This is frequently a higher overhead than writing the original code being tested!

When used on new functionality, if a fault is found, there needs to be a check whether the fault is with the code being tested, or the automated test, or both are simply different interpretations of the same spec. Having automated testing doesn't reduce your testing investment. If anything it increases it!

There is no doubt that automated testing does have its benefits especially when it comes to running regression tests on stable parts of the code to check that the new functionality hasn't inadvertently broken anything. It is particularly efficient when working at an API and unit level and can run multiple tests combinations and undertake a full regression test overnight. However, this assumes that you have stable parts of the code! If everything is always changing then you may find that more effort is put into script maintenance than into writing new scripts or even new code. You'll have to look seriously at the extent of your investment in automated scripts.

It's important to maintain test team independence, so that means the team developing the automatic testing harness must be different from the team developing the code. Therefore, if you are going to follow the automated test route your test team will need highly skilled automated test script developers. This increases the investment as you will need a different calibre of staff in your testing department.

I'd also question whether the overhead of developing automated UI testing is worth it. Can an automated UI test really replicate a real user's actions? As the functional intelligence coded into the browser increases so does the risk that not all browsers will behave or display identically. How do you keep the maintenance cost of these scripts acceptable?

There are some functional UI tests which can be successfully automated using recorders. However, where there is subtle user interaction you will need real live humans testing it. The advantage of these real live humans is that not only can they test functionality, but they can also monitor the softer side of testing the UI. Does it flow? Is it easy to use? Does it display correctly?

Accept the fact that you will need manual testing somewhere in the process!

Manual Testing and Agile

I previously mentioned that the Agile process assumes automated integral testing is developed alongside the code. The problem is that this doesn't reflect reality. Even if you are focusing on automated testing there will be a need for some manual testing unless your product doesn't have a UI or has a simple UI.

Additionally, if you have existing code that does not have automated testing then regression testing and testing of new functionality based on the existing code will need to be manual. You will need to adjust the whole development process to fit this in.

What you do not want is a development process that treats testing as an optional extra rather than an integral part of the process.

Where there is a significant element of manual testing, development and test management need to work closely together to ensure maximum efficiency and resource utilisation. For example, testers may be waiting for code to test and, once under test, developers may be waiting for bugs to be identified[98]. The process needs to be closely managed to ensure that one party isn't waiting on the other party and always has something to do. Likewise there is a danger that the process breaks down because all testing is left to the end of the Sprint, so either the testers are under pressure to minimise testing as the Sprint is ending or the Sprint is closed before the testing is completed.

It's really important that the process reflects the reality and that it is adjusted to ensure that adequate testing is performed. This requires flexibility and creative process design which accommodates all parties and allows them to complete their tasks.

Risk Based Testing

Given the complexity of modern software, comprehensive testing of every aspect is simply not possible. The number of combinations of parameters is huge and even with automated testing not all bugs will be found. This is

---

[98] There is an argument that while developers are writing the code, testers can be developing the test script. However, at best, all they can do is produce preliminary or outline scripts.

especially true when you have various set-up and configuration options all of which should theoretically tested in all combinations.

Thus testing becomes a risk management process. In all code there are simple and complex areas. It goes without saying that a majority of testing should be concentrated on the complex areas. This is where the CTO, development manager, test manager and even individual developers need to sit down and plan a test strategy. Which areas of the code are the highest risk? Generally it's the level of complexity rather than the volume of code which determines the associated risk of inaccuracies.

No automated script can substitute for a knowledgeable human tester who has an understanding of what and why they are testing. Experienced testers get a feel for the software and what is likely to go wrong and where. The culture needs to focus on and reward quality which is the responsibility of both the development and test teams.

Support

Support is a critical part of customer satisfaction and yet is a tough area to get right. How much resource do you throw at it? What level of support do you provide for how much?

Regardless of delivery mechanism of your software (i.e. an online service or on-premise) you want the client to actually use it and build their business processes around it. This ensures annual renewal fees and additional licenses that are necessary to grow the business. So it's in your interest to provide comprehensive start-up support to get the clients up and running.

We've already discussed my approach to professional services under Pricing, and I am excluding the provision of professional services from support. However, I do address where support finishes and professional services start!

The first thing to decide is whether you are offering technical support and or a helpdesk and set client expectations accordingly. Let's examine the difference:

A helpdesk (aka helpline) suggests that you have a team of user specialists on hand (on the end of a phone, chat, email or other such facility) to explain to users how to use the system. This is generally aimed at end users of the software.

Technical support provides the more in-depth technical assistance to get the system up and running and thereafter running smoothly and is not designed to be a user handholding exercise. This is especially needed in an on-premise environment, although for cloud services there may well be hooks to IDaaS[99] type services and others to configure. It is typically offered to nominated client super users and IT support staff.

The challenges associated with helpdesks, if you are operating internationally, are time zones and languages. It is also expensive having staff on hand to answer the phone or chat service. The necessity to offer a helpdesk will depend largely on the environment into which you sell. If you

---

[99] Identity as a service (IDaaS) are cloud-based solutions for standard corporate user management functions such as single sign-on (SSO). The point is that in a corporate environment it's rarely as simple as a single, standalone system with no interaction with other third party systems.

are selling into the SME market (this is unlikely to be international), these companies are less likely to have internal IT support and therefore will require a much higher level of end user type support.

As this will be priced as a service and the support element won't be broken out you just need to be explicit about what support is provided. This doesn't mean you have to offer a helpdesk but it may mean a high investment in self-help tools such as videos, etc. You may well decide to offer access to a support team for an additional payment or as part of a premium account. The key is to set client expectations and remember that the support service received is all part of the user experience and will have a major impact on user satisfaction.

At PleaseTech, we offered technical support to nominated <u>trained</u> users and set expectations and contractual terms accordingly. However, we never turned away anyone requesting support on the basis we needed customers to have happy users. This didn't mean we were inundated with support calls as most large corporates have their own internal help desks and generally discourage their staff from contacting vendors directly.

The approach we encouraged was for the client to have internal superusers who were the people supported by us. We also provided, as part of the software's in-built help, a comprehensive self-help portal, training videos (which customers were able to download and add to their own internal help/training portals), and so on.

Ultimately, in providing support you want to throw the least amount of resources at it as possible whilst ensuring happy clients who will sing your praises from the rooftops. It helps if you as the CEO take a personal interest in support and everyone is aware of how important it is. In PleaseTech, I emphasised it's importance by ensuring I was on top of all support queries. Every incoming and outgoing support email was copied to me personally. I didn't necessarily do anything with them but I could keep an eye on developing situations and it had several beneficial effects:

1. The support staff knew I was watching and, if there were a few emails bouncing backwards and forwards, I would occasionally get a pre-emptive email or chat from the head of support which said something along the lines of 'I know you are watching and will be getting concerned, but ....'.

2. I was able to monitor the status of important clients and got a feeling how they were getting on with the software.

3. I got an instinctive feeling for which areas of the software were causing grief and needed to be addressed.

So, my advice to you is to be on top of support and understand what is going on. Don't just rely on monthly stats which show how many calls were dealt with within an agreed timeframe.

In the rest of this section I cover some additional thoughts on support and how to turn it into an asset rather than a perceived overhead and liability.

Early Days

In the early days it's all hands to the pump. Before we had a dedicated support person and then personnel, we had the support system automatically broadcast all incoming support emails to all technical staff (and me) with the understanding that anyone (including me) with the time and ability to respond should do so. I personally responded to usability questions (i.e. how do you do this …..) as the more deeply technical questions were outside my competency. Obviously for the frequently asked questions we had stock answers available and that meant techies weren't always required for technical queries.

It worked particularly well in dealing with the USA and associated late night support queries. There was usually one of us sitting in our home office in front of a PC who would respond. Frequently that person was me and, if I picked up a deeply technical question and it seemed that the client need an immediate answer, I'd ring around the techies until I found someone able to pick it up.

This approach enabled us to provide a high level of customer service which was above and beyond that expected from a small UK company. Some of our west coast clients found it hard to comprehend how we provided better support from eight time zones away than they got from their local suppliers. This did us no harm and we used it in our sales pitches. For example, I (and as we grew, the sales team) regularly told clients that such was our commitment to support that I (the CEO) got copies of all incoming support emails. The message was: we take this seriously.

As we grew we graduated away from the broadcast to all approach and implemented a formal ticket management system, the developers were only involved when they had to be. However, I still received a copy of all support emails and everyone in the company understood that support was important!

SLAs

As you grow clients will start demanding formal Service Levels Agreements (SLAs).

A typical support SLA will cover the agreed response times for support contacts and associated penalties for failure to meet the agreed service level. When considering SLAs you need to be realistic. There is no point in setting yourself up for failure and therefore a penalty.

For example, at PleaseTech we always based SLAs on UK office hours regardless of where the client was. We were able to get away with this as we had a unique product and it was a question of explaining to the client they either lived with it or didn't buy it[100]!

In this respect, it's absolutely necessary to understand the difference between a 'response time' and a 'resolution time'. Agreeing to a fixed resolution time is a bad idea. Modern software is extremely complex with multiple interactions and changes to third party systems outside of your control. A resolution may not be that straight forward.

If the client insists on fixed resolution times (some are fairly intransigent in this respect) give yourself a fighting chance in the contract. For example, you may want to specify that it applies to specifically validated environments with a precise version of each third party software you interact with, thus ensuring that if it's a change in a third party piece of software which has broken the system you are not penalised. In short, if you absolutely must accede to a fixed resolution time make it as difficult as possible for the client to comply with its terms.

Remember that, once the contract is signed, such contracts are generally filed away and never referred to again unless there is a break down in relationships between you and the client. The IT support staff managing your

---

[100] Usually. There are always exceptions for very large deals!

system and or the interactions of third party software with your system, may be aware of the high level aspects of the agreement but may not know the detail and therefore, if it does all end in tears, you should be able to point out a failing on their part to get out of jail free.

Having said all that, the key to a successful support relationship with the client is to not be a slave to an SLA. For example, you may be fully within the SLA in your response times but, if you are simply responding and not addressing the issue in hand, it will be a poor client experience. Therefore you need to drum it into your support staff that they should be actively seeking to assist the client to a resolution and not just responding to stay within the SLA.

Also be aware that a common trap into which many support staff fall is to assume that the client knows as much about the software as they do. So, when they respond asking for further information or a log file or something similar, they shouldn't just ask for the file. They should include an explanation for the poor harassed client support person on how to access the required information. Make it easy for the client.

The key to happy clients is issue resolution and not just response times! This is frequently not helped by the varying levels of technical competence in the IT support operations of your client companies. Some are excellent. Really bright people who understand what they are doing, follow instructions and consider issue resolution to be a joint effort. Others don't meet this standard.

Of course, it always preferable to deal with the able ones, but bear in mind that the less able IT support staff will have a highly developed ability to slope their shoulders and blame all the delays on the vendor, i.e. you and your staff. It is precisely for these situations that you've kept your relationships with the client's senior staff and sometimes you need to have a grown up conversation with these contacts to explain to them that you are doing your best but it's their staff which are the roadblock. Often it won't come as a surprise to your contacts that their internal support staff aren't the sharpest pencils in the box.

Support vs Services

I've already mentioned in the Pricing and Delivering Services section above that in neither of my companies did we sell any significant level services and consequently left money on the table. Having said that we did have services on the price list and a capacity to deliver. You may decide not to leave money on the table and develop a services capacity.

Regardless of the approach you take the question you'll never get away from is: Where does support end and services begin?

Generally, technical support limits itself to explaining to a client how to do something whereas undertaking services involves hands-on implementation. So, if a client is struggling to install something, technical support would be working with the client in an advisory capacity (e.g. reviewing log files and suggesting alternative approaches, etc.) whilst hands-on troubleshooting would be the provision of implementation services.

As I have previously suggested, you'll find that the technical ability of some client's support staff is poor. These clients require a high degree of support and sometimes it would be easier for our support staff to get a remote log onto their system and just solve the problem.

You would be right in thinking that therein lies a slippery slope. However, ultimately, my objective was always to have a happy client. I believed that with a happy client, use of the software would grow and we'd reap the benefits in the future. Therefore we were fairly generous with our interpretation of what constituted technical support regardless of whether the client had purchased implementation services or not.

In these cases, we made the point to the client that we were going above and beyond the support contract. This was worth doing as it laid down a marker for future work (i.e. we had an expectation that they'd pay) and it built goodwill. If you are going to do something nice for them make sure they understand that is what you are doing!

In order to achieve this you need to have good communication between all members engaged with the client. The head of support needs to judge when such additional support is needed and communicate with the account manager. The account manager then needs to have the appropriate words with the client and bank those brownie points.

If you see the client purely as a money making exercise and extract your pound of flesh every time you can, sooner or later this will come back to bite you. Building up a reserve of good will is never a bad thing.

Other Support Miscellany

Some other support thoughts for you:

1. There is always a need to provide more support early on in a client's use of the software. As they get familiar with it the amount of support required tends to die away. Obvious? Perhaps, but be aware of this and have a plan to cope if you have several clients going live in the same broad timeframe.

2. Be prepared for the Friday night rush. It makes sense when you think about it. People suddenly spot that there is a deadline on Monday and decide to clear the action on Friday. If you are dealing with the USA this is Friday night for you! It may have been quiet all week but suddenly your support line will fill up with support queries just as your team is heading off for the weekend and, because your clients are trying to meet a deadline, all queries are urgent!

   Note: You can change out 'Friday night' with any other deadline such as a public holiday (e.g. Christmas or Easter in the UK, Independence Day or Thanksgiving in the USA) or similar.

3. A small team can be sold as a positive. When clients asked how big our support team was, I generally told them the truth (it was always a lot smaller than they were comfortable with) and added that there was a good reason behind that. We didn't need a massive support team because we produced high quality software and suggested to them that if they didn't believe me, to ask an existing client if our support was up to scratch. It never lost us a deal!

In The PleaseTech Story I mention the case of a prospect who had spoken to five of her industry contacts prior to making an enquiry. If our support hadn't been on point we would not have got her call and the resulting business. Support is a key factor in client satisfaction and by placing great support at the heart of your operation you'll get the renewals and license rollouts which will enable you to grow the business.

Quality Management System (QMS)

Depending on the industries you address, you may need to expand your development and test policies and procedures into a more formal QMS.

A lot of the constituent parts of a QMS are simple good practice. We've already discussed the need for control and full traceability in the development environment. This will need to be addressed via managing documents and records to provide appropriate audit trails. In following this good practice you have the basis of a QMS. All you need do is 'top and tail' it with a formal policy statement, some objectives and a commitment to continuous improvement, and you are done and dusted.

I may sound facetious, but the point is that you do not need to spend your hard earned money on quality consultants who will 'borrow your watch to tell you the time'[101]. There is plenty of information available on the web and there are even free complete template sets.

It is up to you whether you believe that having a formal ISO certification is worthwhile. I've never seen it as necessary. As far I was concerned the important things were that the software was of high quality and that the company was efficiently run. Having ISO certification wasn't going to change anything.

However, in both my businesses we did operate in the Life Sciences market in which having a formal quality system was mandatory. Note: Having a quality system was mandatory – it was not mandatory to have a formal certification. Our clients and prospects would audit us regularly.

Our approach at PleaseTech was to internally develop a QMS which we then improved every time there was an audit. The way it worked was quite simple; the auditors would often find things we could do better. Afterall they were auditors and liked finding failings or aspects which could be improved. Typically, the auditors would present their findings and we'd have to agree to rectify and improve certain aspects of our QMS within six months. The extent of the improvements was always a matter for negotiation, but they were pushing at an open door. We weren't defending what we had – just

---

[101] We discuss dealing with Consultants and Independent Experts below.

trying to minimise the extra work! The main purpose of the QMS was to pass audits – we already delivered quality software and had a well-run company!

The way I saw it was that we were getting free consultancy. By taking onboard the 'advice' from the auditors, we moved the QMS forward without spending anything on a consultant. Furthermore, the incremental enhancements we implemented were the important enhancements as they were at the top of the auditor's list. As we grew, we recruited a part time Quality Manager to keep the whole show on the road, but it was very much a home-grown system.

The key point is that you don't need to go out and spend a fortune on consultants. As long as you are delivering a high-quality product and the company is effectively run, you can adopt an incremental approach to implementing a QMS – if you need one.

Finance, Admin, Legal et al

These topics have a natural grouping as they are all, to one extent or another, bound by law and typically fall under the CFO's remit. There is a considerable amount of recruitment, financial, and associated legislation that all needs to be considered. Additionally, it's the main area in which professional advice is sought especially with respect to legal and tax matters.

When I started my first business life was relatively simple and, with the help of a few books (no internet then), I kept the financial records and didn't use the services of an accountant for a while. However, these days, life is less simple and, whilst there are areas a well-read amateur can handle, things like the Making Tax Digital (MTD) initiative in the UK means you have to use an accounting package. Therefore the use of an accountant or of a self-employed part time book keeper is more or less mandatory[102].

The other thing to bear in mind is that, by establishing a formal limited company, you have adopted a number of responsibilities associated with reporting, etc. None of these are particularly onerous and can mostly be achieved online by the aforementioned well-read amateur but you will probably find that your time is better spent trying to make sales!

As with all administration having a well organised and efficient system makes life so much easier. It makes day-to-day operations easier, it makes growth easier and, if you are successful, it makes exit easier. It is therefore not an area you should neglect!

General Finance

There is a considerable amount of legislation around the financial management of a company with which any competent accountant should be familiar. This legislation is constantly changing and best practices are continually evolving. It goes without saying that your accounting policy should be in accordance with current legislation and good accounting practice.

The first thing you need to be very aware of is the distinction between the company's formal accounts and its internal management accounts. Management accounts should reflect the financial reality of the business on

---

[102] I found the self-employed part time bookkeeper I am using for my current companies by posting the opportunity on the local community FaceBook page.

a month-by-month basis (focusing on the business's key financial parameters – see below) whilst the formal profit and loss (P&L) and balance sheet reflect a historical snapshot of a previous period.

Whilst a monthly P&L and balance sheet can be interesting, they are not really pertinent if your sales are lumpy. I have already mentioned that both PleaseTech and CDC were a Q1 and Q4 business and therefore a monthly P&L was not really that useful.

Ultimately you need to focus on and have an intimate knowledge of the three key financial ingredients of any small business: sales, cash and costs!

Cash Flow

As previously noted, cash is the lifeblood of the business. Costs reduce the cash balance and sales eventually increase it! Cash enables you to meet your commitments whether they be to the staff via the payroll or the landlord for rent, or services vital to the delivery of your products.

The cash flow forecast was the financial parameter to which I paid the most attention, especially in the start-up years. The key metric is cash cover[103]. In other words, if you sold nothing more and maintained the same overheads, how long before the cash runs out? We used to monitor two forms of cash cover. One was actual cash in the bank and the other was cash in the bank and monies owed to us. Having a healthy cash cover gives you time to react to events if need be.

As the business grows you will need to make decisions regarding how much you invest in growth and how much you hold back investment to increase your cash cover. I've come across businesses that cut cash cover very fine. So fine that sometimes on the first of the month, they don't even know how they will make the monthly payroll. In my view this is simply stupid. All that energy running around desperately chasing cash is energy which could have gone into more sales! Ultimately, only you will be able to judge the correct level of cash cover for your business. Personally, once out of the early start-up phase, I used to get nervous if the cash cover was less than six months.

---

[103] In VC land this is called your 'cash runway'.

This compares with Bill Gates who always liked to have 12 months cash cover[104].

When considering cash flow projections you should always take a conservative view. Assume that costs happen instantly and that clients pay slowly (which they do). It's also worth remembering that, especially in the early days, it's not a smooth progression. An extra head can significantly increase overheads and decimate cash cover!

Revenue Recognition

One of the areas non-financial people find trickiest to understand is revenue recognition. It's not as simple as: we've sold £100K and been paid so our revenue is £100k! There is the sale event (i.e. the receipt of the PO) but it only becomes revenue once the software or service sold has been delivered. Note that the receipt of the cash is immaterial and doesn't affect the accounting.

So, for example, if you sell a software service to a client for £120k for a year's worth of the service, there are several aspects from an accounting and financial reporting perspective which will happen. Once the order is received the £120k will be shown in the management accounts as sales but not revenue. Once the £120k has been invoiced and payment received, your cash balance will improve by £120k but it's still not recognisable revenue. From an accounting and formal reporting perspective this order can only be taken to revenue as it is delivered. This means that, assuming the service is being delivered in accordance with the contract, £10k is taken to revenue every month.

If your financial year is the calendar year and it so happens that you sold the contract in December for commencement on 1st January, you will get the revenue from the deal in the year after the sale. You may have met your sales target (in so far as the PO has been received) for the year in which it was sold but it won't impact your formally reported revenue for that year[105].

---

[104] Source: Question and answer with Bill Gates at the launch of the Harvard Campaign, 2013: https://youtu.be/cBHJ-8Bch4E

[105] This is why it all pays to place close attention to the wording of a company's announcements regarding their performance. Are they talking about sales, revenue, etc.

Alternatively, if you sell the same system partway through the year, it follows that you will get a percentage of the deal as revenue. For example, if the deal was sold in March for go live on 1st April, 75% of the deal (£90k) will be recognised as revenue in the remaining nine months and that's what will be added to your formally reported revenue.

It's worth noting that the sums are very different if you are selling a perpetual license with annual support (a standard on-premise license). In the £120K deal let's assume that £100k is the license fee and £20k is the annual support. Once the software is delivered[106], £100k can be recognised as revenue immediately and it's only the £20k support which is recognised incrementally as it is delivered over the course of the forthcoming year. In other words, much more is recognised much earlier. This is why moving from selling perpetual licenses to annual renewing term licenses has a negative impact on top line (i.e. revenue) growth.

The key point is that the receipt of cash is not pertinent to whether the revenue is recognised. It's whether the goods or service have been delivered. Cash is accounted for separately. It's vitally important but it's nothing to do with revenue recognition.

The other thing you'll have to do is unbundle sales (if appropriate) for revenue recognition. This means separating out the elements and allocating 'fair value' using equality of discount, where applicable. Let's assume our previous example of the £120K service sales included a chunk of 'free' training. Let's also say that this free training was worth £12K at list price and that there has been no other discounting. This means that the training should be separated out in the calculations. So, assuming the second example of the sale in March for a 1st April go live, and further assuming that the training took three months to complete, the revenue recognised in the nine months of the financial year will be £93K (rather than the £90k previously). This is because the £12K allocated to the training is delivered separately from the service and is taken to revenue (adjusted for discount)

---

[106] Having a clear definition of when an on premise license is delivered is very important. Providing download details and a license key is typically all that is required. It is not necessary for the software to be installed and working. The software has been delivered and, unless there is a claw back clause or some other right of cancellation in the contract, it can be recognised.

once delivered leaving the service itself (worth £9.1K per month adjusted for discount) which will be taken to revenue as it is delivered[107].

You may ask why all this is necessary. The answer comes in three parts:

1. It's actually not at all important for the day-to-day running of the business. As noted above you need to be monitoring sales, cash and costs. Clearly it's necessary to have confidence that what is sold can be delivered and therefore invoiced and therefore the cash collected. It's also important to ensure that your sales are profitable - unless you are in VC land when profit is sacrificed for growth.

2. It's important that you file accurate end of year accounts (however small you are) because these will have an impact on your company's tax position. There are big fines for getting tax wrong and therefore this is to be avoided.

3. It's vitally important if you are dealing with venture capitalists or other investors. What is the basis of the targets set (and the forecasts you made)? Is it sales, is it revenue? Remember the distinction and that there can be a significant delay between the actual sale and the ability to recognise the revenue especially in respect to an online service which is taken to revenue monthly. Be very sure to be clear what your business plan is offering and understand what the VC investors will be judging you upon.

If the three arguments above aren't enough to convince you that revenue recognition matters, consider the exit. Your revenue recognition policy will be examined by your acquirer and any anomalies will be problematic.

At the time of writing the UK civil court case between Hewlett-Packard ("HP") and the Founder and CEO of Autonomy (Dr. Mike Lynch) and its former CFO (Sushovan Hussain), is underway. It's the fallout from HP's acquisition of Autonomy. I'm sure that you are aware of the case and its background (if not, look it up). The bottom line is that one of HP's central claims is that Autonomy artificially inflated its revenue especially via

---

[107] To go through the maths: £120K is deemed to include £12K training. Thus the total list price is £132K. The deal was £120k implying a discount of 9% which means that what is delivered is 9 months of the main deal (£120K*0.91*0.75=£81.9K) plus the training (£12K*0.91=£10.9k) = £92.8K which for our purposes is £93K!

hardware sales and sales via resellers. Trust me, your revenue recognition policy is important[108].

Costs

A software company typically has high fixed costs. These are the salaries and associated overheads (the main cost) and other overheads such as rent, electricity, connectivity, cloud services, search advertising fees, etc.

When projecting costs it's important to remember that the cost of an employee is not just their annual salary. There are additional fixed costs such as pension contributions and national insurance which the employer has to pay. These can add significantly to the cost of the salary. These change all the time (with legislation, tax rates, etc.) and searching will provide you with the current standard metrics. There are also some excellent online tools which can assist in the calculations. Adding staff also comes with start-up costs; a new PC, desk, chair, etc. These costs add up. So when you are planning, especially in the early days, be sure to be realistic.

In the early days, costs are all about cash management. Will you have enough cash to cover the bills? As you grow you need to become more sophisticated in your treatment of costs. For example, you will want to split out hosting costs between internal overheads and service delivery. This will ensure that you will be able to calculate the real contribution (i.e. gross profit) from your services and understand what internal services really cost.

There isn't much more to say about costs except for one bit of advice which becomes pertinent as you grow. I absolutely refused to talk about 'budgets' or allocate anyone a budget.

I had two main reasons for this;

Firstly, I believe that if you give someone a budget they will spend it whether they need to or not. Indeed, this is why most B2B businesses are Q4 businesses. Most corporates budgets are issued on a 'use it or lose it' basis and, to compound the need to spend it, if it's not used the budget may be

---

[108] There is an interesting 2018 article on this on FT.com (https://tinyurl.com/y7bepc6g) which notes that "revenue recognition has been a US preoccupation for years, but British auditors have tended to give companies a much freer hand". So it's especially important if selling to a US company!

reduced the following year[109]. When you relate that to your business, do you really want someone spending money just because it's in their budget?

Secondly, I haven't run a large enough or stable enough business where allocating budgets makes sense. Small software companies operate in a dynamic environment and, to repeat one of my favourite mantras, the only constant is change. Therefore you need to manage dynamically. If you need larger servers, more security, additional people or whatever, you need it whether or not you foresaw that in the previous year when the 'budgets' were set!

By all means have spending projections (it's what we called them in PleaseTech) but be sure to personally sign off on all important financial commitments. I always took the view that if someone could justify spending the money and we could afford to do so (this is where the cash flow forecasts and management are key) then I'd give the go ahead regardless of whether the expenditure was forecast in the spending projections. Budgets are a form of secondary financial control. At the size of company I'm talking about you need to be exercising direct financial control.

It all comes back to being on top of your business and understanding what will improve things. If that means spending money and you can afford it, then it is sensible to do so. Likewise if the spending is gratuitous you can stop it.

Expenses

In addition to salaries, one of the key costs will be travel expenses. This will be especially true if your business model includes attending shows and visiting clients i.e. you have people 'on the road'.

There are a lot of myths around expenses and, unfortunately, abuse of expenses is not unknown. Once there are people other than the principals travelling, it's important to have a clear written policy of what is acceptable and what isn't acceptable.

---

[109] To be fair, many corporate managers avoid spending money in the first half of the year in case there are changed circumstances and only release the budget as the year draws to a close. This is because corporate budgets are rigid and don't reflect changing circumstances.

I've always been clear that the expense policy applies to me just as much to anyone else in the company. This is important not only from a cultural perspective but also because with a clear company-wide expense policy that applies to everyone, your policy is less likely to be challenged by HMRC. Clearly, your policy should be in accordance with HMRC guidelines and expenses incurred purely for business purposes.

If you cannot show that the expense is purely for business purposes, HMRC may consider it a benefit in kind and it will become part of your taxable income. Therefore I strongly recommend that you keep detailed records and file formal expense claims on a regular basis.

For example, if claiming mileage, record the postcodes and who you visited, if claiming for foreign spending include both the foreign receipt and a redacted credit card bill showing how much you paid in GBP.

Ensure a clear division of entertainment vs other expense types. This is because, currently, entertainment is not an allowable expense against corporate tax and will need to be accounted for separately. Rules do change so keep track of them and update your policy appropriately.

Some words of hard won advice with respect to expenses which can be a very contentious area:

1. Do not issue company credit cards. Make people use personal credit cards and get them to reclaim the cash spent from the company with a formal expense claim form and receipts. It's amazing how much more compliant to the policy and willing to submit formal expense claims people are when there is a personal liability and their credit card bill is due. Clearly, there will be some circumstances when the company needs to provide an advance or purchase something like an airfare on behalf of an employee but this should be the exception rather than the rule.

2. There are very few advantages and many disadvantages to subcontracting travel arrangements to a third party. We did experiment with this in the later days of CDC but it was extremely unpopular and I recall it was abandoned. It's much better that everyone makes their own travel arrangements. Travel was so important (and a major overhead) throughout the PleaseTech days

that I've added a section on my travel tips to the book's website (www.softwarecompanybook.com).

3. Be very clear on what is and isn't acceptable and, within reason, be tight on expenses as sooner or later someone will try it on. For example, be clear on things like valet parking, parking tickets (the company doesn't pay them), travel to and from the airport, airport parking, taxis, hotel class, shared hotel rooms[110], laundry, etc. You don't want someone swanning up late for a flight and decide to stick their car in short term parking and expect to reclaim the cost. Most people treat the company's money as they would their own but there is always one[111].

4. If an employee is likely to be entertaining clients (and if attending conferences, this will be more-or-less mandatory), be clear on what level of entertainment is acceptable. For example, ordering a very expensive bottle of wine in order to show off to a client is completely unacceptable in my view.

5. Be careful of someone who wants to take a holiday either side of a business flight. If audited, HMRC will almost certainly consider that the expense was not incurred wholly and exclusively for business purposes and, if this is the view, there will be a benefit in kind to be charged and potentially a fine.

With any degree of travel, expenses will be a major cost. As with all costs it is essential that the cost is controlled and detailed records are kept. These detailed records will be necessary in the event of an HMRC audit (and they

---

[110] You may be tempted to try and reduce costs by asking people to share hotel rooms. I consider this a very bad idea. Even in the really early days of CDC when we were existing on loans, sharing a room was not an option. We just went to a cheaper hotel. I would reiterate that I've always been clear that the expense policy applies to me just as much to anyone else in the company. I wouldn't share a hotel room with anyone but my wife and I don't expect my staff to have to do so.

[111] I know of one single (as in not married) salesman who boasted that he would pack all his laundry and then have it done in the hotel at the company's expense. I don't think this abuse lasted and he soon disappeared from view.

do happen) and during due diligence prior to exit to assure the acquiring company that there is no hidden tax liability[112].

Finally, I'll drop it in here as there is nowhere else it logically goes, and is an important point; if you are asking employees to use their own personal car for travel (for example, to and from meetings and or the airport), make sure that they have included such business travel in their car insurance.

Foreign Currency

If you are dealing internationally (and, if not, why not?) you'll have to deal with foreign currency. As I noted earlier, I believe that it's your responsibility to deal with the foreign currency risk. It certainly isn't your client's job to take the risk so that leaves it as your risk. Clearly there are limits. You can't quote in every currency and the reality is that companies in countries with minor currencies will be used to buying software in the default currency, US dollars. In PleaseTech we had a pricelist which included US dollars, pounds and euros as options. We occasionally quoted in other currencies making sure that we had a healthy margin to cover the costs and risks.

The risk is of course the movement of currency between quote, order and cash receipt. In other words, if selling in dollars you can never be sure of how many pounds will actually end up in your bank account.

The first thing to do is ensure that you are in control of the transaction costs and have separate bank accounts for your major currencies (i.e. in our case GBP, USD and EUR). You then need to make a decision on currency policy. Do you hold the money in the foreign currency converting when you need the cash or when the rate appears to be good, or do you convert instantly?

This obviously has an impact on your cash flow and as you do more and more foreign currency sales, you may need to have a separate currency cash flow forecast and your currency management will need to become more sophisticated. For bigger contracts, there is always the option to hedge or buy forward. It's never a good idea to use your bank for currency exchange or hedging. Specialist currency brokers exist for a reason.

---

[112] We will be covering this in the section on exit but, in brief, you'll have to provide a seven year warranty against tax liabilities so it's in your interest to ensure that there are no potential tax bombs anywhere in the business. In other words, play by the rules.

You may want to go with the flow during the year but cover everything towards the year end so as to avoid a surprise in the year end accounts. Currency gains and losses should be accounted for separately.

At a practical level, there are several things to consider:

1. Ensure your clients understand that the contract currency is the currency in which they pay. You do not want to be paid in GBP at their bank's exchange rate. Nor do you want to have the client decide to change the payment currency during the contract.

2. Make sure the invoice has the correct bank account for the contract currency and state very clearly on the invoice that the sums are to be paid in (for example) USD and not GBP. Despite this, one issue we regularly had was that when receiving an electronic transfer from the USA an intermediator bank (generally not the sending bank) would assume it should be sent in GBP and convert it at their rate and forward GBP. This meant that despite the client sending USD and their bank sending USD, we got GBP in our USD account and another conversion fee! Sometimes it's not worth the effort to unwind this transaction and other times it most definitely is.

3. We found that many companies in the USA still send physical cheques and you'll need a mechanism to convert them to cash at as low a cost as possible.

Ultimately, you need to remember (and remind your CFO) that you are a software company and not a currency trader. Therefore low risk currency management is generally adopted!

Overseas Considerations

If you are selling internationally there are certain considerations which need to be explored as things like withholding tax can seriously damage your wealth and make dealing with a particular territory very marginal, especially if you've had to adjust your price (aka discount) for the local market.

Some considerations which come to mind (not a comprehensive list):

1. Is there a tax agreement which means that the client does not have to withhold part of the payment in lieu of tax (withholding tax)?

2. Will you need a license to operate?

3. What is the status of Sales Tax/VAT? For example, in the USA each state has a different rate. Make sure that your contract places the onus on the client to pay any local sales tax to the appropriate authority (this is not always possible and you may have to register yourself and fight to get the tax refunded).

Obviously, there are a load of further considerations if you decide to set-up a subsidiary especially if it is for sales activity. Generally a foreign sales subsidiary is a massive financial and administrative overhead and certainly to be avoided if at all possible. Think of it as having a whole additional company with added complications such as tax issues and remote management operating in a jurisdiction with which you are not familiar. Your accountant should know the types of questions to ask. These will be around tax treatment and transfer pricing, reporting, and any specific local ownership requirements (which we covered under offshoring) and so on.

Sourcing of Financing

I have very little experience with respect to sources of financing other than venture capital and that I address in a separate section which also covers business angels and crowdfunding.

My experience of loans is limited to special UK government backed loans issued under the now defunct Small Firms Loan Guarantee Scheme (SFLGS) which appears to have been replaced by the Enterprise Finance Guarantee (EFG) scheme. Loans under these schemes reduce the risk to the lending bank as the government underwrites the majority of any default.

All I can say is that when I used the SFLGS in the 1990s, it worked very well. There was no requirement for me to put up any personal guarantees[113] and this reduced the personal risk of undertaking a start-up.

My general advice to people is never to put your house on the line and always have some savings which can pay the mortgage for a few months if it all goes pear-shaped. I believe that, if you have too much to lose, you'll make the wrong decisions and your decision making will be skewed towards

---

[113] Whilst I had personal assets which could cover the loans (the equity in my house), conveniently my wife refused to allow the joint asset to be collateral. This meant I could not put up collateral and therefore qualified for the loan.

short term cash issues rather than a balanced view with longer term investment.

If you do approach banks for a loan, they will look at it from a risk minimisation perspective and some bankers will want to extract every penny in collateral they can. This is why the EFG type schemes are so beneficial. The more intelligent bankers understand that too much personal commitment is not conducive to the success of the business. You can try and explain to the less intelligent ones that you have plenty of skin in the game. You may tell them that you have given up a decent paying job, you are not taking a salary and working eighteen hours a day to get this thing off the ground. If that isn't skin in the game, what is? However, don't expect them to understand. As far as I can tell, they simply turn up for their overpaid jobs and haven't got a clue how much commitment a start-up takes!

Another source of financing you'll come across is factoring. Factoring is getting advanced payment on your invoices by a third party (a factor) at a cost. Typically, you still have to chase the debt, etc. but you simply get the money earlier. If the client defaults you will have to cover the default. I have no experience of it and question whether it's sensible (or even possible) for the provision of enterprise software and services despite us getting endless mailshots on the subject. If you do consider it remember the old maxim: you never get something for nothing. Be absolutely sure what you are signing up for. Read the contract, don't just rely on what the salesperson told you!

Remember there are plenty of ways of cutting back on cash out whilst you are waiting for an invoice to be paid. In the early days of CDC, despite having got to a point where I was paying myself a salary, there were a number of occasions when I didn't pay myself for a month or so to ensure that we had sufficient cash to pay the important bills.

If such cash flow interrupts are not one-offs, then you may be over expanding and your overheads are simply too high for the current level of sales. Examine all overheads and expenses very closely and work out what can be removed. There will be no easy solutions and factoring certainly isn't an easy solution.

Other Financial Considerations

It goes without saying that you need to keep your accounts up-to-date and constantly adjust cash flow forecasts to reflect reality. As you grow you need a comprehensive system which provides good management information and full traceability (e.g. make sure deferred income can be traced to specific contracts) because, in due diligence, you'll have to prove the numbers.

Software companies can grow very rapidly and, without a solid system in place chaos can reign. It's also worth noting that, especially when dealing internationally, many aspects will be outside the experience of most accountants. Therefore, you need to encourage your CFO (or other financial advisor) to get external advice when it is required. It won't be free but timely advice resulting the correct decisions and set-up will pay for itself over time.

Finally, remember that as William Bruce Cameron so eloquently put it: Not everything that can be counted counts, and not everything that counts can be counted.

In short, whilst you do need an efficient finance system which underpins growth, it's a condition for success. Getting it right won't in itself make you successful.

Admin

Following directly on from my statement that you need an efficient finance system that underpins growth, the same is true of administration. If the administration of the business isn't controlled, growth will be chaos.

Administration isn't simply about insurance and compliance with (the nightmare that is) GDPR and other such legislation, it needs to be proactive in putting in place the systems and tangible assets to support growth. For example, it's very easy to forget the practicalities of expansion; office space, infrastructure, PCs, telephones, etc. Many of these items have relatively long lead times, suck up a huge amount of effort and it's important to have someone competent dealing with them as they can be expensive to get wrong.

I'm not going to major on admin as it covers everything from building administration (utilities, janitorial suppliers, insurance, etc.) to legal compliance with the ever changing laws, especially the health and safety laws associated with office premises and your duty of care to your employees. As with all disciplines you'll want to ensure that you get value for money and meet the minimum legal requirements without gilding the lily.

However, recruitment and employment is one of the major challenges of growing your company and I do have a fair amount to say on that subject!

Recruitment and Employment

The recruiting challenge for a small, growth company is to consider both the immediate need but also the need in the longer term, where the longer term may be only 12 or 18 months away. Do you try and get an experienced 'senior' manager and then rely on them to get their hands dirty doing the job for the immediate requirement, or do you go for someone who is proven at the job but without management experience in the belief that they can grow with the company and into the management role.

If you do go for the experienced senior individual expecting them to do the hard yards for the first year or so, choose wisely. Think carefully whether it's so long since they did any hands-on work they've forgotten how to do it or even whether they've ever had experience of doing things themselves[114].

---

[114] Read the section on Growth which explains how some people are a fish out of water in small companies.

Furthermore, are they used to large budgets and have no understanding of cash flow constraints or other such niceties? You need motivated people who are able to roll up their sleeves and get on with it themselves and who understand and can cope with a small company environment.

Unfortunately the VCs do like a good solid CV from a nice large company. So, if you are VC backed they're likely to be impressed by all the wrong stuff. Who knows, maybe time has moved on and they have learnt their lesson but I doubt it. I do give you some ammunition to argue your case in the 'A model for growth' section.

Sifting the Wheat from the Chaff
There is an old saying which is: Recruit in haste repent at leisure.

Never has a truer word been spoken! The financial and emotional cost of having to fire someone is high. It's also very disruptive to the business. Therefore be absolutely sure that the person you are recruiting is suitable. Test, interview, interview, interview, take references and interview again. If in doubt don't do it!

One of the challenges people in technology companies face is that one person's idea of expertise is another person's idea of basic knowledge. Someone may say that they are a spreadsheet or Word expert and, to their peers in their present company and therefore in their own minds, they are. To you and your peers their knowledge may seem extremely basic. So, if it matters, test it[115]!

In PleaseTech we had a laptop with Microsoft Office on it and regularly tested candidate's competency[116]. It's worth noting that if we were going to

---

[115] If a CV has been submitted by an agency always check with the candidate at the initial interview that it does offer a true representation of their career. It's not unknown for the CV to have been massaged or even a completely wrong one supplied!

[116] In Word can they format a document properly? Format a table? Do they understanding Styles, Tabs, Indents, Hanging Indents, Borders, Headers and Footers, etc. In Excel, can they format, create formulae, link between sheets, can they hide and unhide rows and columns, understand IF statements, what about pivot tables (something I confess I've never got my head around), etc.

test they were forewarned as the idea was to test their expertise not to surprise them.

The techies invented their own tests. Writing a bit of code or whatever they did (I never really knew or cared)[117]. Salespeople went through a telephone interview, a face-to-face interview, had to give both a remote and in person presentation on a software product of their choosing. We always sent a lot of emails to them to see how they responded and followed up.

For most prospective staff, after a first successful interview, we asked them to supply a user manual for their house. The idea was that they were going away and we were going to babysit their house so we needed a user manual. We, of course, stressed we didn't want actual alarm codes or to know where the spare key was really hidden. Candidates would ask us about the level of detail we wanted. We never specified that and always told them to simply give the level of detail they thought correct.

Our reasoning was that they were unlikely to have such a document to hand, couldn't copy it from the internet and therefore would have to prepare it from scratch themselves.

We used to learn a huge amount from this exercise. Was the document well presented? Was it delivered as a Word file or PDF? If Word, was it correctly formatted using the correct Word constructs? Were the spelling and grammar correct? Was it easy to follow? We learnt whether they were detail or broad brush people. Some candidates didn't get around to doing this and dropped out. That was fine, they clearly didn't want the job that much!

I've always said, only half in jest, that I'd never have managed to get a job in PleaseTech and that is not a bad thing! There is absolutely no point in having a recruitment approach in which you end up as the most accomplished person in the company. It's a well-established fact in many walks of life that the successful leaders are those who surround themselves with the most capable people.

---

[117] In Malaysia one candidate was found trying to find the answer on the web on his phone! The interview was terminated.

Of course, the ability to fit in the company's culture is equally as important as technical skills. This is difficult to judge but over a couple or so interviews you will get a feeling for whether the individual has the personality to fit in.

Everyone has their own interview style. Mine is conversational. I like the candidate to tell me their story. I ask them to explain why they are sitting in front of me at this point in the space-time continuum. You can learn a lot from where they start and how detailed their explanation is!

We never used personality tests mainly because I always thought that they were a waste of time and money. I think it's better to ensure that a broad selection of their future peer group in the company meet them and, if there is any doubt as to their suitability, it's a rejection. It's much better not to hire than hire the wrong person. You may not meet that headcount target but you may be saving a considerable amount of heartache.

Not all people take being rejected well. If you do reject someone, it's advisable to keep interview notes and make a record of why they were considered not suitable. Be sure that such interview notes don't contain anything incriminating. In the event of any court action, these records will be demanded by the opposition (and you will have to provide them) and, if they contain, for example, something discriminatory it won't go well for you.

It follows that everyone interviewing staff and making such notes should be aware of the anti-discrimination law and the potential consequences of ignoring it and especially the potential consequences of including discriminatory comments in interview notes.

This is an extremely serious matter. The financial penalties are huge. One unguarded note (for example, a suggestion that the individual looked too old and tired - as opposed to just tired) combined with a rejectee who feels hard done by and wants to get revenge could cost you your business whether or not, in our example, age was any factor in the decision which, of course, it's not legally allowed to be!

If you are VC backed it is tempting to just recruit to meet the headcount target and be able to report that you are on target in the monthly board meetings. My advice would be to resist. If I had my time again at CDC one of the key things I'd do differently is not recruit just to get the numbers up. Do not compromise on the quality of staff.

At PleaseTech, our more cautious approach paid off handsomely. We built a fantastic team of bright intelligent people (of all ages!) who enjoyed working for us and enjoyed the culture and helped us as a company punch well above our weight.

Making your Company Attractive to Recruits

When you are interviewing it is, of course, a two-way street; you are trying to sell the company to them just as much as they are trying to sell themselves to you.

This is especially true when you are a small company and may not have a fully featured benefits package to offer or name recognition. I've never thought of this as a negative. The first thing to remember is that, for some, the fact that you are a small company is in itself attractive as they've been there and done that with large corporates. They know that with a small company they'll be involved in a wider range of activity and that no two days will be the same.

If you get the culture right they'll also know that a small company offers a great sense of purpose and togetherness with everyone focused on a clear objective with few internal politics. That's not to say that everyone is best mates, it's just that there is a common drive and fellowship not found in larger companies.

I used to describe PleaseTech as a company where bright, intelligent people who liked a bit of banter enjoyed working with other bright, intelligent people who liked a bit of banter. It's about giving them a feeling of the culture and making them feel that they want to be part of it.

Of course, different levels and types of people will respond to different messages. For a techie the idea that they won't be shoehorned into one specific technical area and will have exposure to a wide range of exciting new technologies may well be the deciding factor. For others it may be the opportunity to attend conferences in the USA. For many the chance of a part time job or 'school hours' job (i.e. from 9:30am to 3:00pm) is a real incentive.

I absolutely believe that offering part time roles is a win-win. In both my companies, we found that part time staff were highly productive and did just as much as people working full hours. Not only were they highly focused because getting a decent part time job is so rare, the staff who took the part time jobs were extremely loyal and desperate for the company to succeed as they knew finding another similar job would be very difficult.

It's also worth noting that hiring part timers is also conducive to your cash flow as you'll be paying them less. That doesn't mean you underpay them. We never penalised part timers and always paid a market FTE (full time equivalent) but, by definition, the fact that they aren't full time means they earn less and therefore there is less cash out! This can be very useful especially in the early days when a new headcount can mean a significant percentage step up in overheads.

I'd make a couple of other points about offering part time roles:

1. Some people think that when you advertise a part time role you are somehow suggesting that that the role is somewhat diminished and not pressurised. You need to ensure that potential part timers understand that the role isn't a soft option and that they will be under just as much if not more pressure as a full time employee.

2. If you are dealing with the USA, you may want people (such as support) to work part time in the evenings remembering 5:00pm UK time is 9:00am on the West Coast. I can't recall having a serious attempt to recruit for such hours but have no doubt that such roles will be a lot less popular than school hours roles. They may even require you to pay a premium.

3. There needs to be flexibility on both sides and part timers need to understand that they too may need to occasionally go above and beyond the call of duty and turn up outside contracted hours and be able and willing to make appropriate arrangements. An example of this would be QA staff. If you are being audited and the client will be on site from 9:00am to 5:00pm then they will need to be there regardless of their contracted hours.

I'd recommend that you undertake an analysis and consider which roles could be part time. Are there any reasons people in administration, marketing, quality, compliance, etc. can't be part time? If you do offer part time roles I'll wager you get more high quality applicants resulting in highly motivated and productive staff regardless of the benefits you offer.

Returning to benefits, obviously the temptation is to adopt the 'Silicon Valley' workplace approach and start offering fridges packed with free colas and other such goodies. I address my thoughts about such West Coast frippery under the development section where I made it clear no bean bag would ever darken the development floor of a company with which I'm involved. It won't surprise you to learn that I have a similar feeling about such refreshments. I can't think of one person in my entire business career who has turned down a role at one of my companies because the fridge wasn't stocked with soft drinks!

Having said that, to a certain extent it's 'whatever works for you' as the key point of being a small company is flexibility. As I note below in the 'working from home' section, at PleaseTech, the UK staff had the option of working from home on a Monday and Friday. This policy was very attractive to a lot of people and, I have no doubt, much more attractive than a fridge full of carbonated drinks.

In summary, you should not underestimate the attractiveness of the jobs you offer and there is absolutely no need to offer a range of expensive benefits (other than the legal minimum) until you are considerably larger. However, as you grow and start making profits, offering a bonus scheme tied into the results of the company will endear you to a lot of people.

Share Options and Bonus Scheme
I mentioned previously, be parsimonious with your offers of share options. Only offer these as a benefit for important senior positions or company lynchpins. You won't know if someone is a lynchpin or goes above and beyond for a while so, if asked by candidates during the interview process about the availability of share options[118], you can hint that as the company grows you do anticipate offering share options to a cross section of key staff.

Although not all staff in PleaseTech had share options, all participated in the bonus scheme. This was a very simple scheme which started as a means of distributing profit to those initial employees who could have easily got a better salary elsewhere. Once we had started paying market salaries across the board it morphed into an informal profit share scheme.

---

[118] Remember that options issued under the EMI scheme have a 10 year validity so their issue implies an exit within 10 years!

Towards the end of the year we worked out what our profit was expected to be and then decided how much of it we were going to give back to staff, and how much we were going to keep for growth. Having established that, we then divvied up the allocation amongst the staff broadly in proportion to their salary but adjusted for their contribution.

There was no qualifying period, although new starters would get a pro-rated bonus and could expect that to be near the lower end of the scale. There was no set formula, although as we got larger we did start introducing an unofficial methodology to ensure it was fair. I saw it as a way of rewarding all staff but especially those who had gone above and beyond the call of duty in the preceding year. It was also useful as a means of levelling up any salary anomalies we felt existed. In a good year bonuses for some individuals could be in excess of 30% of annual salary - well worth having.

I believe that our generous approach to bonuses had several benefits:

1. It genuinely did make people more careful with their spending because ultimately they could be spending their own bonus. So, whilst the bonus culture became a bit of a standing joke as all requests for expenditure (for example, for a new server) were met with affected concern least it diminished the bonus pool, it did engender a shared sense of responsibility and understanding of profit throughout the company. Our profitability mattered to our staff.

2. It helped people buy into the view that we were all in this together. The fact that the management wasn't creaming all the spare cash off the top for themselves and ensured that there was plenty for everyone was a major motivator. This helped create that commonality of purpose and focus which stood us in very good stead.

3. It meant that, in a good year (and most of them were), our employees were paid right at the top of industry norms. This certainly helped with loyalty but, because it was non-contractual (i.e. only available if the company had done well), it didn't increase our overheads so our rolling cash cover was unaffected.

A critical part of success is creating the right culture and attitude. Having a 'we are all in this together and taking on the world' approach certainly worked for us. Sharing the financial rewards of the business was a key part of that equation.

The Employment Contract

All employees should have an employment contract signed before they start. There is a considerable amount of information available on the web regarding what should be in an employment contract and it is possible to purchase proforma contracts for not a lot of money. So there is really no excuse.

You should also have a new employee form to gather standard data such as national insurance number and bank account details. This form should contain a statement to the effect that the CV and other information they supplied regarding their qualifications and previous employment is true and accurate[119].

In addition to the basics such as job title, salary and benefits, sick pay, location, holidays, disciplinary policies and procedures, notice periods, termination, anti-bribery, etc. you need to ensure that the contract has a very strong confidentiality and intellectual property clause. This is vital to protect your business, and it worth spending the time getting it correct.

Other clauses I'd recommend you include are a gardening leave clause and non-solicitation clause. The key point of a gardening leave clause is it means that you have the option to exclude someone from the office whist they are serving out their notice period. It's not always necessary to enact this option (in fact, you really want an employee to leave on good terms and hand over during their notice period) but it's useful to have it. The non-solicitation clause simply stops leavers going to another start-up trying to poach their ex colleagues i.e. your staff.

It is sensible to separate company policy and procedures from your employment contract and have the employment contract reference these policies and procedures. For example, you don't want to have to update all

---

[119] As we became more established, we also had a policy of checking qualifications claimed on the CV. We did catch the occasional person being 'overzealous' in their claimed qualifications.

employment contracts if the disciplinary policies and procedures change. You should include a catchall (i.e. 'policies or procedures as they are introduced from time to time') because, as you grow, there will need to be an ever expanding set of such rules that your employees are expected to obey.

Be sure to have a formal probationary period and a probationary process with regular reviews. A six month probationary period should be adequate for you to establish whether your recruitment process was successful. Surely no one can hide incompetence or a personality flaw that long?

You may have heard of the so called 'two year' employment rule which you may understand as meaning that if an employee is let go within two years of their initial employment they have fewer rights with respect to claiming for unfair dismissal, etc. This is broadly true but be aware of two key things:

1. There are a lot of 'get out' clauses. For example, if the dismissal is considered discriminatory the length of employment is immaterial. There are many other such caveats which a basic search will reveal.

2. Don't take the two year rule as waiver on the need to follow any written disciplinary and termination procedures you have in place. This can be considered wrongful dismissal which brings it under the caveats discussed above.

In short, there is a vast amount of legislation in place around employment and it is a minefield for the unwary. The simple fact is that as your company grows and becomes valuable, you must assume that it may be a target for the unscrupulous. Your only defence is making sure that your recruitment process is exhaustive, your employment contract strong and your procedures comprehensive and detailed. It goes without saying that your staff all need to be aware of the danger of and the need to prevent workplace harassment. In short, you need to understand that getting your recruitment wrong is as much of a threat to your business as a security breach or being hacked.

The good news is that, in my experience, the vast majority of your potential employees are not unscrupulous, they simply want to be treated fairly, paid and enjoy working for you.

Finally, remember that there are different rules and employment practices in different countries and be sure to adjust accordingly.

Working from Home

In the early days of both my companies we didn't have office premises and everyone worked from home. Skype was our friend.

The good news is that this keeps admin to a minimum but it does raise a few points to watch:

1. We found that working from home was challenging for some. Specifically, those living alone suffered (especially if they weren't in a relationship) as it could be several days between real human contact for them. Research has shown that the buzz of a coffee shop is better for creative thinkers than a quiet home office[120]. I don't have an answer but it is one of the factors in a decision whether to get a physical office and is something to be aware of.

2. No matter how good modern communication technology is, nothing beats face-to-face meetings when discussing complex software. Brainstorming around a whiteboard simply can't be replicated online. So be prepared to meet up somewhere where you have use of a whiteboard. Having a small office and treating it almost like a drop-in centre is not a bad initial approach.

3. Decide whether you are providing company kit (i.e. laptops, etc.) or whether each person is providing their own. If the latter, ensure that the employment contract covers your ownership of the data and that you have a central data repository (i.e. cloud) where your data can be stored[121].

In PleaseTech, once we had a physical office we offered people the option of working from home on Monday and Friday if they had adequate broadband

---

[120] Whilst researching this I found the website https://coffitivity.com which "recreates the ambient sounds of a cafe to boost your creativity and help you work better".

[121] I suspect that thanks to GDPR it won't be possible for people handling client data to use their own kit.

connectivity[122]. 100% of the staff took advantage of this! On the whole this worked well but I'd offer a further couple of pointers:

1. As you grow, beware of people starting to abuse the system and start working from home on other days of the week because 'they have a delivery' or something similar. Make sure that your employment contract specifies the place of work as being the office and that the ability to work from home on Mondays and Fridays is a concession not a right. You can then have a quiet word explaining to the appropriate people that they are expected in the office mid-week and to schedule deliveries on Mondays and Fridays.

2. We offered a £500 per annum contribution to their broadband and telecoms bill. This was paid in addition to the salary but part of the salary so there were no benefit in kind issues.

3. This approach is especially beneficial when dealing internationally. If work was required in the evenings (which it always is when dealing with the USA), individuals were fully set-up to deal with it from home and there was no need to stay in the office.

Personally, I'm a great fan of working from home. However, I'm lucky. I have a separate office isolated from the rest of the house and if I ever need to concentrate on something (such as writing a book) I disappear into the home office. However, not all people have this luxury and you need to be sure that people are productive at home as there are multiple distractions.

Letting People Go

If you run a business there will be times when you need to fire people. There is no easy way to do this but, at the same time, you are doing everyone a favour as there is nothing worse in a company than having someone who is so obviously out of place that they create a tension that overpowers everything good. It can turn a great atmosphere poisonous.

I'm fortunate to have never had to make someone redundant because the company was underperforming or because of cash flow issues. Everyone I've let go has deserved it because either they weren't performing or had the

---

[122] This was limited to the UK.

wrong attitude (or weren't performing because they had the wrong attitude), or it was a case of misconduct.

Unfortunately, if you create a relaxed, laid back vibe some people seem to think that no-one cares about their performance or what they do. I always used to stress to new recruits that they should not let our laissez-faire attitude fool them into complacency. The company was staffed by enthusiastic professionals who were deadly serious and cared passionately about what they did. They just did it in a relaxed manner!

Ideally you catch the issues early and that is why your employment contract should come complete with a lengthy probationary period. However, regardless of the timing, there is an adage to which I subscribe which goes something like this: if you have to cut, cut quick and cut deep.

I don't necessarily agree that dismissal should be the last resort. The question you have to ask is whether you can really afford to nurse someone with the resources at your disposal. If they are a fish out of water no amount of nursing will turn them into a high performer and surely it's better to face reality for everyone's sake?

Several points regarding employee rights have been addressed in the employment contract section, specifically with reference to the two year rule. It's also worth noting that there are different processes to which you need to adhere in respect of dismissal for conduct and performance reasons. In the event you need to dismiss someone because of misconduct, you should acquaint yourself with the differences between misconduct, serious misconduct and gross misconduct.

Once it's clear someone has to go do not delay the inevitable. You'll have to decide whether you are going to go via the performance or misconduct route and go through the appropriate process or let them go on agreed terms which will involve legal advice and a Settlement Agreement (aka Compromise Agreement). This latter approach is not inexpensive and only emphasises the need to ensure that your recruitment process and your probationary process is thorough and you take decisions sooner rather than later.

Once your legal ducks are in a row and you've addressed the situation, if you've created the right culture, everyone will know you've acted in the best interests of the company and, in many cases, in the best interests of the individual being dismissed. You may be surprised at the palpable release of tension and the sense of a boil having been lanced.

Finally, remember that you have a duty of care to an employee even if you are firing them. This means that you should take reasonable steps to ensure their safety and wellbeing. Practically that means there should be someone there to support them, make sure they get home safely and so on. Do not just leave them in tears in the conference room with a black binbag for their personal effects.

A Final Word on Employing People

The first thing to say is that, as an employer, never forget you are messing with people's lives. The people you employ have mortgages, families to support and will make other such commitments on the basis that their salary will enter their bank account every month.

If you can't guarantee the future, be honest. In the early days of PleaseTech, I recruited someone who had just been made redundant. I promised them that I'd pay them for six months but couldn't guarantee what would happen after that. The lady in question accepted on the basis that, in six months, if the worst came to worst she'd be in the same position. We still laughed about it five years later.

Therefore, if you can't afford to recruit someone or think that there is a reasonable chance you'll have to let them go shortly (if, for example, a large contract doesn't come in), think very carefully whether you should go ahead. I accept that sometimes the decision is marginal and you need to staff up in anticipation of success and, alas, you can't predict the future. Just remember that in making the decision it's not all about you!

It follows that I abhor with a passion the 'rank and yank' appraisal approach (aka stack ranking) which says that you should seek to rank your staff every year and fire the worst performing 10% regardless of absolute performance[123].

---

[123] This 'rank and yank' approach was advanced by Jack Welch, Chairman and CEO of General Electric (GE) as a way to ensure a process of continuous improvement and is allegedly still in use by some in the IT industry.

I have always been strongly sceptical of any formal performance ranking scheme as I think they simply do not work[124]; they fail to recognise when people go above and beyond the call of duty and, in many cases, they ignore the softer touches an employee may bring to the company. I can think of people who may not be top performers but who are the heartbeat of the company and are instrumental in creating that all-important sense of purpose and togetherness. How do you measure that? As your company grows some base assessment may prove necessary but I'd resist it as long as possible.

Finally, a word of warning: By running the company, no matter how small, you are perceived as being powerful. Power is attractive to some. Even in this day and age there is a possibility staff will come on to you. Furthermore, you work long hours, you spend a lot of time with your colleagues and, when attending shows with a lot of socialising and not a lot of sleep, you can enter an intensely rarefied atmosphere where time is compressed and norms seem to belong to a different world. There will be temptations.

Don't do it! Just don't do it.

Policies and Procedures

As noted above, as you grow you will need to establish an ever-expanding set of rules that your employees are expected to obey. Many of these will be associated with the employment of people and are alluded to above.

As a basic minimum, in addition to your standard employment documentation and associated policies, you should have in place a health and safety policy and clear policies on the use of social media, email and the internet. If it sounds like a lot of work to get all these policies and procedures in place, don't be too alarmed - most are fairly standard, and you can obtain templates from many websites.

A brief search turned up numerous free basic policy templates and even free employee handbook templates. Additionally, there are many sites which provide comprehensive sets of policies and procedures for a modest fee. So, there is really no excuse not to have the fundamentals in place.

---

[124] The only time I've been involved in such a scheme was in my second job as an engineer with a mega American corporate. I've considered them a complete waste of time ever since!

A critical policy to establish early on and to drum into all staff is your social media policy. Again, templates are freely available on the web and can be tailored to your specific needs. However, the most important part of the policy is to ensure that staff do not break confidentiality agreements by publishing the names of your clients. This is closely followed by making sure they understand that all company information is confidential and nothing which originates from within the company should be published without formal approval!

Standard policies go on to cover aspects such as workplace harassment, bullying, etc. These are all necessary and it is important to ensure that employees are aware of the standards of behaviour expected.

It's all too easy to give administration, policies and procedures and all the associated 'nonsense' a low priority. However, you must remember that having a solid underlying system underpins growth and prevents chaos. Make sure someone is focused on it. It needn't be expensive. A part time employee and the judicious use of websites (paid or otherwise) will establish a firm foundation that will allow you to concentrate on growing the business.

Legal

In this section we cover some of the legal matters you'll come across. Before reading it I would remind you about my disclaimer and repeat that I am not a lawyer, this is not formal legal advice and I am merely explaining my layman's understanding of such matters.

Non-disclosure Agreements, etc.

It's typical to exchange non-disclosure agreements (NDAs) with prospective clients and partners. Standard documents are available on any number of websites for a small fee and differ slightly according to their main purpose.

The important thing is to get a two way NDA so both parties are protected. Some very large companies refuse to sign two way NDAs[125] and, if that is the case, you should consider how much information you do disclose to them. If anyone other than a massive company refuses a standard two way NDA I'd be questioning their motives.

All two way NDAs should have the same terms for both parties. Always try and offer your NDA. NDAs are normally standard and not a subject of negotiation. If you have to sign the other party's NDA check it out and ensure that they haven't slipped in more onerous terms for you. It's not unknown. If this is the case question their motives and go back to them. Some seem to have different levels of NDA and try it on with the tougher one first.

It's important to understand that an NDA doesn't stop people from ripping you or your ideas off. Going to court is expensive and time consuming so, regardless of what confidentiality documentation you have in place, be careful with whom you share your IP, especially your real core IP. I've addressed this in more detail in the 'Protecting your IP' section below.

Clearly, judging when an NDA is required is the tricky bit. If it's a potential partner that is easier and generally the rule is the sooner the better but, if it's a prospective client, that is harder. You don't want to stop the momentum of the sale by stalling everything to go through a legal process.

---

[125] Their information is confidential but not yours. This is typically a policy decision so they are not responsible for any leaks of your information.

This is where marking your documents 'Commercial in Confidence' can be useful.

Without an NDA in place the 'Commercial in Confidence' text itself doesn't have any legal weight. However, by including it you've nothing to lose and everything to gain. Business recipients generally assume that a document so marked may be shared within the business but not outside it which is generally your precise intention when you send them the document. They may not know whether you have an NDA with their organisation and generally play it safe and assume one is in place.

Some NDAs place an obligation on the disclosing party to mark the documents as confidential if they are covered by the NDA. Marking your documents 'Commercial in Confidence' meets this obligation, so my advice is that anything you send prospective clients, which isn't publicly available (i.e. on your website), is marked with the 'Commercial in Confidence' moniker. You've nothing to lose and everything to gain!

Software Licensing, Custom Development et al

If you are selling on-premise licenses you will need a Software License and Maintenance Agreement (SWL). If selling an online usage as a service you will need a SaaS Agreement. Standard templates for these licenses are available from various online portals for a small fee.

A well formatted agreement should have the terms and conditions in the main body of the document and the actual software or services being provided as addendums incorporated by a suitable clause into the main agreement. This means that if the client decides to purchase more licenses or otherwise alter their initial usage, it can be dealt with by an addendum and does not require a whole new agreement.

The next question is whether the agreement needs to be signed by both parties. I am aware of companies who play the 'last terms game' or 'terms tennis'. The game goes something like this:

1. Your proposal offers your software or service subject to your standard SWL or SaaS terms.

2. The client places an order, subject to their purchasing terms which include a statement to the effect that no action on their part

whatsoever will constitute agreement to any other terms and conditions (T&Cs).

3. You accept the client's order with a statement to the effect that the software or service is supplied to the client on the terms of your standard SWL or SaaS terms and you do not accept the client's T&Cs.

So, in effect, every item of correspondence rejects the other parties T&Cs and specifies their own, and the theory is that the latest one to reject the other's terms is the winner. This, of course, is complete rubbish and the effect is legal uncertainty. In the event of a dispute, a court would have to determine the actual legal position and, if you are selling to the right sort of clients, your (presumably soon to be ex) client will have much deeper pockets and therefore a much better legal team than you. It's far better to have an agreed contract signed by both parties with a sensible arbitration clause.

You may think that your liability is automatically limited to the initial license fee. You should think of it the other way around. Your liability is unlimited unless limited by an agreement. So, in addition to the license terms, your software license should specify your maximum financial exposure by limiting your liability and exclude consequential loss. I think we all know that your client's standard terms and conditions will strongly favour them! If your client believes that they are entitled to consequential loss, and a court agrees, that is your business finished - all those years of work gone.

In PleaseTech, except for our entry level SaaS service, we always went to the trouble of having an agreement signed by both parties. Of course, it's a pain to get such a document negotiated and agreed, and it can take a long time but we felt it was always worth it as there is no uncertainty which can come back to bite you, especially at exit. Any acquirer will want to see a nice set of signed agreements which limit your liability and make it clear what the client has purchased and on what terms. If this isn't available you may need to provide an associated warranty (which we discuss under the exit section).

What about standard click licenses? The answer is that any corporate worth its salt will have a policy that prevents individuals signing up for software services under a click license. If you are intent on using click licenses, there are various steps through which you can go to make a click license a legally valid agreement - search for and read the legal precedents based on case law. However, be prepared to have to supply the terms to a corporate in advance and be prepared that they may want to negotiate those terms[126]. I cover such negotiations in a separate section below.

Moving onto other considerations in respect of software licensing, if you service the B2B market it's likely that at some point you will need to add client specific functionality to your product. We've already discussed that you should make this as generic as possible (while meeting the client's requirements) and here I explain how I've dealt with the legalities of this in the past.

What you absolutely want to avoid is an individual client having any perceived ownership rights over any part of your software. The question with custom software is always: who owns it - the client or the developer? The answer is that it depends on the contract under which it was developed. So, to avoid such legal uncertainties and the need to negotiate a custom development software contract, my recommendation is you that avoid charging the customer specifically for the development.

This is where the concept of a 'disruption fee' comes into play. If you quote any custom development fee as a disruption fee and make it clear to the client that they are paying not for the custom development but for the disruption the development will cause to the business, then the question of ownership doesn't come into it. The development is simply an enhancement to the product and is therefore covered under the standard SWL or SaaS agreement.

To be clear, this doesn't mean that you should not have a clear written agreement as to what enhancements the client expects. It simply means that you've agreed to enhance your software to meet the client's requirements and the client has agreed to pay you a disruption fee for doing so.

Some other considerations with respect to software licensing:

1. As noted under the development section, you'll almost certainly have third party libraries (both open source and commercial) and

---

[126] When you design your SaaS system, it's worth including a setting that allows you to turn off any mandatory acceptance of a click license, and have said license terms replaced by a notice to the effect that the service is supplied subject to the service agreement entered into by the client.

potentially will have sub-licensed some specialist technology. Some of these will require you to add specific license terms and attributions to your agreements. This is where full traceability comes into play, especially when you exit. You will need to be able to show that the license terms of each third party library have been met and be able to show where in your SWL/SaaS agreement the terms are enacted. As the required attributions[127] will typically change from release to release of your software, I'd recommend that your agreements refer to an attributions webpage/document (on a non-public url and not linked from your website but referenced in the software and documentation). This can then be incremented for every version.

2. You must think very carefully through the realities if you are licensing software through third parties such as another independent software vendor incorporating your software or reselling it as part of a package. In my experience it was almost impossible to get the reseller to get the client to sign a separate SWL. The only way we found it worked was where we had our T&Cs incorporated as a standard addendum to the reseller's own license[128]. If they are reluctant to do this you may want to keep the prerogative of negotiating your own license with the customer in your reseller agreement.

3. To some extent you will have to localise your agreements. For example, the company name and address format in the USA is very different from the UK, which is different from Europe. Also be cognisant of the fact that some currencies are displayed differently and have a comma where we would place a full stop and vice versa. So 100.08 may be displayed as 100,08 and 1,100.08 may be 1.100,08.

4. Be absolutely clear with whom you are signing the agreement. Is it the main corporate body or some valueless subsidiary. It's not

---

[127] Attributions may also be required in the software interface.

[128] There is an interesting corollary to this. If you suddenly find a partner who is poor at paperwork wanting to get all the paperwork for the last few years in order, there is a high probability that they are going through due diligence and are about to be sold!

unknown for large corporates to try and limit their liability (for example, for IP theft) by placing contracts through a subsidiary with no assets which can be terminated with little or no pain.

As a final note, I'd remind you that you actually want to sell your software and you want the client to find your T&Cs acceptable. It is therefore a lot less painful all round if your SWL is fair and reasonable rather than onerous. I've never understood companies who take pride in having an onerous software license or SaaS agreement over which they then go to war with the client's legal team. Starting with sensible, standard T&Cs which protect both party's interests is a sensible approach and one that makes things happen so much quicker.

Contract and Software License Negotiation

If you are selling B2B you will end up in contract negotiations with your clients. After years of such negotiations my advice is to always start with your own (fair and reasonable) agreement and then argue only over material amendments.

It seems that online service agreements are less likely to be targets for heavy client amendment than on-premise SWLs which are almost always subject to negotiation. Some clients are extremely difficult to deal with. Their lawyers don't approach such negotiations in the spirit of wanting to get a reasonable agreement sorted out as quickly as possible and are constantly trying to get one over on you. In these situations you need to be on your toes and make extensive use of document comparison functionality as they don't always remember to track their changes!

Some corporate negotiators will cover your agreement with mark-up but change nothing material. If that is the case it doesn't matter, and you can accept all their changes and go for signature. They will feel they've done their job and you don't care as none of your red lines have been crossed[129].

---

[129] It's worth creating and storing a document comparison with your standard agreement alongside the signed agreement. This will come in very useful during due diligence!

From a practical perspective these negotiations are generally carried out by email and with a Word document using tracked changes and comments[130]. Generally, etiquette is not to accept your own proposed changes unless they have been specifically agreed with your opposite number and you make an appropriate comment on the paragraph.

Make sure you understand what proposed new clauses and or amendments really mean. We found that reading difficult clauses aloud to someone else with a logical mind really helped get to grips with them. Generally, agreements should be balanced, so do not let the client add a load of obligations on you without corresponding obligations on them.

If you are finding it difficult to agree on changes with a client, sometimes it's worth asking the intent behind their changes. Once both sides understand the intentions and concerns of the other, it can help with the drafting.

If you have to start with a client's agreement start by comparing it to your own agreement: What is missing? What has been added? Can you match the client's clauses to your own? Is it a balanced agreement or is it overly onerous on the supplier (that's you)? Are all terms defined? Are there any legal inconsistencies? Again, make sure you understand what the clauses really mean. If you get an unbalanced, inconsistent agreement be extremely cautious.

Sometimes it's better to walk away than sign a bad deal with a difficult client. I can only think of one time we decided that the size of the deal and the terms of the contract that the client was mandating was not worth the business risk. It doesn't happen often, and the fact that you are prepared to walk away can change the client's position, but it does sometimes happen.

As I indicate above, such negotiations are about business risk. You have to make sure that the person negotiating the contract understands the implications of clauses and your red lines (for example, never agree to remove the standard consequential loss exclusion clause and ensure your liability is capped). I suggest that you, your CFO, or another senior commercially minded person lead the negotiations and only resort to taking advice from your lawyers when absolutely necessary. That way you'll build

---

[130] Even though we sold document review software this is the way we did it in PleaseTech! Some battles are not worth fighting and it's best to go with the flow.

up internal knowledge of such contracts and be able to keep your legal costs reasonable.

Protecting your IP

It's important to understand that no number of NDAs and software license agreements will stop people from trying to rip off your software or ideas. Clearly, if you are offering an online SaaS service you are mainly concerned about your ideas as expressed through the interface. The end users, partners and or implementors will not have access to the nuts and bolts of your software. The reality is that it is a simple fact is that a good idea doesn't mind who originally has it, and it's almost impossible to protect ideas - especially in the software environment. The only protection is to stay ahead of the competition.

When I say "it's almost impossible to protect ideas", I mean in Europe and the world outside the USA. In the USA software patents have historically been permitted. As the USA is the world's largest software market this has posed a problem for British companies who make too much information available on their website. Unscrupulous US operators have been known to take good ideas from other parts of the world and patent them in the USA. This prevents the originating company from selling in the USA without paying said unscrupulous operator a license fee!

I know of one British company that naively had this happen and even believed that they had identified text lifted from their user manual in the patent application text. However, they were unable to prove that their information had been in the public domain (and therefore it was prior art) before the patent application was submitted. It didn't end well for them and they eventually ceased to exist. The unscrupulous operator flourished. I discuss patent protection below.

When it comes to on-premise software the risk of IP theft is much higher as not only do you have the ideas issue as discussed above, but you are also shipping the detail of your valuable IP to a third party and have zero control over what they do with it. Going to court is expensive, time consuming and in some countries simply not possible, so regardless of what documentation you have in place, be careful with whom you share your IP, especially your real core IP.

I've previously mentioned that, although India has on the face of it reasonable IP protection its courts are notoriously slow. This is reinforced by the UK India Business Council which notes on its 'intellectual property in India' webpage that 'courts can take years to come to a final decision'. It also notes that (i) you need to register your IP rights which could take several years owning to the backlogs at the IP registries, and (ii) "Small players account for a large number of IP infringements. This means that seizures tend to be small, requiring a sustained and costly effort in order to make any significant impact"[131].

Likewise in 2017, the US-based Commission on the Theft of Intellectual Property said, "China remains the world's principal IP infringer, driven by an industrial policy that continues to prioritize both acquisition and development of science and technology"[132].

So use your judgement. Research the company, especially if they approach you out of the blue and want an evaluation or have an urgent customer requirement which conveniently means they get access to your technology.

In PleaseTech, unless we were dealing with a major Western corporation we thought twice and usually declined to engage. In fact, even when we were dealing with a subsidiary of a major western corporation based in a developing country we insisted that the contract was signed with their HQ based in a jurisdiction in which we had recourse! To say that this was not universally popular is a bit of an understatement and our approach did elicit more than one accusation of racism but, as I used to explain patiently to the upset individual on the other end of the phone, the laws of their home country provided no practical IP protection and we had a policy of only dealing with companies in jurisdictions with such IP protection.

Copyright and Trademarks
When it comes to your IP, it's important to understand basics as well as the more advanced stuff.

Familiarise yourselves with the nature of copyright and what it means. There are countless websites available to explain the detail. However, the executive summary is that copyright automatically covers all original works

---

[131] Source: https://tinyurl.com/yybgdedy
[132] View the press release here: https://tinyurl.com/yx96czxo

which could be considered as intellectual property. So, literature, music, art, films, etc. are covered. Perhaps more importantly from our perspective, it also covers "original non-literary written work, such as software, web content and databases"[133]. Copyright prevents others from using this original work in any way without a license to do so.

However, enforcement of copyright is expensive. So, unless you have the means to sue the infringing party, it offers only a very basic level of protection from people who follow the rules.

Unlike the UK which has no copyright registration process, it is possible to register copyright in the USA. Registration is not necessary because, like the UK, copyright is automatically applied under US law and there is no need to register copyright to have protection. However, the registration process provides a number of benefits which include eligibility for statutory damages, attorneys' fees, and costs[134].

I've never registered copyright in the USA and have no opinion as to whether it's worth doing. However, having read up on it for the purposes of this book, I'm tempted to register the book via the online process. It seems fairly straight forward, costs around $50 and it will be interesting to see how complicated it is. It will also be nice to have a formal copyright certificate to hang on the home office wall!

The other basic IP protection to understand are trademarks. There is a difference between a Registered Trademark denoted by the ® symbol and an unregistered trademark which is denoted by the ™ symbol. As the International Trademark Association puts it, "the symbol ™ is used to provide notice of a claim of common-law rights in a trademark. A ™ usually is used in connection with an unregistered mark, to inform potential infringers that a term, slogan, logo or other indicator is being claimed as a trademark"[135]. In short, you can use ™ to suggest that you are using something as a trademark. You should, of course, check that the text you are claiming is not being claimed elsewhere.

---

[133] Source: https://www.gov.uk/copyright
[134] Source: The United States Copyright Office, specifically https://tinyurl.com/mc9pvo4
[135] Source: The INTA factsheet here: https://tinyurl.com/yxspa4x2

A registered trademark means exactly what it says; the trademark has been formally registered and approved by an appropriate government authority. Trademarks are territorial meaning that they only apply in the territory in which they are registered. It is possible to register for an International Trade Mark (valid in countries signed up to The Madrid Protocol) but, to do this you need to have registered the mark in your own country first which must be a member of said protocol.

Registering a trademark need not be expensive (you can do it yourself) but the question is: is it worth applying for a registered trademark? We didn't apply for any with PleaseTech and I can't recall if CDC ever made such an application. I think it's a nice to have rather than mandatory.

In my opinion, domain possession is nine-tenths of the battle. The UK government website is quite clear on this saying "Being the owner of a registered trade mark, does not automatically entitle you to use that mark as a domain name. The main reason being, that the same trade mark can be registered for different goods or services and by different proprietors. Also, someone may have already, and quite legitimately, registered the domain name, perhaps with its use being connected with unregistered goods or services"[136].

If you name a product and own the domain name then, assuming the product name isn't being used elsewhere in your field[137], I'd think you've gained the high ground and taken what I see to be the mandatory steps.

Patents
There is a lot of misunderstanding around patents, especially software patents. You've almost certainly heard about patent trolls and have probably read about so called patent wars being played out in the mobile phone sector.

If you think that patents are only the domain of large companies you'd be very wrong. Patent trolls, more formally known as a 'patent holding company' (PHC), or a 'non-practicing entity' (NPE), or a 'patent assertion

---

[136] Reference: https://tinyurl.com/yyhlksht
[137] If your product name is similar to another in your field (regardless of domain ownership) you may be accused of 'passing off' by the other party. In the USA this is termed 'misappropriation' and has a slightly different context.

entity' (PAE – which is what I will mostly call them), are a fact of life for even the smallest company.

The sad fact is that in the USA patents, which were originally created to encourage innovation by protecting those who had invested in developing new technologies, are now, especially in the software industry, seen as a major roadblock to innovation. In this section I explain my understanding of it all and hope that it helps you in yours.

Software Patents

It is generally accepted that it is not possible to obtain a software patent in the UK or Europe. There are some aspects of software technology which in certain limited circumstances could be patentable but anything addressing a business method is un-patentable.

This is not true in the USA which is awash with patents affecting software and technology. Patents are issued around the business method implemented i.e. what it achieves and how it achieves it. Some of these patents are at incredibly high level and have nothing innovative in them whatsoever!

A considerable number of these patents are in the ownership of the PAEs whose sole reason for existing is to extricate license fees from companies which they assert have infringed their patent. Unfortunately, the cost of defending a patent case is high and, in the USA, historically claimants (i.e. the trolls) only paid their own costs even if they lost a case. This, coupled with the existence of 'no-win, no-fee' lawyers and the fact that cases are tried by juries leading to potentially large compensation awards, not only encouraged claims but made the cost and the risk of defending said claims high, too high in most cases.

Therefore most companies approached by the PAE simply negotiated a license fee that was carefully judged by the PAE to be lower that the sums which would be spent in a court case. Thankfully there are people who fight back. In my research for this section I came across a chap called Austin Meyer (the author of a flight simulator called X-Plane) and his 'The Patent Scam' YouTube video[138]. It's just over 21 minutes long and, if you want to understand how the game is played and the ecosystem around it, is well

---

[138] It is here: https://youtu.be/sG9UMMq2dz4

worth watching. He makes the point that most NPEs are shell companies with no assets and it costs around $3million to defend a case. The kind of good news is he won. The bad news is that the PAE then simply shifted the focus of its attack[139]!

The USA has, therefore, been a minefield for British software companies. We have already alluded to the problems in the 'Protecting you IP' section above and raised the fact that unscrupulous US operators have been known to take good ideas from other parts of the world and patent them in the USA.

If your immediate thought is that prior to designing your software you'll undertake a patent search and make sure you are non-infringing, think again. There is a very good reason not to undertake such a search!

If you have knowingly breached a patent any compensation award against you can be tripled. Simply being aware of the patent would generally be considered knowledge of it and therefore any infringement would be considered deliberate. Any search will throw up hundreds of potentially infringing patents and you will need to ensure that you are not knowingly infringing them.

Therefore, frequently, ignorance is bliss. If you haven't searched you don't know about any potential infringements and therefore cannot knowingly infringe!

It follows that this all changes if someone (however well meaning) draws your attention to a patent that they think you may be infringing. You now are aware of the potential infringement and need to take steps to understand the patent in question and either be clearly non-infringing or obtain a formal legal opinion on whether you infringe it!

At this point you will need the services of a patent attorney. If you are lucky, you will be able to obtain from them a formal non-infringe opinion. It's important to understand that this opinion doesn't prevent anyone taking action against you but it serves two purposes: (i) it can deter action as these opinions are issued by patent attorneys who know what they are doing and

---

[139] The YouTube video ' Austin Meyer of X-Plane Fights Patent Troll & Wins' (https://youtu.be/NbyW_QS8Ef8). I'd also recommend you watch 'Last Week Tonight with John Oliver' (HBO) who covers patent trolls here: https://youtu.be/3bxcc3SM_KA

therefore the simple existence of such an opinion can deter a claimant from making a claim, and (ii) it protects you from knowingly having infringed the patent because, if you have a non-infringe opinion from a recognised patent attorney, legally you have not knowingly infringed.

The good news is that recently the tide has been turning against the trolls.

Post-Alice, post-Octane and Venue Shopping

The tide has been turning because of three key US Supreme Court decisions.

In 2014 there was a landmark decision at the US Supreme Court (regarding Alice Corp. vs CLS Bank International) which found that the implementation of an abstract idea[140] on a computer system is not enough to make an idea patentable - commonly known as the 'Alice' decision the subsequent era is known as 'post-Alice'.

In practice, this has meant that well established business methods, even if they were originally performed manually by a human and not a computer, are not eligible for patents. This immediately allowed many patents to be challenged as invalid as they were based on standard business practices being performed with the aid of a computer rather than a human[141]. Result!

In 2015 there was a further US Supreme Court Decision (Octane Fitness LLC vs ICON Health & Fitness, Inc) which also radically altered the patent litigation landscape.

In the section above I noted that claimants (i.e. those bringing the action) usually only pay their own costs even if they lost. This assertion was true in practice although, theoretically, costs could be awarded against the claimant in the event of a bad faith completely baseless claim. However, the hurdle of proving a claim was brought in bad faith and was baseless was so high that there was never a realistic chance of recovering the fees incurred in defending a case.

In the Octane decision, the Supreme Court redefined the hurdle and thus made it much more dangerous for PAEs to bring weak cases to the courts.

---

[140] The case also determined that known ideas are abstract.
[141] To be clear, many such patents were awarded on the basis that the innovation claim was that a well-known standard business process could be done with the benefit of a computer! Unbelievable!

This was reinforced in 2016 when a decision held that the law firm representing a 'frivolous' and 'unreasonable' claimant was jointly and severally liable for costs awarded to the defendant in light of the Octane decision (Gust, Inc vs AlphaCap Ventures, LLC).

This suddenly increased the risk of being a PAE's law firm and had the effect of greatly reducing the number of actual claims and consequently suppressed the license fees sought by claimants.

However a more recently Federal Circuit ruling reversed the Gust decision[142] but, despite this, there is no doubt that vexatious patent litigation is increasingly unfavourable and risky, so that the practice of shell PAEs filing claims and demanding settlements is declining.

Finally, there was a US Supreme Court decision in 2017 (which reversed a 2016 US Court of Appeals decision), meaning that the practice of 'venue shopping' will increasingly be a thing of the past.

Venue shopping allowed claimants to bring cases in favourable jurisdictions. The US District Court for the Eastern District of Texas became the favoured court to register a claim because it dealt with claims very quickly and the juries were considered to be sympathetic to claimants often awarding an extremely high level of damages[143]. It used to receive around a third of all filed patent infringement suits in the USA. It no longer does!

The Supreme Court's decision was based around the word 'resides'. Previously it was accepted that if you did business in a particular court district you resided there! The Supreme Court decided that a company resided in the state in which it was incorporated. This has led to the epicentre of patent infringement claims moving to Delaware as that is where a lot of US companies are incorporated.

The bad news is that if you are a UK or other foreign company doing business in the USA but not incorporated there, no such reside restriction applies and therefore it's likely to be East Texas for you.

---

[142] Source: https://tinyurl.com/sokbdak

[143] The Bloomberg Opinion article 'The Town That Trolls Built' is interesting: https://tinyurl.com/y4u4cm94

However, be aware that the position on patents is constantly changing. In January 2019 the US Patent and Trademark Office (USPTO) revised their Patent Subject Matter Eligibility Guidance[144] which will make it easier to patent software. This could take us back to the pre-Alice environment although the full implications of the revised guidance are yet to be understood.

Received a Letter Alleging Infringement?

If you receive a letter alleging that your product is infringing a patent there are four things you must do:

1. Do not ignore it. If you do the claimant will simply obtain a default judgement and you'll probably be arrested next time you try and pass American immigration.

2. Do not deal with the PAE company or their law firm directly. They may well ask you to call them to discuss the matter. You'll simply be an innocent lamb to the slaughter. Remember, they play this game every day. It's their job.

3. Lawyer up. Get yourself a decent American Patent Attorney who understands the rules of the game and also plays it every day.

4. Sit down with your CTO and any other technical people you need and crawl over the patent and the alleged infringement and prepare a document explaining how your software works and (hopefully) why your software is not infringing to share with your patent attorney.

Your patent attorney will then advise you what to do. There are basically three ways to address the issue:

1. Prove prior art and to this end you must always keep details of what you published on your website and when and what you showed at conferences[145]. Also keep notes on any details of similar products, when they were launched, etc. In the early days at PleaseTech I was on the show floor at a conference and an 'independent consultant'

---

[144] It is here: https://tinyurl.com/y357cdhc
[145] For a good explanation of what is considered prior art read this Ius Mentis article: https://tinyurl.com/y2rsg6nf

came round and showed a high degree of interest in what we did and made a large number of notes. He clearly wasn't an independent consultant as he had almost zero market knowledge and I was immediately suspicious. I therefore noted his name and the date and time of the visit on a copy of the flyer he'd taken. The point of doing this was, of course, to ensure that should he have put in a patent application we'd be able to demonstrate prior art and ultimately invalidate the application.

2. Try and invalidate the application by proving it should not have been awarded in the first place. In the post-Alice era this is considerably easier. In 2018 (four years since the Alice decision) the Electronic Frontier Foundation suggested that there were more than 400 patents claims found invalid because of Alice[146]. There is a (currently) ongoing patent case regarding the ubiquitous software digital assistants such as Siri, Alexa and Cortana which illustrates the application of this defence[147].

3. Prove that you are not infringing! The downside of this final option is that you'll probably have to do this by defending a court case which, as we have already discussed, is not inexpensive. However, in the post-Octane world, providing sufficient evidence that you do not infringe with a non-infringe opinion may be sufficient to deter the claimant as they will not want to be found to have brought a frivolous or unreasonable claim.

The point is that your patent attorney will understand the best approach in the current patent litigation landscape which, as previously mentioned, is constantly changing. If you want a patent attorney recommendation please feel free to drop me a line via LinkedIn or the website and I'll happily respond.

Should you Apply for a Patent?

The first thing I'd say is the presumption has to be that we are talking software patents here and that means an application in the USA. I wouldn't (and haven't) and I suggest that you think very carefully before you do. In

---

[146] Source: EFF article 'Happy Birthday Alice: Four Years Busting Software Patents' here: https://tinyurl.com/y77u7ydz
[147] Source: For an overview as at January 2019, see: https://tinyurl.com/y7yx6s7g

this section I try and explain my position and bring to your attention the pitfalls associated with a patent application.

If you are considering a patent application there are three key thought processes you need to go through:

1. Can a patent be obtained, and if so, will it give you any protection?
2. Can you afford to get the patent, and is it a sensible investment?
3. Can you afford to enforce the patent?

Point three is the nuts of it. If you can't afford to defend your patent why have it in the first place unless you have ambitions to become a PAE!

It will cost you at least US$15,000 to get a patent and a whole lot of work. It will cost you a whole lot more to defend your patent. Patent attorneys are not cheap!

For example, the British technology company Dyson is said to spend millions of pounds every year defending their patents yet the number of different high pressured air type hand dryers seems to grow every year.

The problem with patents is that, unless they are very broad like the software patents we have been discussing which are being invalidated, they are easily worked around. Take the sad story of Obit Trevor Baylis who invented and patented the wind-up radio. He died in poverty after other manufacturers sidestepped the patent by including a rechargeable battery in the device[148].

The rechargeable battery probably wasn't even invented when Mr Baylis filed his patent application, and that is the key point, the pace of technological change means that by the time your application is granted technology is likely to have moved on.

However, don't let me stop you! As I have regularly mentioned, the only constant is change and this is equally true in the patent world. It may be that aforementioned USPTO's revised Patent Subject Matter Eligibility Guidance will make software patents worth the effort. If in doubt consult an expensive patent attorney!

---

[148] Source: The Register article: https://tinyurl.com/y3kk3mrm

Dealing with Professional Advisors and Consultants

Sooner or later you are going to have to spend money on professional advisors. These advisors range from the professions such as lawyers and accountants to so called independent experts aka consultants. These are very different animals and that is why I'm going to address them separately.

Before we do that it's worth bearing in mind one of Larry Ellison's quotes: "The most important aspect of my personality as far as determining my success goes; has been my questioning conventional wisdom, doubting experts and questioning authority. While that can be painful in your relationships with your parents and teachers, it's enormously useful in life."[149]

The bottom line is that advisors (whether they be lawyers, accountants or whatever) can advise, but you have to decide. It's your business, your responsibility and that means your decision. So, whilst I do offer some advice below, the overriding message is that what experts tell you is their opinion and is not the gospel truth.

Accountants and Lawyers

The first thing to say about professional services firms is not to be intimidated! Treat them just like any other supplier. Explain what you want them to do and have them quote. They may not be able to give a precise figure but should be able to provide a reasonably accurate estimate. Make it clear that you care about costs and want to understand how they will be contained and that, if there is any danger of the estimate being exceeded, that you will need to be advised in advance.

It's probably helpful if you explain your ambitions for growth and, if possible, how quickly you are growing. They'll want to work with you and may possibly quote with one eye on future business!

You should be thinking of different horses for different courses. You'll almost certainly get the best value from smaller specialist firms. Larger firms may offer a 'one stop shop' but the convenience is unlikely to be worth the additional cost.

---

[149] From Wealthygorilla.com, https://tinyurl.com/yypo2o7z

Take references. At the very least taking such references may put you in touch with some useful industry contacts!

I think dealing with accountants is more straight forward than dealing with lawyers. Accountancy rules are fairly well defined and there is less interpretation required. Therefore in seeking advice from an accountancy firm, it's generally a matter of employing a specialist to follow the frequently complex rules and understand HMRC's interpretation of said rules.

Lawyers are a different kettle of fish. Unless you are using them to provide you with something standard such as an employment contract (and, if so, I'd ask why when there are lots of places you can get one on the web[150]), you are likely to be dealing with lawyers primarily in matters of commercial law and employment law.

Occasionally, you get a cross over. Both lawyers and accountants will be able to offer advice on tax matters and, if you need tax advice, you'll need to discuss your requirements with both and understand which one is best placed to advise you. Share options is another cross over area. In PleaseTech we used lawyers to draw up the scheme documentation and our tax accountant for the HMRC approval.

Some other thoughts with respect to dealing with lawyers:

1. Make sure that you can work with the lawyers in question. Meet not only the partner (who will probably do the selling) but also the associates who will actually do the work. In most standard steady state businesses you'll typically be dealing with the lawyers when something has gone wrong. These are stressful times and you need to rely upon and trust your chosen advisors.

2. Lawyers will always advise you of the worst downsides. This is understandable as it's important you are aware of the downsides and it protects their backside. However, ultimately you have to judge how likely the downside is to occur and how bad it will be. If I'd always worked on the basis that the worst downside would

---

[150] As you grow and get to a sensible size, it's as well to have any such contracts you are relying upon (e.g. employment and licensing, etc.) formally reviewed by a competent law firm occasionally.

happen[151], I'd be working as a corporate salaryman. I can't say this often enough: make your own judgement.

3. If doing something out of the norm (such as setting up a joint venture or similar), do talk to your lawyers. It may sound like they are trying to stymie the deal but they will be simply advising you on what could go wrong. It's as well to understand such issues and address them head on up front rather than trying to repair the damage when it's all gone pear-shaped.

The key with lawyers is to ensure you have a clear business purpose behind everything. If you are working on a contract and you need formal legal input, you need to make sure that the Heads of Terms is explicit and agreed at a business level and it's just the particularly obscure points on which you need advice. Whatever you do, in the event of a dispute, don't let the lawyers argue it out. They can argue forever, at your expense, over the location of a full stop.

Consultants and Independent Experts

The key thing to remember when dealing with consultants and independent experts is the maxim that the sole purpose of a consultancy assignment is to secure the next consultancy assignment. As the Americans say, ain't that the truth.

I've dealt with a wide range of so called independent experts in my time and, in general, I've been very disappointed in their output. Or is that input? The idea that consultants borrow your watch to tell you the time and then charged you for the pleasure is not that far out.

I've had my fair share of consultants who pad their report out with information you gave them and with a load of banal generalities and then fail to address the issue on which you specifically engaged them to advise. Their reports never failed to include a section called 'next steps' which generally advised spending more of your hard earnt cash with the same consultant for, presumably, more prosaic drivel.

---

[151] If you want to look at downsides just study the possible adverse reactions in the patient leaflet in any medicine you take. It's a wonder that (i) anyone takes medicine and (ii) that they survive when they do!

When you engage a consultant think about what is in it for them. For example, let us assume you engage a consultant to help you understand and prepare for some new legislation being introduced. Ask yourself how likely it is that the consultant will recommend a minimal implementation. Are they not going to be tempted to recommend a 'belt and braces' approach which would keep them occupied for a while for a nice fat fee?

One of the problems is that you will know a lot more about your business than any consultant. Unless the consultant has been retained to advise on specific technical points, they haven't got a clue what you do, and want you to pay them to undertake an exercise to help them understand it and put it all in context before they advise you.

We once engaged a marketing consultant to determine if there were any tricks we were missing. We wanted suggestions for practical, cost effective marketing programs. We agreed on a one day workshop with the intention of saying: this is what we are doing in respect of marketing are we missing anything? Perhaps it was our fault for a poor choice of consultant but the individual concerned completely ignored our question and wanted to go through a whole strategic marketing exercise redefining our message and defining our target market. Suggestions for anything practical were not on his agenda. Needless to say, we didn't continue the relationship but it did cost us a day of his time at his exorbitant rate!

I think at the root of the problem is that most consultants aren't generic experts. They have a set methodology of doing their thing and are therefore a one trick pony. I guess that means you need to establish if their particular trick is the one you are interested in! Clearly the marketing consultant we engaged was a strategic messaging guy and not a hands on practical guy. I'm not sure that's how he sold himself but you live and learn!

I'm glad to see that I'm supported in my views by Jack Ma the billionaire co-founder of Alibaba who is on record as stating that he "hates hiring people who come in as experts" and goes on to point out that "there is no expert of the future, there is always an expert of yesterday"[152]. The point being that so

---

[152] Reported here (in addition to other places): https://tinyurl.com/yapuzgj5. His quote appears to be based on that from David Ben-Gurion the founder and first Prime Minister of Israel, who is quoted as saying: "All the experts …are experts on

called experts may understand what has succeeded in the past but that doesn't mean that it will succeed in the future.

So my advice is be very wary of so called experts and consultants. If you use them make sure that the brief is tight and make sure that there is absolutely no misunderstanding what you expect to be delivered.

what was. There is no expert on what will be." To become an 'expert' on the future, vision must replace experience.' Source: https://tinyurl.com/y62ba5fk.

Partners

When you are selling B2B there is no escaping partners. Regardless of whether you're selling on-premise solutions or cloud services, you'll need to co-operate and interact with other third party products and companies. Some of these third parties will help you, some will hinder, some will be easy to deal with, some will be complete pains and some will actively work against you. You have to deal with them and you have no choice because, ultimately, at some level, dealing with them will be necessary to unlock corporate accounts.

By way of background, I've previously mentioned that it's a simple fact that there is a constant pressure on corporate IT departments to minimise the number of disparate systems staff have to use in the course of day-to-day jobs – this also feeds into the number of systems the IT department themselves have to maintain and support. This is why, in B2B software, integration is the name of the game. The easier you make it for end users in the context of the major systems they use day-to-day and the easier you make it for the IT department to manage and maintain, the easier your sales process will be!

You may be able to integrate your product into another environment (cloud or otherwise) seamlessly or you may simply need to receive data from third party systems, or pass data to them. At the very least you'll almost certainly need to support your client's Single Sign-on (SSO) infrastructure whether this is Active Directory or an IDaaS type service[153] or something else.

In addition to the purveyors of other software products there will be various other contractors, integrators and or outsourcers to consider. The one thing in common that these third parties have is that they only have your interests at heart when they coincide with theirs. If there is nothing in it for them, they are at best neutral, at worst, they can attempt to kill the deal, replicate your IP and so on.

---

[153] User management is a major overhead for corporate support organisations. Imagine a large corporate and all the coming and going of staff and then the number of systems each must be given access to or have their access terminated. This is potentially hundreds of transactions per day. This is why centralised user management is vital for efficiency. If you want to play with the big boys you have to use grown up toys!

This means that the partnership landscape is complex. You may well be competing with a 'partner' on one account and co-operating on another. Some will appear to be on your side but will be dripping poison in the client's ear! In fact, you could write a whole book on partnerships and how to handle them. In this section I've tried to provide an overview of the third parties you are likely to come across and my advice on how to deal with them.

'Ecosystem' Partners

If you read The CDC Story, you'll understand that we ended up building our products based on Documentum and a large part of our success was because we were part of the Documentum ecosystem, as Documentum grew so did we. In PleaseTech, we were partners with a number of ecosystem providers (Documentum, OpenText, et al) and that greatly contributed to our success.

To be clear, I don't advocate building your products on a single ecosystem as it gives the owner of that ecosystem too much power over you. However, I do strongly advocate getting involved in one or more ecosystems. It is a simple fact that in all such ecosystems there are functionality gaps and areas of functionality that the lead product doesn't cover particularly well. These gaps and upgrades are the opportunities for third party partners such as yourselves.

Mature Ecosystem Partners

Mature ecosystem providers are the larger dominant companies and will generally have a well-developed partner program to which you can apply. Before you jump in with both wellies and start applying, it's important to understand the different options.

Unless you have a very strong sales team and want to resell the partners' products, I'd suggest you sign up as a Technology Partner (or whatever they call the equivalent). If you attempt to sign up as a resale partner expect a Partner Manager to crawl all over you and expect to have to justify to said Partner Manager your raison d'être and to convince them that you will be able to add value, create demand and therefore resell their product. This is because their remuneration, at least in part, will be based on your performance. Therefore this can be quite an onerous process, especially if they already have resale partners in your space or there is a danger you'll end up competing with their direct sales force. Successful resale partners tend to operate in niches which the ecosystem provider doesn't directly address themselves. These may be geographical or specialist industry niches.

It's not only the sign up process which is a pain, when thinking about whether a resale partnership is suitable, consider why you would want to sell their product at low margin when you can sell your own product at 100% contribution. Surely, you'll be better off concentrating your scarce sales effort to maximise your value, not theirs! Unless you have a compelling reason to resell someone else's infrastructure/ecosystem, I'd avoid it.

The option I've always taken is to sign up as a Technology Partner. As I see it, Technology Partners are the lowest of the low – the mushrooms in the system[154]. Relatively little effort goes into the Technology Partner program because it doesn't bring the ecosystem provider any direct measurable benefit! However, dealing with independent software vendors (ISVs) such as yourself is something that is mandatory for the ecosystem providers. This is because, whether they like it or not, clients are always going to want some ISV's product integrated into the ecosystem, and the ecosystem provider needs a way of legally giving the ISVs access to their platform. From their perspective, having an 'open' platform with a strong Technology Partner program is a useful marketing tool and gives clients confidence that they are not being locked in!

Signing up as a Technology Partner is generally a less onerous process than as a Resale partner[155] and, once you've paid your annual membership (typically circa $10,000) you'll be left alone to get on with it. This type of partnership typically gives you a license to use the ecosystem software for development and demonstration purposes so that you can develop and demonstrate your integration. Don't expect much support and expect zero interest in your integration unless one of their sales opportunities depends on it and then, suddenly, you'll be flavour of the month!

However, it's your ticket to the user conferences where you can take a booth and sell to their client base! You'll soon find out if there is wider demand and whether there are any other functionality gaps you can fill.

---

[154] Kept in the dark and fed manure.

[155] It's generally helpful to have a client of theirs interested in an integration. This covers the inevitable need to demonstrate demand for the integration and provides a client reference.

You'll also meet lots of other small companies filling (hopefully) other functionality gaps. Spending time with the ones which have been around the block to understand the ecosystem and the machinations of the host ecosystem provider is generally time well spent[156].

Of course, once you've signed up and have your integration available, you want the sales team in the ecosystem provider to be aware of you and what you bring to the party. This is easier said than done. Sticking your products on the partner portal generally achieves very little! Don't get me wrong, it's worth doing as the link to your website will come from an authoritative source and, if you've read the marketing section, you'll know that's a good thing! Just don't expect any leads.

Your first instinct may be to attempt to woo the salespeople - mistake[157]. The people in the ecosystem providers you really need to cultivate are the pre-sales techies. It's the pre-sales techies who wield the real power and who are always looking for solutions for the clients. The problem is that all other partner companies know this and therefore the pre-sales techies, who are busy people anyway, are inundated. So how do you get their attention?

It helps if you are the best of breed in your niche but these things take time to establish and you need their attention right now. I've found that the best approach is via the pre-sales techie assigned to a mutual client. Assuming you have a happy client, a working integration that adds value and that is applicable to others, use it (officially or unofficially) as an internal case study and make sure you bring it to said pre-sales techie's attention. Ask them to circulate this success story in their peer group, follow up, etc.

Over time you need to develop a reputation as a solid partner with a solid, reliable product that adds value to both existing clients and in sales situations. There is no substitute for marketing to the ecosystem's personnel and, as you grow, you may want to recruit business development personnel dedicated to this role!

---

[156] The other thing I'd strongly recommend you do is to attend the partner days wherever possible. Some of the industry insights and research shared on such days can be very valuable.

[157] The salespeople will be focused on one thing, meeting their quarterly target. If you are not directly contributing to that goal you won't get the time of day.

The only other piece of advice I can offer is that, within these companies, the only constant is change. There are re-organisations, the partner program is 're-imagined', people leave and people join, and generally there is a constant state of flux. So be prepared. It's not a case of once you've cracked it you can sit back and let the benefits roll in. Only you can judge how much work you put into each partner. My approach has always been to market and sell to the client and not rely on the partner for anything other than a client base and partner program!

Immature Ecosystem Partners

I've differentiated immature ecosystem providers from the more mature companies because these companies are the ones aspiring to be the larger ecosystems and won't have a mature partner program or won't have worked out how to deal with ISVs and may not have a complete API. They also may well have a rather inflated view of their own importance! I've decided to call them AESPs in this section as constantly writing 'the aspiring ecosystem provider with an inflated sense of their own importance' is a pain.

I've had a number of unfortunate dealings with AESPs, one of which I've discussed below but, ultimately, what makes you win is your relationship with the end client. This means that that the AESP can't bully you.

The immaturity of said ASEPs is not always a bad thing. If they don't have a developed partner program, and they want/need to work with you, you won't have to pay a partnership fee. Furthermore, because they will be smaller, you'll be able to easily identify and build a good working relationship with the really important pre-sales techies and product managers in the company.

With some, this initial activity can develop into a long term relationship which carries on for mutual benefit as you both grow. A point of danger in such a relationship is when the AESP gets large enough to introduce a formal partner program. Typically, they'll recruit partner managers from other companies. These new partner managers will arrive with absolutely no knowledge of the existing partners, their relative importance, the day-to-day working relationships already established or, in many cases, the industries and clients pertinent to their new employers! Be prepared to have to fight to be recognised and appreciated, and do not hesitate to get the individuals with whom you have day-to-day working relationships with to weigh in on your behalf.

Ultimately, it depends on the strength of your position. In one such case I recall, the new partner team came in all aggressive and tried to formalise everything and stitch us up for a large partner fee. I simply refused to pay and explained to them (and all the people within the company with whom I'd established good, long term relationships) that it was now up to them to explain to their clients why the critical bit of software we provided was no longer available. And, by the way, if they didn't explain this to our mutual clients I certainly would! It's amazing how quickly exceptions can be made in such circumstances!

However, at some stage you'll need to work with a new AESP in which you don't have existing relationships and their partner team will see you as fair game and try in on. They will demand outrageous partnership fees to deal with you and or come over all arrogant and actively work to convince the client your solution is not needed. In the worst cases, they'll pretend to co-operate and then try and understand your solution so that they can develop it themselves.

The only solution I've found to address these bullying AESPs is to have a good relationship with the client and be prepared to be open and honest with the client. In one instance, a client asked us to integrate with an AESP's infrastructure in which they were heavily investing. The AESP wanted to charge us an annual fee of something like £15,000 to be in their 'catalogue'. It simply wasn't economical. I tried to reason with the AESP to no avail. They were arrogant and self-important. No problem. I simply explained to the client that we couldn't economically undertake the integration due to the AESP's demands. The client went ballistic! It transpired that the client had spent a couple of million with this company and, to cut a long story short, not long afterwards the AESP was all sweetness and light, the integration went ahead and we were in their catalogue for nothing. It had all been a big misunderstanding!

There is an unwritten industry code of conduct that vendors should sort out their own squabbles and not worry the client. As far as the client is concerned everything is smooth and harmonious! Poppycock! The only entity you need to worry about is your company. If involving the client saves you some cash and ensures cooperation from a bolshie third party, have no hesitation! You'll see that this is a perennial theme on so called partnerships!

Infrastructure Partners
I've called this group infrastructure partners to try and differentiate them from the ecosystem providers although most are, in their own right, ecosystem providers as well. I'm mainly thinking of companies like Microsoft and Oracle here. Companies which provide the underlying infrastructure to the large corporates.

Microsoft has a great partner program that allows you to sign up as a developer for a pittance (currently circa £350 per year) and receive lots of freebies in the form of licenses for use in your business – the so called internal use rights (IUR) benefits. You just have to be developing on, or be doing something with, the Microsoft platform. It's almost criminal not to sign up.

Unfortunately, these perks are common knowledge and recently (Q2 2019) Microsoft made an attempt to cancel this benefit. The uproar in the partner community was immediate and the change itself was cancelled although I suspect the IUR benefits are living on borrowed time!

The point is that, even if it's no longer Microsoft, there will be other such programs that greatly benefit your business and save you a lot of money. Identifying them and where appropriate signing up for these benefits is always a good thing! Don't sign up in anticipation of partner support, leads or other such niceties, sign up purely on cost/benefit grounds!

System Integrators
Systems Integrators (SIs) are frequently charged by clients with implementing major projects. They may well have sold the client an ecosystem and be charged with rolling it out. I've been in the situation where the client has purchased licenses and then handed over to an SI to implement our software as part of a larger project. I've also been in a situation where the SI has proposed my software as part of a larger complex project.

This makes the relationships interesting. The SIs won't know your software and it can be hit or miss whether their project team is any good technically. In addition to the standard qualifier (which, to remind you, is: third parties will only have your interests at heart when they coincide with theirs), there are a number of things to bear in mind when dealing with SIs.

Firstly, some SIs will want a margin or a referral commission on any of your software they resell or recommend. Others, some would argue at the more ethical end of the spectrum, won't as their pitch to the client is that they are basing their recommendations on merit rather than the amount they make in margin! We cover this in 'Your Partner Program' below.

Mostly, SIs make their money by charging an hourly rate for consultancy and implementation services. However, if they are on a fixed price contract they can become dangerous! Fixed price contracts are notoriously difficult to deliver and are frequently sold as a loss leader – especially when dealing with the UK government it would seem! So, to avoid losing money, the SIs will be looking for extras from the client. To justify said extras they may well end up casting aspersions and blame against everyone but themselves.

The answer to this is, once again, to ensure that you have a good relationship with the end client and make sure you understand what is going on and what people may be saying about you and your software! There have been a number of times in my career when I've had to spell out in plain English to a client exactly what has gone on, and why the complete pigs ear of a project in front of them was nothing to do with us, our software or our support. Indeed, there have been several times when I've had to throw valuable resource at a client's failing project simply to ensure that we were not only doing, but being seen to be doing, everything in our power to assist in getting the project back on track!

When this happens make sure that the client is aware that is what you are doing and that you are doing it out of the goodness of your heart to rescue their project. They will be grateful and while you may not get any immediate benefit, you hope to get your rewards further down the track. If you manage to rescue the project and it's ultimately successful they are normally only too happy to give you stunning client references!

What if you don't have a direct relationship with the client and the SI sold your software? The answer is to use the sale to establish a direct relationship with the client. The SI won't like this because they want to control the client and make sure that their version of events is the only version available. Remember, your duty is to your company and therefore don't worry too much about treading on their toes. And, if it helps salve your conscience, SIs have little long term memory.

I say SIs have little long term memory because they are almost entirely project based. This is both good and bad. The good is that annoying a particular SI because you explained to the client in words of one syllable that it was their fault and not yours, is unlikely to come back and bite you as you are unlikely ever to work with that same team again.

The bad, is that even if you've had a good experience, you are unlikely ever to work with that same team again and therefore all that knowledge they have of your software and any relationships you've built up go out of the window and therefore every project is a clean sheet.

Having a long term, repeatable relationship with a pure play SI is almost impossible. The bigger they are the harder it is. In my experience they think and act on a purely tactical basis!

The exception to this is when the SI develops a 'product' or service offering which attempts to package commonly used functionality (typically based around a mature ecosystem's platform) to make it available to other clients on a more cost effective basis. The general pitch is along the lines of its 80% product and 20% customisation which means the costs are considerably less than a fully custom project.

This approach can work for the SI if they adopt a more product based mentality. Not all do. If you are dealing with an SI in this mode then think of them more like an immature ecosystem provider than an SI, although they will exhibit characteristics of both. I warned you at the start of this section that the partnership landscape was complex!

Consultants

There can be a very grey area between consultants and SIs. I see it as a spectrum. At one end are the real hands on integrators and at the other are the pure play consultants. In the middle of the spectrum it gets very messy! Some consultants are very much like SIs and vice versa except that consultants rarely get their hands dirty. Whereas SIs will tend to do actual implementation and data migration and so on, consultants will identify a need and may even produce a high level specification but avoid any real work.

Given that, I'd apply almost all the same caveats to consultants as I would to SIs.

As with all such third parties, work out what is in it for them and then work out how to align your interests. This is generally easier with small one or two-person consultancies than with larger consultancies which tend to have a similar turnover of personnel as the SIs.

Outsourcers

These are the companies that take over implementation services and or run the IT department and or support for a major corporate. There is an SLA in place and the contract is supposed to align the outsourcer's interests and the client's interests.

I'm going to give it to you straight! I have a very low opinion of outsourcers. In my experience it rarely works as a business practice and the end user clients you will be dealing with will dislike the arrangement just as much as anyone! It's like handing over your house maintenance to someone on a fixed price contract with the consequence that they are always trying to do it on the cheap.

Firstly, you need to understand the nature of the contract between the client and the outsourcer. In some of the contracts, the client is solely responsible for specifying the requirements and it's the outsourcer's job to deliver by whatever means they decide. The client can suggest your product but, ultimately, it's the outsourcer's decision. So, if they think they can deliver the requirements as a custom solution because they'll make more that way, they will[158]. In my experience, if they conclude that they have to provide your product they'll demand ridiculous margins to resell to the client.

The only way to deal with this is not to play their game. Stand back, ensure that the client has a definitive statement of requirements (which you've created for them and which major on your USPs and the really difficult stuff you do), and let the outsourcer have a crack at the custom solution. Keep in touch with the client to follow the unfolding disaster and hope that at some

---

[158] The people who write these contracts on behalf of the clients seem to have no appreciation of the real world.

point in the future the client will have a new budget, will have learnt their lesson and that there is an opportunity for you.

If you are able to sell directly to the client and learn that there is an outsourcer involved for implementation and or managing the infrastructure or in any way at all, my strong advice is to include a large implementation support fee. In my experience the outsource personnel are rarely the brightest sparks and will either mess it up and you'll need to rescue it or, if you are lucky, expect you to do the work for free. At least with this second option you don't have to waste time undoing the mess they previously made!

I'm sure that there are decent, reliable, trustworthy outsourcers out there – it's just that our paths never crossed!

Purchasing Outsourcers

There exists a little known genre of company which exists to source software for corporate purchasing departments. They mainly specialise in sourcing what used to be known as shrink wrapped COTS licenses[159]. You may come across them for two reasons:

Firstly, if you are selling to a very large corporate and you are selling a trial license or low value pilot project, the purchasing department may not consider it worth their while setting you up as a separate vendor on their system so they will sub-contact the purchase to what is the equivalent of a purchasing outsourcer. The purchasing outsourcer may require/request a margin on the deal.

This has only happened to us once and we dealt with it by supplying the software through the purchasing outsourcer at the same price we'd quoted the client and the client then paid a purchasing premium to the outsourcer. This was a perfectly happy experience (significantly helped by a sensible client and a purchasing outsourcer essentially doing the client a favour) and I would certainly not attach the same caveats to purchasing outsourcers as I would to the IT outsourcers addressed above. However, my experience is strictly limited.

---

[159] The software hasn't been shrink wrapped for years but there doesn't appear to be a modern term to describe this type of lower value off-the-shelf standard software.

By the way, this did have a happy ending. The client decided to roll out our product, set us up as a direct vendor and became one of our bigger clients over the next few years.

The other interactions I've had with these type of companies is when the corporate purchasing department decides that they want or need three quotes for the software. Knowing nothing about your software they typically put it out to their standard suppliers. The first you know of this is when you get emails and calls asking you to quote for X licenses and requesting a standard reseller discount. As these companies are not generally au fait with anything other than COTS licenses frequently the detail is missing (i.e. different license types, etc. if you have them). The more aggressive ones call you and intimate that unless you give them a healthy margin you'll never get to sell to the client as all software sales to the end user client go through them. Don't fall for this rubbish!

If you are on top of your sales you'll know or be able to easily work out who the prospective client is and you can then explain to the client and all parties involved that you do not sell via non-value add resellers – which these companies are as they are not adding any value.

If the companies won't accept that as an answer you make it clear your policy is not to sell through any non-authorised resellers and, if they ask, be sure to make the terms for being authorised particularly onerous!

Whilst we are on the subject, as a matter of principle with any non-direct selling, you need to think about how your licensing works if you are selling through third parties. Considerations around this are covered under the software licensing section and below under 'Things to consider with respect to resellers'.

Informal Partners

In every market there will be a number of small companies who aren't your partners but who aren't competitors either. They simply coexist in the same ecosystem and are people you just rub along with. You'll probably have common clients and you'll bump into them at the same shows and get chatting.

Not only do you meet some wonderful people in these informal partners (as the relationship is informal you probably keep in touch and chat because you get on with each other), these informal relationships can be very useful.

Market knowledge, information on what is happening at mutual clients or prospects, the latest shenanigans at the ecosystem provider and other useful gossip can all be exchanged.

With the ones you know well, they can also have their uses when a client needs three quotes. Being able to call someone and say: 'would you mind if I gave your name and contact details to XZY Inc as a partner who can provide a quote?'. You then give them the information they need to provide a quote to the client. The client has three quotes. Yours is the same or cheaper than the others (they have their margin to consider) and everyone is happy. You buy them dinner when you next meet!

Your Partner Program

No matter what size you are, having a section on your website talking about your partner program is never a bad thing! It doesn't really matter how formal your partner program is. Pretending you have one suggests that you are bigger than you may actually be!

The companies discussed under this section are different as you are the principal and the partners you work with hereunder are trying to leverage your client base or your software and see an advantage to be working with you! Naturally, I'd strongly suggest that you don't have an inflated sense of your own importance or act arrogantly. That doesn't mean you need to let them tread all over you; it just means that you are approachable, decent and honest.

In reality, as the principal you'll need to work with several types of third parties:

1. Sales Partners: These are organisations or individuals who approach you believing that they can help you sell your software because they have an 'in' with a particular client or group of clients or address a market you don't. Not all are opportunists. Some may be independent consultants who really do have an in at a particular client. Others may want to cover a territory you aren't covering directly or find it difficult to cover. If based in the UK, Australia

comes immediately to mind! Naturally, they'll want a margin or a kickback of some description.

2. Integration Partners: These are typically other ISVs who approach you to integrate your product with theirs. You are the ecosystem provider in these cases. They tend to be smaller companies competing in the market and believe that an integration with your product will help them compete with or give them an advantage over their larger competitors. As you grow and become recognised there will be more and more of these.

3. Systems integrators: They'd love to be able to sell lots of professional services implementing your software. These services may compete with you if you provide implementation services and are building a professional services capability or may be necessary to complement your limited capacity.

Let's deal with them one at a time.

Sales Partners

We are going to split sales partners into hangers-on or potentially genuinely useful people in your home markets (i.e. the ones you expect to sell to directly) and resellers in markets you do not sell to directly, or will have difficulty in selling to directly.

Home Market Sales Partners

The reality is you will come across a number of people who try and convince you that they are the key to unlocking a client. They are some sort of magical gatekeeper and the client will only purchase if you secure a recommendation from them. Some are genuine. Most are trying it on.

Assuming you determine that they are genuine, ultimately, you want to sell to the client directly and, if appropriate, pay off the 'consultant'. This is where the introductory commission comes in. Typically set at 5% - 10% of the initial software license or a negotiable fixed fee, it should only be payable when you have an order from, and have been paid by, said client and should be strictly limited to the first year, the initial contact, or whatever. Stick a time limit on any agreement (i.e. you receive the order within X months of the introduction) otherwise, if the first sales attempt doesn't work out and then a couple of years later, after hours of your time cultivating the client, there is a sale you really don't want to pay for the initial introduction!

In short, it needs to be a genuine introduction to a genuine opportunity with a brand new client with whom you've not previously interacted which can be closed in a relatively short time frame. It's not just a: 'here are the contact details for Joe Doe, I've known him for years and he may be interested in your stuff'.

In terms of the introductory commission, you want to pay as little as possible and, as it's something for nothing for the introducer, there is generally scope for haggling.

It's worth noting two more things:

1. The ethical consultants advising a client will not expect an introductory commission as they are being paid by the client for their expertise. In the rare occasions we paid an introductory commission to such a consultant, we'd always make a point of dropping into the conversation with the client (after we had the order) the fact we would be paying the consultant an introductory commission. If the consultant was double dipping, they'd soon have an irate client to deal with.

2. You will get people calling you saying things like: 'we are working with [insert major corporate name] on sourcing [insert a generic term which could be used to describe your product]'. Ignore these people. They are not working with a major prospect at all. They are usually selling advertising and want you to advertise in their guide or other publication addressing the [generic term] market.

Resellers in non-Core and Difficult Markets
Resellers in non-core markets (either geographic or industry) can be a major bonus. I have to be upfront and say that I've never really cracked the resale market as our stuff (both in CDC and PleaseTech) was fairly complex to sell and we were busy concentrating on selling directly to our core markets. We did get some sales through such channels but they were never more than a small bonus.

The key to success is a clearly defined market with clearly defined limits and clearly defined margins which are based on the amount of sales effort you have to make compared with the reseller. From memory, we had something like:

1. 10% margin: where we did a majority of the selling.

2. 15 – 20% margin: where there was a joint sales effort and the margin depended on how much we did.

3. 30% margin: where the reseller did all the selling and we were involved purely in software license discussions[160].

You'll need to define who is providing what level of support and this will be reflected in the margins. Who is paying for translations? Consider both UI and documentation, training videos, etc. When considering UI translations, be sure to set expectations. In my experience is one thing to translate the main UI and a completely different investment if everything (including the system admin interface and obscure error messages, etc.) needs to be translated.

It's also worth discussing whether you get a margin on any services the reseller is able to sell with the contract. We never did. Whatever the deal, expect to have to provide a very high level of sales support for the first few sales.

If looking for such resellers, it's worth approaching the resellers of your major ecosystem providers. As they resell the ecosystem they'll have the client contacts and can add your offering to the mix. However, it's not a given and you'll have to convince them that they can make money out of your product. The challenge is, of course, to decide how much effort to put into pursuing resellers when you could put the same effort into making direct sales.

I included 'difficult' markets in the title as there are some markets to which it's almost impossible to sell to directly. The example which comes immediately to mind is the US government. The US government spends a huge amount every year on software and, in our naivety at PleaseTech, we attended a couple of US Government centric shows. These shows are exclusively attended by government employees and feature vendors

---

[160] Obviously, occasionally it is necessary to give higher margins but, if it were me, I'd go there kicking and screaming and only based on performance!

wanting to sell to government departments. We soon learnt that in order to do almost anything in the government market you need a GSA[161] agreement.

What these GSA agreements do is provide a pre-agreed framework contract between the government and the vendor (including pricing) which a purchasing government agency or branch can leverage[162]. It's very simple for a US government body to purchase with the aid of a GSA agreement and very difficult for them to purchase without one.

Therefore, for such markets, it's worth teaming up with a reseller who has a GSA agreement as it's a lot easier for such a reseller to add products to an existing GSA agreement than it is for you to establish such an agreement. Some companies simply act as a GSA facilitator and seem to exist simply to allow companies such as yours to leverage their broad GSA contract – at a price obviously.

You need to think of these resellers purely as facilitators. You will have to find the prospect, do the selling and give them a margin, and for that they do very little, if anything. The reason you are giving them a margin is because they facilitate the sale via the GSA credentials.

Integration Partners

You may think this is where I explain to you that you can charge a nice annual fee to sign people up as Technology Partners of your own. Unfortunately it doesn't work like that! Initially you'll be too small and, once you start gaining traction you have to make a strategic decision as to whether you want to encourage others to integrate with your software[163]. Charging them a partner fee discourages them.

My position on integrations has always been very simple; if I thought it would be in our interest to undertake an integration with another product

---

[161] The General Services Administration (GSA) is a United States government agency.
[162] It's worth noting that these GSA contracts are public domain (i.e. published and available on the web) and thus any confidential information therein (e.g. your pricing) is no longer confidential.
[163] I always wanted to encourage such integrations as I saw it strategically beneficial. If you make it difficult and a competitor makes it easy you'll just be pushing business to the competitor.

we would look at developing one[164]. This is when we'd sign up as a Technology Partner as covered above. However, the reality is that as you will have extremely limited development capacity and such integrations tend to be complex. It's therefore necessary to carefully pick and choose the integrations you do.

As you become established you will be approached by the smaller competitors of the ecosystem providers and you'll need to make a decision on how to handle them. If you aren't going to do the integration yourself, I'd suggest that you sign them up as your partners and assist them to undertake the integration by providing a technology partner type relationship with a license to use your software, documentation and access to advice and guidance. Don't just throw your software over the wall at them because it's important to you that the integration is done well. You don't want them out in the market showcasing your software with a poor integration. First impressions tend to linger in the client's mind!

In working with these partners you need to be very clear how the solution is going to be sold. As they developed the integration one assumes that they will own it. Is it an integral part of their software or a cost option? If a cost option, will it price your solution out of the market as, don't forget, the client still has to purchase your software? Who is going to sell your software? Are you working with them to sell it directly or are they acting as resellers? If acting as resellers, what is the margin? How will their sales force be trained?

However signing up everyone who approaches you is not sustainable in the long run as you'll soon learn that even providing advice and guidance sucks resource. It's at this point that you may start to think about charging a partnership fee to cover the expense!

---

[164] It's worth observing that you may not sell a specific integration but it's still required strategically. For example, a number of our clients were investing in Microsoft SharePoint. They didn't buy our SharePoint integration but the fact that we had one meant that we fitted in their strategy and overcame objections.

Systems Integrators

We discussed SIs above from the perspective of them driving the business and having the relationship with the client and you being part of a bigger project which they are implementing. This section discusses dealings with them with you driving the partnership.

The first thing to establish is that unless your product requires extensive professional services to implement and or configure, it's unlikely that SIs will be interested. They are only attracted to products that leverage professional services. Unless you really are unique and bring a significant competitive advantage, it's highly likely that they will propose a competitive product – one that leverages more professional services.

So, in summary, unless your product leverages professional services, don't go around wasting your time being nice to SIs trying to sign them up as partners to promote your wares! Not only do they not have any long term memory (see above) but your interests are not aligned.

Occasionally, a project will come along where your interests are aligned and the only sensible approach will be for them to resell your software. In these one-off circumstances you'll be forced to give them a margin. Just try and keep it as low as possible and read the section below on things to consider with respect to resellers before you sign anything!

Reseller Considerations

In whatever circumstance a third party resells your software there are a number of things to consider and cover in the contract.

Firstly, responsibilities. Who is delivering what? Who is undertaking any implementation services? If the third party, will they be technically competent? Who is responsible for end user client support? First line support? Second line support? Is the reseller able to commit you to anything? I strongly suggest this should not be in their remit!

Secondly, make sure there is a clear understanding on margins especially with respect to support and renewals. Does the client renew with you or the reseller? If the client renews with you does the reseller get a kickback?

Thirdly, who is responsible for pricing and discounting? Go to strenuous efforts to avoid giving away any responsibility for discounting. All discounts need to be approved by you in writing.

If that isn't possible because the reseller is selling your product as an integral part of their own, make sure that there is a very clear 'equality of discount' clause. Equality of discount prevents the reseller discounting your software and not theirs. You don't want to discover that they found it expedient to discount your software by 90% but only discount their own by 10%[165].

It's worth noting that even an equality of discount clause isn't ideal and can leave you out of pocket because, if the reseller routinely discounts their product by 60% and you don't (having read my diatribe on discounting in the Sales chapter), you can see how, with the equality of discount, your software could always be discounted by 60%!

Fourthly, what are the software licensing provisions? Will the client sign your software license? If so, whose responsibility is it to get that signature? I'd strongly recommend that you retain the responsibility and have a clause which means that you can withhold software or license key provision until you have a signed license. The reality is that getting a signed software license from the client is hard work and the reseller almost certainly won't bother.

If your software is going to be covered by the reseller's license make sure that it really does cover your software and has clauses covering all the aspects you need covered. Specifically, you may have special licensing conditions for third party software incorporated in your software for which generic licensing conditions won't be adequate. You may have to demand a special addendum for your software. This will be strongly resisted by the reseller. Ultimately, software licensing on other people's paper is a nightmare and you should try and avoid it.

Finally, another couple of points which I'll add here as they need to be covered but they don't really fit in anywhere else.

1. If you are lucky enough to have multiple resellers all trying to sell your software to the same client as part of the same deal in competition with each other, how do you play it? Don't agree to work with the first one who brings you the opportunity and discard

---

[165] You calculate the discount by adding up the list price of all software and services sold and comparing it against what the client actually paid. This gives you the overall discount. You then apply this discount percentage equally to all products and services in the deal.

all the others. This doesn't do you or the prospective client any favours. I've always simply played it with a straight bat. Everyone gets exactly the same terms, the same discounts (if any), the same information and the same support.

2. When dealing with larger companies, just because you are on a third party's price list or integrated as part of their software and they have a resale agreement with you doesn't mean that their sales team understands or even knows about your product. It'll just be a price list item. If you want the dollars to roll in you'll have to make the effort to educate their sales force. Again, the pre-sales techies are a good place to start!

And, as a very last point in this Partners section, if you are ever tempted to greatly discount your software because someone offers you an OEM deal and explains that what you'll lose in top line price you'll make up in quantity, don't believe them. By all means put an escalating discount to them depending on quantity, but the one time I was tempted the promised volume never materialised and we ended up giving away cheap software. Luckily we had a break clause and were able to escape the trap. People will promise you the world. Only believe them when it is delivered!

Growth

Growth is a natural consequence of success and, I would argue, essential for its continuation. It allows you to provide a better service to your customers, gives you a fighting chance in the technology race and, not least, increases the value of your company.

We've obliquely addressed growth throughout the book and mentioned some of the resulting issues. This chapter will cover in more detail the cultural and staff challenges growth brings, but first I want to address the naive belief that it's possible to grow to a certain size, stop growing and enter into a permanent steady state. As your company develops and you contemplate the next stage of expansion, it can be tempting to look around and think: you know what, life's pretty good! Why don't we just stay as we are?

The answer is that you simply can't do that in the world of software. Remember that the only constant is change and if you are not keeping up and constantly updating and expanding your products, there is someone in a garage somewhere who has designs on your customer base. It's the equivalent of an arms race in which the best defence is growth because this gives you the resources to throw at the problem. Attaining some sort of steady state nirvana is a fallacy. A company is either growing or dying and, let's be clear, dying is no fun. Most choose growth.

The problem is that the realities of growth are not always pleasant for the staff or yourself!

The Realities of Growth

Setting aside the cash side of the equation, growth has a significant impact on company culture and staff composition which is important to understand.

I've already alluded to this when discussing the management of development when I note that, as the company grows, you need to introduce more formal reporting and management controls and that this is seldom welcomed by the start-up team. Along with this, the culture changes from a small informal group of like-minded people pitching in as and where necessary, into that of a more structured organisation.

Many people won't like being hemmed in and no longer knowing about or being part of everything that is going on. To add to the challenge, new recruits won't understand the history or the problem. Whereas the start-up team may be having to adjust to the new reality, for the new recruits it is all they know and they won't understand what all the fuss is about. You therefore need to be careful a 'them and us' mentality doesn't start to gain traction.

Additionally, you have to accept that the company will outgrow some people. Not every member of the start-up team (however that is defined) will have the ability (or, in many cases, desire) to fit into the evolving structure. A further danger is that you give people responsibilities beyond their capability simply because they were in at the beginning.

So tough decisions have to be taken even if it means that some feel hard done by and subsequently seek fresh pastures. You may even have to take proactive action and let an individual or two go.

It is always regrettable when you can't take some people with you on the journey but the simple fact is that you won't be able to please everyone. It is this natural attrition which reemphasises my points made in the initial chapter regarding ownership, shareholder agreements, options, etc. The reality is not everyone will last the course, and having anticipated this and addressed it in advance will be a major benefit at a time when you can do without other distractions.

When observing high growth companies, I've noted that things start going pear-shaped when they recruit lots of new people who hit the ground running. The basic problem is that these newbies have no idea in which direction to run. I alluded to this when I addressed the issue of new partner managers in some growth companies setting up partner programs with no knowledge of the existing partners, their relative importance, the day-to-day working relationships already established or, in many cases, the industries and clients pertinent to their new employers.

Partner management is but one example. Consider that this happens across the company in areas like product management, marketing, etc.! The problem is completely understandable. The new employees feel they don't have the time or, in many cases, guidance to understand their new employer's peculiarities and so fall back on what they do know, which may be inappropriate and can inadvertently take the company in a different direction.

Worse still, different elements of the company can end up pulling in different directions. The reason I mention this is that you do not want this to happen in your company. Invest time in your new staff to ensure that they do know in which direction your team is focused.

The speed of growth is obviously a critical determinant of the size of the problem. In PleaseTech our steady organic growth alleviated many of these challenges. However, at CDC when we had headcount growth of 275% per year, it was a different story.

Growth will not only challenge your staff, it will challenge you! It will raise all sorts of questions. Are you competent to take the company to the next level? Do you want to?

In the next section I'll outline a model that went some way in helping me understand growth from a theoretical management perspective and thereby helped me rationalise some of the decisions taken.

A Model for Growth

Throughout my business career I've been an avid reader of business books. Some are really good and others a complete waste of time. Every now and then one contains a real gem. In the '90s I read a book called Accidental Empires by Robert X Cringely. A copy of the 1996 reprint[166] is still on my bookshelf and on page 236 there is a large corner turned down which is where the book outlines a growth model which I'll call 'commandos, infantry and occupation troops'.

Cringely suggests that the growth of a company can be thought of as a military operation given that both involve strategy, tactics, supply lines, communication, alliances and people. I'll paraphrase my understanding of the model he outlines.

Companies are started by commandos (the first wave). They are the first to see action. Commandos are multi-skilled, work expeditiously and, while they

---

[166] I noted that my edition was the 1996 'TV Tie-in' Edition. Sure enough, if you go to YouTube and search for 'The Triumph of the Nerds: The Rise of Accidental Empires' you'll find the three part series. A fascinating insight into the history of the industry narrated by Robert Cringely (aka Mark Stephens) himself.

have an overall objective, make it up as they go along as they react to constantly changing conditions on the ground.

Companies are grown by infantry (the second wave). The infantry builds on the initial success of the commandos. It is well organised, well supplied, has clearly defined tactics and objectives, and overwhelms the opposition. It needs a lot of support and structure: reporting lines, communication lines, middle managers, specialists, front line staff, back room staff, etc.

Finally there are the occupation troops (the third wave) who are essentially passive. They are risk-averse, resist change and rarely, if ever, engage the enemy. In fact the enemy is just as likely to be seen as another department in the same organisation as it is a competitor. These companies are typified by the dominant or monopoly supplier in their industry.

If you accept the basic premise of the above then there are certain learnings which can be applied:

1. Always ensure that the right commander is in charge of the right troops. If you get this wrong you are doomed to disaster. For example, if you put a commando in charge of infantry, the commando will expect infantry to react like other commandos and therefore there will be chaos. Likewise having an infantry commander leading commandos will fail.

2. Always place the right troops in the right regiment. Placing natural commandos in the infantry will lead to pain. It follows that an infantryman will be a fish out of water in a commando unit! This is why I emphasise that when you are recruiting it's best to avoid the corporate people as they will be out of their depth without their support network.

3. The transitions between the stages are especially difficult. Keeping the commandos engaged whilst the infantry take over is tricky. If you've got it right, the start-up team (including yourself) are natural commandos. Some are able to make the transition into the infantry, and many are not.

Hopefully you can see how this model applies to a growing business and how it explains some of the challenges of growth which we have discussed. For instance, it explains why there is generally a steady supply of people with start-up experience who are available for no reason other than the company they were with grew beyond them. These people are the commandos someone lost in their transition to infantry.

I'd argue that you generally want to keep the commandos on board for as long as possible, especially the technical ones! Therefore, as I previously noted, a certain degree of obfuscation may be necessary to maintain at least a semblance of the environment with which they are comfortable as the company formalises in other areas.

You will not be immune either! You have to look in the mirror and ask yourself if you (i) are capable of, and (ii) want to make the move into running an infantry battalion. Many, myself included, are not convinced that such a move plays to their strengths and therefore this is a classic time to sell.

It's also worth noting that if you are VC backed, it's not just you who will be asking those questions. Your investors will be well aware of the need to make the transition and will be considering their options. It's not for nothing that there is a common belief that, after a venture capital investment, the first job of the board is to appoint a new CEO and the first job of the new CEO is to fire the founder!

However, before we address the whole VC game let's talk about exit!

Exit

Exit

You've done the hard yards, worked your socks off, built the business, seen the value of the business grow, fretted that a costly error or market step change could rob of that value and decided it's time to cash in. All you need now is a successful exit.

The reality is that there are many reasons people decide to exit and, if we are honest, it's rarely a purely financial decision. It's normally a combination or accumulation of factors that bring you to the conclusion that it's time!

Certainly the transition from commando to infantry can be a factor[167]. You may start to feel that you aren't really enjoying it anymore. The exciting innovation has largely gone, it's all a bit repetitive and you are spending your time in management meetings and they bore you to tears! You used to be a road warrior and now you are a meeting junkie drinking too much coffee. You then realise with a shock that this is your new life in the infantry!

In my case, there is no doubt that fatigue was a factor. I'd been working flat out on the business for almost 15 years and I was drained[168]. In such circumstances, you examine the options and realise that there aren't many! You either continue, sell or recruit someone else to run the business and move yourself to Chairman. I'd suggest that the latter option is full of risk and, anyway, isn't an exit!

If you are VC backed these thought processes don't really apply as your wishes are immaterial and you mustn't show your investors any sign of weakness in any respect. You just have to keep peddling with a smile on your face until the VCs decide how and when they'd like to exit. If you are lucky and it's a trade sale they'll need to keep you on board. If it's an IPO, well … I refer you to my experiences at CDC in The CDC Story!

Whichever route you chose to take it's worth noting it is not entirely without risk. The preparation for any exit is onerous, the associated expense is massive and there are no guarantees of a happy ending. You will incur

---

[167] If you are wondering what I'm talking about it's because you skipped the chapter on growth!

[168] I subsequently found that, due to an undiagnosed health condition, I'd been operating on only 50% lung capacity. Therein lies another lesson – don't neglect your own health!

significant legal and other professional fees which are not success dependent. I'm aware of one company that went through the IPO process and was extremely close to a successful listing when there was a sudden collective market confidence collapse resulting in the IPO being pulled. The bill was, I understand, around £800K.

It's not just IPOs that go bad. Corporate financiers will tell you that trade sales can - and do - fall apart at the very last minute. Indeed, the CDC exit took six months from the Heads of Terms and there were a number of times it looked and felt like it would fall apart. It's always more complicated when you have VC investors trying to protect their position, especially when there is an earnout involved. It wasn't until exchange happened in the small hours of the morning that we knew the deal was secure.

A failed trade sale will be less expensive than a failed IPO but you are unlikely to have a bill below six figures and the further along the process the deal falls apart the higher the bill will be!

There are two primary exit routes (i) trade sale and (ii) IPO, although I'm going to argue that an IPO isn't an exit at all. I have absolutely no experience of MBOs (management buyouts), remain unconvinced that they are relevant to growing software companies and so chose to ignore them!

IPO as an Exit

Let me start by making it clear that I have no direct experience of IPOs. I've chatted with a number of CEOs of businesses preparing for IPOs, some of which have been successful and some of which have been pulled! I've also witnessed the subsequent pressures on those CEOs who did manage to float.

I'll therefore limit myself to the observation that an IPO is not an exit for the management team and especially the CEO. So if you are uncomfortable running the infantry or are in any way burnt out, don't even think about it. All you do is change one type of pressure for another.

If anything, running a quoted company is considerably harder than running a private company, even one with VCs. Your focus will be on managing the investors rather than the business and you'll need to have a COO running the operational side of things. You need to be the smooth-talking, suit-wearing beguiler wowing the city boys.

Of course, your business may be under control but your share price will be subject to forces completely outside your influence and, if you think VCs get upset when you miss your numbers, you ain't seen nothing yet!

Once floated your shares have an intrinsic value and you can put a real figure on your net worth (which may fluctuate wildly) but you are not free to realise your new found wealth. You will be prevented from selling the shares for a lock-up period and then will only be able to sell your shares at specific times (i.e. at times when there is no meaningful inside information) and even then the chances are you won't be able to sell them except in dribs and drabs as any major sale will spook the markets.

You only have to follow a couple of smaller market cap companies to understand how the purchase and sale of shares by Directors and especially the CEO, are discussed and dissected *ad nauseam* on the various chat forums. Furthermore, there is endless narrative on the subject of Director transactions as a company performance (and therefore share price direction) indicator in the wider investment press, blogs, etc.

It is true that being listed has the advantage of allowing you to dabble in the M&A market using shares as an incentive or the capital markets as a means to raise more cash to acquire companies to grow your business. I have no doubt that this is some people's idea of a lot of fun, but it's not an exit!

Once floated, to truly exit you need to engineer yourself out of the business over time. Perhaps CEO to Chairman to non-executive Director giving you an excuse to sell shares and realise some of your investment as you go.

For a true exit you need a trade sale.

Trade Sale

You may have heard the adage that 'good businesses get bought not sold'. Not true.

There is no doubt that some businesses are proactively approached by a strategic acquirer prepared to pay top dollar but the resulting deals are, I suspect, a small percentage of the overall M&A transactions made. If you read The PleaseTech Story you'll have learnt how we regularly received unsolicited approaches, several of which were opportunistic in the hope of acquiring the business from naïve owners for a steal. You'll also have learnt that we proactively decided to sell and then marketed the business.

It's a bit like selling your house. You may well get the odd approach when you are not really planning to move but, unless someone makes you an offer you simply can't refuse, when you do decide it's time you'll maximise the value by appealing to the broadest possible market. That means you advertise it for sale and try to attract buyers, ideally bidding against each other.

It comes as a shock to many to know that there is such a market for companies but there is. There are acquiring companies and those looking to be sold. The equivalent of the estate agents are the corporate financiers. They know the market, know what your business is worth, how to present it in a favourable light and who the likely buyers are.

In fact, the M&A departments of acquiring companies are generally so inundated with prospectuses from these corporate financiers that they haven't got the time to proactively go hunting for acquisitions. Therefore the first step in the sales process is to have a chat with a number of corporate financiers.

The other point to make at this stage is that selling a business is not a short term proposition. It's a complicated process that frequently hits 'hiccups', especially if you have anything dubious hidden away. From when you have an identified acquirer who has made an acceptable offer (and that arguably is the hardest part), it can take as little as three months (if your business is as clean as a whistle) or, more likely, six-plus months. So, if all goes smoothly, you should be allowing about a year from start to finish, but that's not including earnouts and lock-ins, etc.

Corporate Financiers, Valuations, etc.
The key to maximising the value of your company is to understand that not all corporate financiers are equal and it pays to retain the services of the good ones. The other point I'd emphasise is that selling technology companies is a specialist field. The generic corporate finance companies which claim to be able to sell any company because the base process is the same are unlikely to have the necessary understanding or relationships to maximise your value.

You will have received regular approaches from some of these generic corporate financiers who seem to mail anyone and everyone. Ignore them. The real good technology industry corporate financiers don't need to resort to such lowbrow tactics.

In fact, the top technology industry corporate financiers are very selective about which companies they chose to represent. They will have established a reputation for only offering top quality opportunities to buyers and therefore will not and do not accept instructions to sell companies that don't meet their standards. The good news is that, if you are a quality company, the top corporate financiers will be keen to represent you, and through them you'll get access to the best buyers and therefore the best deals.

No doubt your next question is: how do I find the top technology industry corporate financiers?

The answer is research and keeping an eye on the market. Once the hard yards are over and the company is growing, most CEOs will have half an eye on the M&A market regardless of whether they are thinking of selling. As you see companies being sold, work out who represented them. It's not hard as it will be in the press release!

Get on the mailing list of a few names you've noted. Go to a few of the seminars they run. This will do several things. It will give you an idea of (i) the company profile the buyer market is currently valuing, (ii) it will put you on the radar of the corporate financiers, and (iii) it will help you understand the multiples and therefore the current value of your company. You'll also get to meet people like me who've been through the process and are happy to share their experience.

The figures which will be discussed in the seminars will be quite generic but they will give you a good idea of the metrics the market values. For example, at the time of writing the market values recurring revenue more highly than non-recurring revenue. Understanding this can help you re-focus the sales team to sell the type of deal that the market is valuing.

Ultimately, something is only worth what someone is prepared to pay for it. Therefore, it's a bit of a guessing game. It's worth noting that, when it comes to the valuation, it's much more about the financial figures than the technology. Unless it is very strategic, technology itself is not separately valued, although having your own IP which creates a decent market entry barrier will deliver a higher valuation as will a blue chip customer base.

Things that will lower your value include being over reliant on a single or handful of clients, disputes or potential disputes of any nature, and working in a competitive niche especially if you aren't the dominant vendor.

The past deal metrics only offer guidance and your friendly corporate financier will be able to give you a valuation 'landing zone'.

When I say 'friendly' I am not trying to be facetious. Establishing an ongoing relationship with a couple of corporate finance advisors is strongly recommended. At PleaseTech, we made a point of buying lunch for Alan Bristow of Icon Corporate Finance[169] once a year (in the summer when things were quiet) to pick his brain on the state of the M&A market, update him about our progress and generally have a 'time out' to think about exits. As with all business, these personal connections and relationships are important and contribute at so many levels to results.

Initiating the Sales Process and Choosing Advisors

You initiate the sales process by signing up with a corporate finance company and getting a set of lawyers ready to act on your behalf. But before you do that there is work to be done!

Hopefully, you've established some relationships with corporate finance companies and can engage in more formal talks with them, obtaining formal proposals that cover costs, etc. Whilst you are engaged in these conversations be sure to ask them which law firms they recommend. You'll then need to talk to the law firms as well and go through a similar process. Don't forget to ask the law firms which corporate finance firms they recommend. You may have missed a particularly good one in your research!

Before you formally engage with these professionals think through your rationale. In The PleaseTech Story, I explain that there needs to be a narrative around the reasons why you are selling at this particular moment. Saying 'it seemed like a good idea at the time' won't get you very far. When a potential acquirer asks, 'why are you selling now?', you'd better have a

---

[169] With whom we had history going back to the CDC days as explained in The CDC Story.

pretty good explanation. It may well be you invoke the commandos to infantry analogy. You may pick a forthcoming milestone birthday (as I did) and use that as an explanation. The key thing is to make it sound positive for the buyer. They need to get the message that they are the lucky people who get to benefit from your advancing years/your lack of experience in managing larger companies/whatever other rational explanation you provide.

Saying something like 'I'm absolutely exhausted, I've been working my butt off for ten years and it's only getting harder', isn't going to fill your potential acquirer full of positive vibes. Saying something like 'I've grown the business to the best of my capabilities but, with the huge potential we see in the market, it's time to hand over to a larger parent company which can provide the structure for managing growth to maximise the opportunity', conveys a very different message!

You also need to be very clear on your personal aspirations and those of any other senior colleagues in the know. Does anyone want to stay with the business other than for an agreed handover period? For me, the concept of working for someone else on any long term basis was a complete non-starter. However, throughout my career I've come across the founders of acquired companies happily working for the purchaser long after the acquisition. So it is a very personal decision and there is no right answer.

Having got your story sorted and established personal aspirations of the protagonists, you've got to make a decision as to which professional advisors you use.

The first critical decision is the corporate finance house. Clearly you want a quality company with a solid track record. However, due to the stressful and high pressure nature of the sales process, you need to ensure that you are able to work closely with the individual corporate finance executive involved. So make sure that there is 'chemistry' and that you feel comfortable with them and their *modus operandi* over a period of time.

The other deciding factor is their reach. What is their buyer universe? Or, in more common terminology, how extensive are their contacts? While many sellers do find their purchaser in their own food chain (i.e. a partner, client company, competitor or other known entity), if the corporate finance company is doing its job, it will introduce into the equation other companies not known to you.

When it comes to lawyers, software and IP are specialist areas so it's important to ensure that they are familiar with selling software companies and have knowledge of what is acceptable and unacceptable when it comes to IP warranties and indemnities. Again chemistry is important.

With both decisions deal size comes into play. Make sure that your advisors are experienced in dealing with your size of company and the likely transaction value. If they are only used to handling much larger deals you'll end up with a corporate finance house not familiar with your buyer universe and a larger law firm that will charge higher fees. Conversely, if used to smaller deals, a corporate finance house may undervalue you and a law firm may be swamped.

When it comes to fees, the legal side is normally a straight forward fee structure with an estimated deal cost. The corporate finance fees, which should be predominantly success based, are an altogether more complicated challenge. Make sure you compare apples with apples. The simplest deals are all cash deals. Complexity arrives when there are earnouts, partial cash/share deals and so on. Make sure you know exactly how much the corporate finance team will be paid (i.e. how is the fee calculated) and when is it due. What happens if, for example, you agree on a deal which has some cash upfront but a majority in shares which have a 25% every six months release clause[170]. Do they get all their remuneration when the deal closes or do they participate in the potential pain or gain as the share price fluctuates?

As with any selection of professional advisors, I'd recommend that you obtain and talk to a number of references. It's a big decision and worth spending a little time making sure that you and any colleagues involved in the sale are happy with your selection.

---

[170] This would enable you to sell 25% of your holding every six months meaning it would take two years to liquidate your holding and you'd be subject to the share price fluctuation in the meantime.

The Pre-sales Process

Signing up with a corporate finance company and placing your lawyers on standby doesn't mean that your company hits the market the next day!

There is a fair amount of preparation you need to do before the 'for sale' board goes up. You'll need to prepare the necessary documentation and your advisors will probably suggest that you embark on a sales preparedness exercise in which you undertake an informal due diligence process to identify any gaping holes. We discuss due diligence below and it's fundamental to get this right as, once you have signed Heads of Terms with a purchaser, you want the due diligence to be as smooth and as quick as possible.

The first thing you'll do is sit down with the corporate finance team and go through all your industry contacts to come up with the A list of potential purchasers[171]. You'll also identify a standby B list. This is where the corporate finance team's knowledge of the market is critical. They should be adding companies not known to you[172]!

The documents which you will prepare with their help[173] are:

1. The information sheet (aka 'teaser'). A single page executive summary that doesn't identify the company. This is sent to prospective purchasers to tempt them to enquire and request further information.

2. The full prospectus. This is a larger document which you should think of as a sales proposal. It covers all aspects of the company and is designed to make the opportunity to acquire you as attractive as possible. It is only sent to prospective purchasers once an NDA is in place.

---

[171] For larger companies, the corporate finance will have their own contacts in the M&A departments.

[172] PleaseTech was purchased by a company not previously known to us. However, it was known to our corporate finance advisors as an acquisitive company and was added to the A list by them.

[173] Don't believe companies which say they will prepare these documents for you. They will provide a blueprint that you'll have to complete because you have the knowledge and they don't.

Once the preparation is complete, the decision must be taken as to when to go to market. This is typically off the back of your end of year results or a major contract win of some other compelling event which radiates good news. Your advisors will have a very clear view on this and it's probably best to listen to them.

The Sales Process

The starting gun is fired and the teaser is sent out to the A list.

A critical point to understand is that, despite the fact that the teaser doesn't identify the company, it's usually fairly easy for anyone with a decent knowledge of the industry to work it out. At this point the rumours will start to circulate that you are up for sale!

Denying these rumours will give you your first taste of being economical with the truth, a skill which, by the end of the process, you'll have perfected! So, my advice is to simply dismiss the rumours and then move on. The maxim 'never complain, never explain' would seem to be appropriate in these circumstances.

What you want from the teaser is serious enquiries and this involves exchanging NDAs. Once the NDAs are exchanged these companies get the full prospectus which names you and reveals many of your innermost business secrets.

It follows that you need to think very carefully about how to deal with competitors. If they are genuinely a potential purchaser you may decide to prepare a separate version of the prospectus in the event they show interest. You'll need to anticipate this, discuss it with your advisors and come up with an approach that explores the opportunity but doesn't give away the crown jewels.

It's worth noting that timing is everything. Companies you assumed would leap at the chance to acquire you may not show interest because you caught them at a bad time. Perhaps they are still digesting a major acquisition. Perhaps they are bidding elsewhere and can't handle two transactions simultaneously. There isn't much you can do about that. It's just the way the cookie crumbles!

Once the NDAs are signed and the prospectus has been dispatched, the next stage will be conference calls and meetings with your potential acquirers. They will explore the opportunity, seek clarification, ask difficult questions and generally try to understand whether this is the opportunity they think it is or whether there is a dark hidden secret which they will uncover and end up wasting their time!

Clearly, it helps if you have done a modicum of research before such conversations as you want to be questioning them and trying to understand whether they are a suitable acquirer! You want to subtly give the impression that the interest from the teaser is beyond your expectations and that they aren't the only game in town. Your corporate financier will certainly be working that angle for all they are worth!

Generally, during this process it pays to be broadly open and honest. If there is bad news or something negative which will come out in the due diligence it's better to address it upfront so neither party is wasting time. It also allows you to put a positive spin on the situation and explain why it's not the deal breaker it may initially appear to be! In short, it's a standard sales process so you need to be honest, but not too honest, and you need to be presenting the positive not the negative.

Meanwhile, in your day job, subterfuge is the name of the game! Remember that this entire process is happening in a parallel universe and is completely unknown except to one or two of your very trusted colleagues. We address the whole aspect of keeping it confidential internally below.

Your corporate financier will be coordinating all activities and sitting in on meetings when they judge it sensible to do so. Ultimately, it's a sales process and at each stage there will be dropouts. However, the output of all these conversations will hopefully be term sheets from multiple potential acquirers.

Term Sheets, Heads of Terms and Exclusivity
The term sheet lists the key aspects of the offer. In summary, how much and on what terms!

Different companies will value the business differently and will propose different conditions with respect to earnouts, lock-ins, and so on. Is it a pure cash transaction? Is there a joint share/cash offer? What are the terms of the earnout, if any? What are the proposed indemnifications, especially around IP? To what value? How long will they last? There will also be sales process terms. Some may want advanced access to and have the opportunity to lock-in key members of staff, others may want to talk to clients, etc.

While the first term sheet landing is an exciting moment, the terms proposed are generally sighting shots. It's the corporate finance team's job to play off the competing parties (taking bids off the wall where necessary) and drive up the price, make the structure of the deal acceptable and have the overly onerous terms removed. If there is a wide spread of interest they may decide to go for a 'best and final' approach. However, frequently there is an obvious lead candidate and it's all about getting that term sheet to the best deal possible on terms acceptable to both sides.

With an acceptable term sheet, the next steps are to convert it into a Heads of Terms with an exclusivity period attached. The exclusivity period is the next step in the process and gives the chosen acquirer a period of exclusivity in which to conduct due diligence and to complete the deal.

Generally, it's not as simple as running with the highest offer. The terms of the offer will be all important as will be the acquirer's track record. If they have a track record of not completing deals because of 'complications' during due diligence or suddenly finding reasons to change the terms, you will want to think twice about whether their offer is all that it seems.

Think carefully about the terms of any proposed earnout. What is its purpose? Is it to bridge the valuation gap between the parties? Is it something expected by the acquirer's investors? Or is it a bit of a ruse to get the price down? Does the purchaser expect to be able to chip away at the earnout, setting onerous terms which are difficult or impossible to meet? This approach seems to be a predilection of American companies and anecdotal evidence suggests earnouts are regularly subject to dispute and that many fail to deliver the promised payments. You only have to spend a short time with a search engine to uncover earnout horror stories. The general advice around earnouts is that a bird in the hand is worth two, or possibly many more, in the bush!

Again, your corporate finance team should be aware of the buyer's reputation and be in a position to advise you. If they are not a known quantity, it may well be worth requesting and taking up references from the principals of other companies purchased by the acquirer. What has been their experience? Was the acquirer ethical or did the experience leave a bitter taste?

The opposite is also true. I'd be somewhat wary of accepting an offer from a company making its first acquisition. I would expect them to be overly cautious as they felt their way through the process. I'd also question how the post-acquisition integration would be handled given that it would be a first for them. So, unless there was a compelling reason to engage with a newbie, I'd stick to selecting a company experienced in acquisitions.

Once the Heads of Terms is agreed and signed, the period of exclusivity and the real fun begins.

Due Diligence
I have mentioned due diligence throughout this book as it is the defining phase in any company sale. The due diligence process is an in-depth investigation into your company by the potential acquirer. This is where any skeletons in the closet will be uncovered[174] and, depending on their severity, may cause the acquirer to drop out or adjust their offer.

There is no point in hiding anything because, as part of the Share Purchase Agreement (SPA), you and the other shareholders will be providing personal warranties which permit the purchaser to claw back at least some of what they paid if, post-sale, they discover any irregularities which are (i) not disclosed and (ii) materially affect the value of the business.

So it is in your interest to disclose more rather than less. If being acquired by an American company it's also worth making sure their attention is drawn to the fact that UK accounting standards are different from US accounting standards, a subject which has been brought to the fore by the ongoing HPE Autonomy trial previously referenced. However, as always, the devil is in the detail.

You will recall that in the section on publicity I warned against publishing the names of your clients on your website without agreement as it would breach

---

[174] Well that's the theory. Search for 'HPE Autonomy trial due diligence' if you want to read how it can go wrong. I especially recommend The Register's April 2019 summary here: https://tinyurl.com/v59w36x

confidentiality clauses. Likewise, in the development and IP software licensing sections, I discussed traceability and the need to understand where you have third party code and the license implications associated with such code. I explained that you would need to be able to show that the license terms of each third party library have been met and be able to show where in your SWL/SaaS agreement the terms are enacted.

To give you an example of the detail involved, Let's assume that you licensed some commercially available icons to use in your interface which you modified. Regardless of whether you are still using the icons you'll need to show that the license for the icons permitted their modification and you have all the rights to said modifications.

Such examples and others I've mentioned throughout the book will very clearly be on the acquirer's radar. This is why I advised against 'terms tennis' and suggested that it was highly desirable to get signed agreements with all clients or otherwise be able to prove that the SWL/SaaS terms had been accepted.

If there are unwelcome findings the purchaser will take a dim view of the associated risk and may well demand the amount of any future legal costs and settlements be covered by an appropriate legal mechanism. These include additional personal indemnities, further warranties, a retention or the placement of a percentage of the proceeds in an ESCROW account for an agreed period.

So, hopefully now you get it. If you don't play by the rules and haven't yet been found out, this is the stage it will come back and bite you! If you disregarded my earlier pleas to get your act together you should now understand why it's necessary and devote at least some of your time to introducing the necessary procedures and safeguards. Ultimately, not doing so will make you poorer. In the worst cases it will kill the sale, leave you with a large legal bill, a set of frustrated corporate advisors and a whole mess to clean up!

Going back to the due diligence process itself, the way it works is that there will be an agreed due diligence checklist that you need to populate in your data room[175]. As each section is finalised, it is opened up to the other side for their review. You will have to include absolutely everything; both historical and current. At the end of the process your acquirer will know your business better than you do!

Due diligence will cover all areas of the business, including:

- Corporate Structure and Organisation
- Financial aspects (accounts, cash flows, tax, etc.)
- Contracts (supplier and client)
- Business assets
- Technical detail of your product
- IP (yours and use of third party IP)
- Internal computer systems and data
- Employee data (including pensions, etc.)
- Litigation
- Insurance
- Internal company policies and audits

There are lots of detailed lists available on the web if you want the nitty-gritty. The documentation in the data room is normally supplemented by meetings which will explore the details of areas such as sales projections including your prospect list, the underlying IP in your product, the detail and structure of the code, etc. Expect them to crawl all over your support requests and bug list to try and understand whether the product has a solid foundation or is built on sand!

It is at this point it all starts getting very serious because you need to start involving more people. They are, of course, sworn to secrecy but, if you have an open culture as is the case in most software companies, then those not in the loop will start to notice something is up!

Keeping it all Confidential
I noted earlier that throughout this process subterfuge is the name of the game. Keeping the whole process under wraps is incredibly difficult.

---

[175] This will be an electronic data room with highly controlled access options and audit trails. Your lawyer may supply one or may recommend a commercial option to which you subscribe.

At the start of the process you will have agreed with the corporate finance advisors a codeword as the project name. My advice is to make sure it's not something that would raise suspicions if one of your colleagues happened to see it in an email subject line!

A random assignation, perhaps 'project Utah', may not be the best option. Imagine 'Utah documents for review' in the subject line of an email. It immediately alerts the casual viewer to a secret project in the company. At PleaseTech, we called it 'KL'. This tied into Kuala Lumpur, the location of our Malaysian development centre and therefore a subject line of 'KL documents for review' would not raise an eyebrow!

In the early stages you can dress up the informal pre-sale due diligence exercise as a QA process or an audit preparation project. You may consider having an external pre-briefed 'consultant' come in and do an 'audit' and then have an executive decision to implement the results. It doesn't really matter so long as it doesn't raise suspicions that it's anything other than business as usual.

As you start having to meet potential acquirers you'll find that most of them will either be existing or potential partners. It's therefore entirely possible to 'hide in plain sight' and be entirely open about who you are meeting. In PleaseTech, I'd would have certainly aroused suspicions if I'd suddenly became coy as to my meeting schedule!

However, as the process gathers momentum it becomes necessary to take more people into your confidence. Once briefed, these people are known as being on the 'inside'. They are inside the process and in the know.

Every circumstance is different. If you and the inside executives are hands on and prepared to do a majority of the work yourselves[176], it will help minimise the spread of knowledge and thus any leaks. However, you can't do everything, therefore you need to be thoughtful about the realities for the people you do need on the inside.

If they have nothing to gain and everything to lose from the process, you may need to cut an individual deal along the lines of a success bonus to

---

[176] Clare Beazley, CFO at PleaseTech, personally scanned all the back copies of contacts, etc. into the system for the data room. She spent so long in the office some staff assumed her marriage was in trouble.

ensure that their focus is on the job in hand and not on securing a new job. If you do cut such a deal, it will have to be disclosed to the other side and the appropriate documentation filed in the data room.

If you think about it, admin staff aside, this is really a test of your options policy. If you've got it right, the people you need on the inside are the very people who have options and stand to benefit from the process.

Closing the Deal

There are two main documents associated with the deal, the SPA and a disclosure letter. The SPA is the definitive document covering the terms of the sale and the disclosure letter qualifies the warranties in the SPA, the idea being that if something is disclosed it cannot be used in a warranty breach claim.

Needless to say, the above documents with the associated indemnities, warranties and disclosures are the subject of detailed negotiation between the parties. It's actually a bit of a legal game as the disclosure letter may make a point that something is not disclosed or legally qualify the disclosure even though the subject is well known to both sides and has been discussed in depth.

Indemnities and warranties usually have an upper claim limit and are time limited. It is my understanding that American companies are more aggressive with respect to these limits than European companies. In other words, with an American acquirer you'll be on the hook for more and for longer! It's also worth noting that the standard tax warranty lasts for seven years. You need to trust your lawyers implicitly as they will advise you on what to accept and when to push back.

It's very easy to get bound up in the process and forget that you must continue to run the business while all this is happening. Keeping the pedal to the metal is mandatory. You will have provided sales projections to the other side and it's important that these are met. Acquirers are skittish animals and missing your numbers or otherwise not delivering something promised will be bad news. Even if they don't pull out, they may rethink their price and propose new terms.

The power balance between the parties shifts throughout the process. Initially, when your advisors are playing the parties off against each other, your side has the whip hand. As soon as the Heads of Terms is signed and the period of exclusivity begins, the power shifts to the acquirer. They can duck out or reframe the terms at a whim whereas all you can do is say 'no' and ensure that your advisors are keeping the other interested parties warm.

What keeps acquirers honest is (i) their genuine desire to purchase the business, and (ii) their reputation in the market. If they get a reputation for dropping out of deals it will hurt their future acquisition aspirations.

However, this is only true if the reasons for dropping out are disingenuous. The corporate finance advisors also have a reputation to protect and if a 'pile of manure' is uncovered during due diligence they won't want to be associated with it either.

Assuming there is no hidden dung heap, your advisor's job to keep the deal moving forward so that it reaches a successful conclusion. Your best side bet is to keep the business moving in a similar direction and meeting its numbers because the acquirer knows that, once the period of exclusivity is over, if the deal isn't closed you are free to open discussions with others. Having missed out, they may be persuaded to up their offer as everything has been going so well with your business!

I think of it like any sales process. Before the deal is signed everything, but everything, is a sales document or communication. You must be in 100% sales mode until the deal is secured! The mantra of 'if in doubt don't do it' which I recommend for recruitment is likely to be the mantra to which the acquirer subscribes for acquisitions.

The process comes to a conclusion when the due diligence is completed to the acquirer's satisfaction, the SPA and due diligence letter are approaching finalisation and final negotiations over working capital and handover are underway. Joint press releases and internal statements, blog posts, etc. will be signed off by both parties and a date and time for exchange and completion agreed.

There will be a lot of communication between the teams on both sides and it's important to ensure that your team understand the need to be on message and not to relax. Your corporate financers will be on guard for this and be warning you that these deals can and do fall apart at the last moment. An unguarded comment can do a lot of damage.

There are also macro events outside of your control to worry about. There may be a sudden step change in the business environment or a change of circumstance for the acquirer. You may get a letter in the post from a patent troll which you will have to disclose and which will throw everything up in the air. As Harold Macmillan observed the thing he feared most was 'events, dear boy, events'.

Hopefully events don't conspire against you and the deal closes. The money gets transferred to your lawyers where it is divvied up and then transferred to the stock and option holders in the appropriate proportions.

It is at this point you realise the enormity of what you have done and have to steel yourself to face the repercussions[177].

The Repercussions
With an event as big as the sale of a company there are immediate and inevitable consequences. Some good, some bad and some simply indifferent!

There is no prescribed post-sale template. I'm aware of one company where, once the deal was closed, the founders were effectively barred from the premises and not permitted to contact any of their former colleagues and clients. I suspect that it is an extreme example but it emphasises that there is no standard post sales paradigm.

Assuming you are not barred from all contact, there is the likelihood that there will be some form of a handover period. Whether or not this involves an earnout is immaterial because the upshot of it all is that you will have to face your staff!

You do so in the knowledge that, while your life may have taken a significant step on the positive side, many of your staff won't be beneficiaries. In fact, despite everything which will be said and all the positives of the new opportunities which you claim await them, for many the immediate

---

[177] If you are interested in listening to my waffling, https://youtu.be/N7SVtA5sSG8 is a post-acquisition interview I did with our corporate finance company, ICON Corporate Finance.

consequence of the deal is uncertainty and longer term consequence could well be losing a job they love.

The fact is that they were quite happy getting on with their lives, content in their well-paid, interesting employment and you, yes you, have thrown a spanner in the works! Don't expect to be met with undying love and affection! Don't get me wrong, for some the new opportunities which come from the bigger company will be exciting, will enable them to progress their careers and gain new experience which your business could not have provided. However, even for those lucky individuals, this brave new world will be preceded by a period of insecurity.

Reassuring staff and customers as best you can and dealing with other such issues are part and parcel of the post-acquisition territory. Your job is to put a positive spin on the new *actualité* and talk up the benefits. This is especially true if you have an earnout to deliver.

However, the reality is that for the acquired company there is frequently a cultural shock that comes from being integrated into a more structured environment. Unfortunately some of your staff will vote with their feet. Others, once handover is complete, will be surplus to requirements and leave involuntarily.

There is little you can do to protect people because you must remember that there is a new master in town and they are paying the piper and therefore they are calling the tune! You may still be there but it's no longer your company – you sold it!

There are also personal consequences to be considered. Everyone (i.e. your family, friends, neighbours, etc.) will be aware of your changed circumstances and, if you sold to a listed company, the details of the transaction value will in the be public domain.

At a practical level, you will be inundated with wealth advisors trying to avail you of their services. Choose wisely. There are inevitably tax consequences. The more complicated the deal the more complicated the resulting tax matters[178]. You will need to take expert advice and be aware of the need for full disclosure to HMRC. Again, choose wisely.

You then need to think about whether you want to do it all over again! The best bit of post-sale advice I got was to not rush into anything.

---

[178] You will almost certainly require tax advice on how to structure the deal tax efficiently and that is typically part of the legal brief. Post exit you will have complex personal tax affairs for which you may require a different advisor.

The Funding Game

The Funding Game

Venture capital is a much misunderstood area around which there are a lot of myths. For some reason, some entrepreneurs see a VC investment in their company as desirable! When you study the form you realise that these people could be considered deluded!

Noam Wasserman's aforementioned book references a 2010 study[179] which finds that, in VC-backed start-ups, 75% of founders received no financial return from their years of hard work! I thankfully am one of the lucky 25% - although that was more by luck than judgement as I explain in The CDC Story.

It's a complicated area. One could write a whole book on the subject and it's therefore a good job someone has. Angels, Dragons & Vultures by Simon Acland[180], a former VC, was published in 2011 and is a book I strongly recommend that you read before taking the leap. Simon is brutally honest!

He notes that, from his personal experience of investing in twenty three start-ups, in only three of the eighteen companies he successfully backed was the original CEO still in place. The remaining five businesses went bust - a majority of those still led by the original CEO. He concludes that in order to achieve success from an early stage investment, it is generally necessary to change the CEO as the company grows and develops.

This seems to confirm the previously mentioned widespread perception that, after a venture capital investment, the first job of the board is to appoint a new CEO and the first job of the new CEO is to fire the founder! I've seen this process a number of times, especially in America, and the reality is that when you take VC investment you have started the process of leaving the company! The only questions are: (i) when will you leave, (ii) on what terms will you leave, and (iii) with how much?

---

[179] Hall & Woodward; June 2010; The burden of the nondiversified risk of entrepreneurship; American Economic Review 100 (3): 1163-94.

[180] I have to declare an interest here. Simon was running Quester when it invested in CDC (see The CDC Story) and, although, he never sat on the CDC Board the initial investment was secured through him. Having not seen him for 20 years, I contacted him to explain I was writing this book and asked for advice. He was very generous with his time and honest in his advice!

Simon's book pulls no punches and I have no intention of replicating it, so the rest of this chapter covers my understanding, experience and the things I think you need to consider if tempted to play the funding game. My knowledge of the fundraising process itself is about 20 years old[181] but I believe that the points I make are still valid in today's environment.

Finally, to be clear, I am not saying 'don't consider VC investment'. It worked well for CDC and I have no regrets pursuing that course at that time. Just go into it with your eyes wide open and with an exit plan!

Business Angels, Family and Friends

Let's start with business angels. Business angels are so called because they invest their own money (unlike VCs who invest other people's money) and are supposed to fill the seed funding gap.

The root of the problem is that VCs have limited bandwidth and there is an overhead for each investment (legal fees, etc.) which makes investing at a level below circa £2million uneconomical. So, with VCs out of the equation, the question is where is a founder going find seed investment? Step forward business angels.

At this point we need to distinguish between an individual angel investment and an angel investment syndicate which pools business angel investments and can invest considerably more. In fact there is a blurred line between an angel syndicate and a venture capital firm[182]. Henceforth I'm going to call them both 'VCs' and observe differences where appropriate.

Individual business angel investments are usually aimed at very early stage companies and are typically cheaper to close in pure cost of capital terms. However, expect angel investors to be particularly unangelic when it comes to driving a hard bargain with respect to their equity stake and the associated conditions. There will be a shareholders agreement or similar which will place a limit on your activities, your salary, your bonuses, etc.

---

[181] As noted in The CDC Story, I raised £11million over three rounds in 1998 – 2000. We also briefly investigated a VC investment in PleaseTech.

[182] There are also early stage VC firms which invest in the hundreds of thousands of pounds.

Experienced angel investors may come up with more complicated investment instruments such as SAFE[183] or convertible notes or suggest different classes of shares with associated dilution protection terms. These instruments will require more specialist legal involvement and therefore the cost of the investment will be higher. There are also downsides which the referenced article in the footnote covers.

Individual business angels have the same problem as family and friends in that their investment is typically just enough to get the company to a stage where VCs may be interested. The problem is that once the VCs get involved the pre-VC shareholders are likely to get diluted out of the picture. The VC will come along, invest their large lump sum on protected terms and it will be a brave business angel or, indeed member of the family and friends group, who refuses to dilute and stops the VC investment by demanding special treatment for their equity stake[184].

Business angels are aware of this which is why they want the more complicated instruments. Family and friends tend to be less sophisticated investors and will see their stake disappear before their eyes when the VCs get involved. This can, I imagine, lead to less than harmonious family and friend relationships! If you want to protect your family and friends you may wish to consider structuring their investment as a long term, interest free loan and alongside that give them the equity for the upside[185]. That way, if they do get diluted out of the picture, at least they have their original investment returned with the potential upside of the equity.

Be sure you do this before the involvement of any external investors and have the loans formally lodged on your books and declare them to investors.

---

[183] Simple Agreement for Future Equity. Read 'Why SAFE notes are not safe for entrepreneurs' in TechCrunch here: https://tinyurl.com/yays9wuh
[184] This inability to prevent the dilution in any meaningful way, is one of the reasons why you won't find me investing as a business angel in software start-ups!
[185] Obviously it would be possible to use convertible instruments but I'd question whether these are worth the extra legal cost at the very early stages. A simple loan agreement sourced from the web and the issue of standard stock will have broadly the same effect although the investors are arguably double dipping. Given the risk of the loan and the fact they are family and friends that's probably fair enough! The loan should have a clause requiring re-payment when there is a major equity event or after X years.

Business angels won't permit any post investment restructuring if it disadvantages them.

The question you have to ask yourself is whether you really need an individual business angel investment. You'll give quite a lot of your company away for not a lot of money! Can you not grow organically or fund the company through a customer project or some other paid for endeavour? Have you really explored all options of loan finance? For example, I mentioned the Enterprise Finance Guarantee scheme which substantially reduces the risk for the lending bank. The government also offers a Start Up Loan for new businesses. Finally, there are any number of financial institutions offering unsecured business loans. I know nothing about them but would treat them with caution on the basis if it sounds too good to be true, it generally is.

I have no experience and little knowledge of crowdfunding but it's obviously an increasingly viable option for ever larger sums either as the basis of a loan or for equity. My gut feel suggests that more suitable to B2C businesses, but who knows? As with all funding options there are pros and cons so you should undertake research before jumping.

There is a common argument that having a business angel involved brings advice and experience into the company. I remain unconvinced that the value of this advice will outweigh the hassle. Is there not some other way of securing such experience, perhaps via an incubator or mentorship scheme? Personally, I'd explore all options before involving a third party such as an angel. The more investors you have in place, especially those with more experience, the more complex it becomes. Funding rounds and exits are complicated enough without external shareholders all trying to maximise their position at everyone else's expense.

The takeaway thought is to ensure that you have drag-along rights with whatever stock you issue so you can't be held to ransom if you want a VC investment further down the road or if you try and sell!

Playing the VC game
Throughout the book I've made some disparaging references to VCs. I've also been clear that the VC investment worked very well for us at CDC. The VC industry is huge and there are winners - it's just not often they include the entrepreneur who founded the company!

The question I have asked myself is whether we'd have gone ahead with the VC investment in the CDC days if I knew then what I know now! Who knows? Sometimes ignorance is bliss. So, for what it's worth, here are my thoughts.

Securing Venture Capital

Traditionally, securing VC investment has been done through corporate finance companies who will have relationships with the VCs and will help in putting your case forward. However, it is possible to directly approach many angel syndicates and, I suspect, many VC firms.

If you read The CDC Story you'll know that we approached our initial VC investors directly after a corporate finance firm blew us off. However, once we had the offer we reconnected, they helped negotiate better terms and that gave us the confidence to go ahead. So, even if you are successful in approaching such investors directly, I'd recommend getting assistance at some stage from a corporate financier as it will almost certainly pay off in a better deal.

Corporate finance advisors will want their pound of flesh and will be seeking a fee and or a percent of the amount raised. They may even try it on and ask for equity in the company. Any such request for equity would be a show stopper for me! I cannot see any reason such an advisor would deserve to double dip. Either they do it on risk (and have the upside of the equity) or they get paid. Not both! If you are tempted to offer them an equity stake I'd say go back and read everything I've written about the value of equity and think again!

Regardless of how much you pay for any such advice, raising venture capital is not an inexpensive pastime. The cost of capital varies but you'll have a hefty legal bill and other expenses[186] and are probably looking in the region of 7% to 10%[187] - more if the amount raised is at the lower end of the scale. In addition, post investment you'll have ongoing fees such as investor

---

[186] In the market research section I explain how in one of the CDC funding rounds we were forced to pay for an expensive market research report in order to give the investors 'comfort'. With such reports there is a quirk which means it's not possible to reclaim the VAT so you are, in effect, overpaying by 20%.
[187] Many fees are contingent on success - try and move as many as possible to this basis.

management fees and other such charges. Be sure to include the cost of funds and such overheads in your business plan.

Don't forget the first rule around raising funding is to never lose focus on business performance. Investors need to see a continual positive progression to invest and a stumble during the process is a sure way to kill any confidence established.

It goes without saying that the more developed your business, the more valuable it will be and the better the deal you'll be able to cut. If you have a proven business with a scalable model in a large market, expect to be very popular. However, also expect to not be around for long after the investment.

Money, Money, Money

Making money is the sole objective of VCs. It's their stated aim and it attracts people interested in the financial side of business. However, this is where real VCs and business angels do diverge to a degree. Business angels are much more likely to be investing out of personal interest and for reasons other than a pure financial return. That is not to say that they are altruistic but they do have different motives.

Real VCs, on the other hand, are not interested in your business except as a means to invest, exit and earn. Your business is just another asset class. This is fine when they are not masquerading as anything else. Unfortunately many like to think they bring something to the table other than cash, but generally they don't. One of main benefits of being a private business with no investors is that you do not have to constantly justify yourself. When you take venture capital investment you gain cash but give up control. That's the nature of the deal.

You will have a VC on your Board of Directors and it will seem that you can do no right. If you meet the targets the Board considers them to have been insufficiently ambitious and simply marks up next year's targets. If you fail to meet the targets because they were overly ambitious then you have failed. No excuses! Best check that exit clause.

Simon Acland makes a very valid point in his aforementioned book to consider whether you really want venture capital. He suggests that one of the main motivations for many entrepreneurs is independence. The reason they stepped out of the relative security of the corporate world is to be their own master.

The simple fact is that by taking a VC investment you will no longer be in complete control. I have previously referenced shareholder agreements (which Simon refers to as "special instruments of torture") and these will greatly restrict your room for manoeuvre. For example, if there is an obvious market step change which means you have to change direction in order to keep up, you can't make that call yourself, you have to convince the external investors that such a change is in their best interests.

In many ways, you've just acquired a new boss who is not emotionally invested and sees you as expendable. Bear in mind that not all of them are particularly bright and some of them have very large egos. As always, it tends to be the less experienced ones who have the most to say and want to throw their weight around.

Their Portfolio Matters

Understand that, while your company is your only bet, it is simply part of the VC's portfolio. Recent studies[188] have shown that 65% of VC deals returned less than the initial capital invested. This in itself is not necessarily a disaster for investors as I explain below, and does somewhat corroborate the previously referenced statistic that 75% of founders get diddly-squat. VCs know that their real returns will come from around 10% of their portfolio and that their downsides are protected (as we will discuss below). Therefore your interests are not aligned with that of the VCs.

The VCs have no emotional attachment and have one focus and only one focus, which is to maximise the return from their portfolio of investments which they generally look to churn every three to seven years. You are part of the portfolio so expect to get churned. Investments frequently have built-in ratchets to ensure that everyone is focused on the need to exit within a defined period[189].

---

[188] Venture Outcomes are Even More Skewed Than You Think, Seth Levine. https://tinyurl.com/ucjqm45
[189] A particularly solid article with respect to all aspects of a venture investment is 'A Guide To Venture Capital Financings For Startups' by Mike Sullivan and Richard D. Harroch at Forbes.com. https://tinyurl.com/vrzd7n7

Being part of a portfolio has other consequences. VC funds may not have the financial firepower to back all their investments as they grow because they invest on the basis that a certain percentage will fail. If their portfolio is particularly well chosen and is a high performance portfolio, they may well let perfectly viable companies die as there are other higher performers on which they wish to concentrate.

If your business is being successful the VCs will need to decide whether to put the wood behind the arrowhead and fully back it. If they do and, in their judgement it will be more successful with a different CEO, it's 'so long and thanks for all the fish'. If your business is failing the VC will not throw good money after bad and it will be 'sayonara baby', and they will look to exit to maximise their (protected) position.

So, not only is your control of the business limited, you also have little control over the timing and nature of an exit or even security of tenure.

Understand Their Raison D'être

Not all VCs and VC funds are equal. There are many different types and each type comes with different investment targets and strategies. It's not possible to list them all as there is an almost infinite variety.

A key driver of VC investment strategies is favourable tax treatment – especially in the UK. Currently individual investors can benefit from schemes such as Venture Capital Trusts (VCT), the Enterprise Investment Scheme (EIS), and the Seed Enterprise Investment Scheme (SEIS). What all these schemes have in common is that they provide favourable tax treatment to individuals who invest in companies that meet specific criteria.

There is anecdotal evidence that the UK currently has an excess of EIS investment funds looking for suitable homes. I understand that such funds are approaching companies rather than vice versa. Why is everyone so keen on EIS? Let's take a moment to understand the scheme.

The UK government has a comprehensive website covering the detail but the salient points of interest to us are (i) the investor can immediately claim back 30% of the value of their investment, (ii) as long as the shares are held for three years there is no capital gains tax on disposal, and (iii) if the business fails or the investment is sold at a loss the part of the investment not claimed back under income tax relief (i.e. the remaining 70%) can be relieved against either income or capital gains tax.

Consider what this means for the investor. Any return greater than 70% of their initial investment is a gain! The upside is tax free and any downside can be offset against other taxes. In fact, if you run the figures, assuming the company fails and the return to the investor is zero, you can show that the total loss for a higher rate taxpayer is less than 40% of the initial investment. No wonder it is so popular!

What does this mean for you? Simple, the investors have a lot less to lose than you do! Not only will they have a protected position in your company (they'll get their money back first) but also their investments are spread across a portfolio and if they only get 71% of their initial investment back they are still ahead of the game whereas you are most definitely not!

Take a scenario where your company is doing OK but not brilliantly and there is an opportunity to sell it for, say, 90% of the sum the VCs have invested. Assuming it's a tax motivated fund, the portfolio driven VC will sell. The entire sale sum will go to the VC (they have a protected position and will get back their investment first) and their investors will be happy because they are 20% to the good having had 30% immediate tax relief.

In short, you and the original investors (family and friends and angels) lose everything and they still win. So, just because 65% of VC deals returned less than the initial capital invested doesn't mean that there is no return for the investors!

It goes without saying that you need to understand the nature of the investing fund, what is going to drive their decisions and their investment strategies. Make sure that they align with your objectives in so far as is possible although your interests will never be fully aligned with that of the VCs.

It's Spend, Spend, Spend then go Again
If it's going moderately well you'll be encouraged to spend your cash as fast as possible to grow as fast as possible. You'll be under pressure to throw money at marketing, to recruit highly paid, experienced staff, to accelerate sales recruitment, etc. Being under this pressure will mean you make

mistakes and waste money. You start to lose your perspective on what things cost and whether they are sensible investments.

Your revenue growth will always lag behind the plan and soon you'll be running out of cash and wondering where all the money went.

If it's all getting a bit chaotic and you try to curtail growth, you'll not receive a favourable reaction. The VCs are not interested in steady state businesses. So, the reality is that before you know it you'll be out on the stump again looking to secure another round.

Raising money takes time. As a management team, you never want to be in a situation where you are running out of cash and desperate for an injection as that places control very firmly in the hands of the VCs who are not known for their generosity. So the general rule is always to go to the market early.

Your VC may be happy to cough up some more cash (aka increase their investment) but will need a co-investor. The point is that, if non-connected VC invests at the same company valuation, it validates that valuation and your original investor can re-value you on their books and in their portfolio. So, not only will you have to go through the whole process to attract another investor, if you are successful you'll have double trouble! Two VCs on your Board to keep happy.

To understand the rationale you have to go back and consider the portfolio. The VCs want those companies which are going to make it, to make it big - it's 'go big or go home'. This groupthink is prevalent despite research which shows quite clearly that highly capitalised companies do not outperform their lightly capitalised peer group[190]. Remember that the VCs have a protected position so that, if the growth fails to materialise and the company gets sold with their investment underwater, they'll be able to get at least something back while the ordinary shareholders (like you, your family and friends) may not get a penny. Their position is less risky than yours.

Once on the roller coaster it's not possible to get off without an exit.

---

[190] Founder Collective 2016 article at Techcrunch.com, link: https://tinyurl.com/v26kcgv

Their Advice isn't that Great

Remember that VCs are extremely unlikely to have ever run a company themselves - unlike angels who typically have personal experience in this respect. This means that VCs advice isn't always that practical or even that good! If you follow it and it all goes wrong they will slope their shoulders and tell you it was just their opinion and it's your business so you have to take the decisions. They are not interested in collective responsibility!

My personal bugbear on this front is recruitment. Watch out if senior appointments have to be approved by the VCs. They do like a good solid CV from a nice large company and, in my experience, are not prepared to consider internal candidates growing into the role as they consider them too 'lightweight'. So the danger is that you waste a lot of money recruiting unsuitable people on unsustainable salaries because they meet the VC's criteria.

It helps if you have support on the Board. The thing we did get right in CDC was to get an excellent neutral Chairman who commanded the respect of the VCs. Having such an experienced neutral third party is a major benefit and will greatly increase your chances of success.

Get it Right from the Get-go

Investment terms tend to roll forward. If you think about it, it makes sense. The terms are part of the valuation, and no investor is going to disadvantage themselves by agreeing better terms for you in the second or subsequent rounds, especially as they will be significantly raising their stake in your business. Likewise, no co-investor is going to jump aboard at the same valuation on worse terms. So you are stuck with the broadly the initial terms.

When considering the terms remember that the odds are stacked against you. You have to assume that you will be fired eventually and therefore you should try and protect your position as no-one else will do it for you.

A reasonable investment agreement should ensure that you can be paid a sensible market determined salary. In his book Wasserman notes that founders receive, on average, $25,000 less in salary than the equivalent non-founder. He calls this the 'founders discount'. If you've read The CDC Story, you'll know that this is the exact problem the founder Directors had as we ramped up recruitment. Our salaries were restricted by the investment agreement yet we were recruiting and having to pay considerably more than we were earning to get the experience the VCs wanted. I'd note that in our case the gap was often considerably more than $25,000 per year.

I don't have any simple solutions to the above conundrums. I'm simply passing on my experience in the hope that it helps. Your corporate finance advisor should have an opinion. Talk to your lawyer, discuss it with the VCs. Who knows they may be grown up and you can come to an arrangement.

Unfortunately the reality is that when you are negotiating you want everything to be smooth and harmonious and don't want to rock the boat. If you just go with the flow you'll end up in a poor personal position. The initial investment is when you have the power to change things because, at this point, you are driving the process and can step away.

When it goes Wrong

You may think I've been overly negative on VCs. I'd argue that I'm being realistic. I've stressed that the VC investment in CDC worked and that there was a return for the founding team[191]. However, I've seen it go wrong for the founders too many times to ignore and, I believe, the statistics back up my cynicism.

In the introduction I explained that equity was a percentage game. When you take venture capital you will be diluted. After several rounds you'll be lucky to end up owning 10% - 15% of the fully converted equity[192]. Let's compare that with being the founder of an organically grown company when you may end up with around 60% of the equity after other founder team equity and share options. It now becomes simple maths to work out that your venture backed company needs to be seven to ten times more valuable than the organically grown one to return to you personally the same amount of cash on exit.

But surely you should achieve that with all the investor's money you are pumping into the company?

---

[191] I suspect that, if you did the maths, there was a significant founders discount compared with a well-paid corporate job for most!

[192] In other words, after the conversation of preference shares and other such convertible instruments.

The problem is what a Techcrunch 2017 article[193] calls 'the marginal-dollar problem'. The basic premise is that every dollar of VC cash is less well spent than a dollar of organic cash. The return on each dollar is therefore lower. Couple that with the fact that, if it's going well, the VCs may block a perfectly good exit to 'hang on for more', you'll find that getting that a seven to ten times higher valuation is not as easy as it may initially seem.

However, it's more than the marginal-dollar problem. This is why the same Techcrunch article describes venture capital as a 'toxic substance' that destroys companies. A brief search for 'VC investments gone wrong' or similar will provide lots of stories about companies with a solid and loyal customer base, and growing revenue which subsequently fail because of VC involvement. Likewise there are multiple stories of companies running out of cash and shutting up shop because they had over expanded (no doubt encouraged by their VCs) and no-one was prepared to back them again.

Who is to blame? Great question. The truth is out there somewhere!

As a final thought on the subject, I want to bring to your attention a classic 'what can go wrong' story which is the sorry tale of ArsDigita. I bring this story to your attention not only because it is the classic case of a successful company which took VC investment which ends in lawsuits, but also because it has been written by the protagonists themselves from several perspectives including a detailed account by the founder Philip Greenspun[194] and a separate account by co-founder Eve Andersson[195]. Eve suggests "the technical and managerial incompetence of the VCs and those they hired drove the company into the ground". Reading these stories convinces you that this is a classic 'VCs gone bad' story.

However, then head on over to read Michel Yoon's take[196] (which is a response to Eve's article which criticises him) and maybe it's not as straightforward. He identifies several cases of the marginal dollar including

---

[193] Toxic VC and the marginal-dollar problem. Techcrunch.com link: https://tinyurl.com/yaf4p2xn
[194] Philip Greenspun's 2001 story 'ArsDigita: From Start-Up to Bust-Up' is here: https://tinyurl.com/wveoksy
[195] Eve Andersson's story 'The rise and fall of ArsDigita' is here: https://tinyurl.com/uu8fteo
[196] ArsDigita: An Alternate Perspective by Michael Yoon is on TheWayBackMachine here https://tinyurl.com/r4xlz88

spending money on artwork and fish tanks, but also notes that the business grew too rapidly opening multiple offices and hiring multiple people. He argues that this lowered their initial recruitment standards and meant that it's cost base was too high to survive the dot-com crash. Interestingly, if you scroll down, you will note that Eve Andersson posted a lengthy response, 'Reflections, a Year and a Half Later'.

If you've got time this all makes fascinating reading and highlights what can and does go wrong in tremendous detail from several perspectives. It certainly reinforces many of the points I've made! If you haven't got the time for the detail, the 2002 Boston Business Journal article 'Equity Notes: ArsDigita VC funds began a battle that everyone lost' by Jeff Miller[197] is a good summary. It's worth noting that not everyone lost! Miller reports that ArsDigita paid Greenspun $7.65 million in exchange for his stock.

In Conclusion

I can guess what you are thinking. It's probably along the lines of 'he's got a downer on VCs, is quoting out of date statistics and the VCs can't be that stupid because everyone's making so much money'. Are they?

A 2012 Kauffman Foundation study[198] noted that "VC returns haven't significantly outperformed the public market since the late 1990s, and, since 1997, less cash has been returned to investors than has been invested in VC". This is backed up by Gil Ben-Artzy, who reported in 2016[199] that 50% of VC funds are underwater (i.e. they return to the investor less than the initial cash invested). 35% return between one and two times the sum invested, 10% return two to three times and only 5% return three times or more.

How does the industry keep going? It would seem to be a combination of hope over experience and favourable tax treatment!

As I mentioned at the start of this chapter, I am not saying 'don't consider VC investment'. Just go into it with your eyes wide open and an exit plan!

---

[197] It's here: https://tinyurl.com/ufxpykr
[198] We Have Met the Enemy … and He is Us: Lessons from Twenty Years of the Kauffman Foundation's Investments in Venture Capital Funds and the Triumph of Hope Over Experience, 2012. Link: https://tinyurl.com/wftxgh9
[199] Money Talks: Things You Learn After 77 Investment Rounds by Gil Ben-Artzy, 2016, Link: https://tinyurl.com/tx8mzsd

A Final Word

I started writing this book in January 2018. It was to be a wet weather project so I had no defined timescale for completion. Here we are over two years later having written the best part of 145,000 words, and it's been an interesting journey.

I've learnt a lot. To ensure I wasn't writing complete bullshit I spent time researching and, trust me, you can spend hours reading up on a topic and following links to ever more interesting websites. Perhaps the most interesting aspect has been finding backup research for the stuff I instinctively knew through my experience. For example, I knew that VC funded companies spend their money less wisely that organically grown companies. But how to explain that? Was that a known thing? A bit of research and I found the article on the 'the marginal-dollar problem'. Bingo!

There are many examples of this type of affirmation of my opinions throughout the book but, at the same time, the research can identify that the situation is not as clear cut as I had thought. To give another recent example (as it's fresh in the memory), I'd planned on using the sorry tale of ArsDigita in the VC section as I'd read about it at the time. My research unearthed Michel Yoon's defence which put a slightly different perspective on my understanding.

I hope I've managed to put a different perspective on your understanding of the various aspects of a software company. It's a complex operation made up of many different skills and different characters, which must all be unified into a single vision to create an output greater than the sum of its parts. Getting the right people in the right place at the right time can make beautiful things happen!

There are few industries where you can start with nothing but an idea or the determination to succeed and I consider myself extremely fortunate to live in an era where software has made this possible. However, the criteria for success is really no different from any other business. You need to focus on making your product or service the best it can be, managing the business to make it the best it can be, and working hard for your clients. Simple, isn't it?

Not everything I wanted to say could be included in the book. Excluding appendices I'm running at around 114,000 words which is pushing the limits of even a business book. So some of my thoughts will be on the website instead (www.softwarecompanybook.com). There I touch on risk, on the personal characteristics I believe that are necessary for success, and company culture. I also include my travel tips on how to maximise your personal comfort while minimising the bill! I'm sure I'll add other stuff from time to time.

I hope you feel that you've learnt something and therefore have had your money's worth. But even more than that, I hope my thoughts will support the next generation of entrepreneurs and produce some bloody good software vendors.

Abbreviations and Industry Terms

AKA	= Also Known As
AMWA	= American Medical Writers Association
API	= Application Programming Interface
APMP	= The Association of Proposal Management Professionals
ARR	= Annual Recurring Revenue
AESP	= Aspiring Ecosystem Provider (my own abbreviation)
B2B	= Business to Business
B2C	= Business to Consumer
BTW	= By The Way
CAB	= Customer Advisory Board
CBER	= The FDA Center for Biologics Evaluation and Research
CDC	= CDC Solutions Ltd (initially Computerised Document Control Ltd)
CEO	= Chief Executive Officer (in the UK, the Managing Director)
CRM	= Customer Relationship Management System
CTO	= Chief Technology Officer (in the UK, the Technical Director)
CFO	= Chief Financial Officer (in the UK, the Finance Director)
COO	= Chief Operating Officer
COTS	= Commercial Off-the-Shelf
CV	= Curriculum Vitae (Résumé in American)
DCS	= DCS-PowerNET – a document management system in the mid-1990s
DIA	= Drugs Information Association
DMS	= Document Management System
EFG	= Enterprise Finance Guarantee
EIS	= Enterprise Investment Scheme
FDA	= The Food and Drug Administration, a United States government agency
FTE	= Full Time Equivalent
FUD	= Fear, Uncertainty and Doubt
GDPR	= General Data Protection Regulation
GSA	= General Services Administration, a United States government agency
HMRC	= Her Majesty's Revenue and Customs - equivalent to the USA's IRS (Internal Revenue Service)
IDaaS	= Identity as a Service
IMHO	= In My Humble Opinion
IP	= Intellectual property
ISV	= Independent Software Vendor
IUR	= Internal Use Rights
KISS	= Keep it Simple, Stupid
M&A	= Mergers and Acquisitions
MMS	= Mystic Management Systems – a US company based in Mystic, CT
MTD	= Making Tax Digital
MVP	= Minimum Viable Product
NDA	= Non-Disclosure Agreement, or 'New Drug Application' depending on context
NPE	= Non-Practicing Entity (relevant to patents)
OEM	= Original Equipment Manufacturer

Abbreviations and Industry Terms

OTE	= On Target Earnings
PAE	= Patent Assertion Entity
P&L	= Profit and Loss
PHC	= Patent Holding Company
PO	= Purchase Order
QA	= Quality Assurance
QMS	= Quality Management System
RDBMS	= Relational Database Management System
RFC	= Request for Comment
RFI	= Request for Information
RFP	= Request for Proposal
RTFM	= a suggestion to read the instruction manual
ROI	= Return on Investment
ROM	= Rough Order of Magnitude
SaaS	= Software as a Service
SDK	= Software Development Kit
SEIS	= Seed Enterprise Investment Scheme
SFLGS	= Small Firms Loan Guarantee Scheme (replaced by the EFG)
SI	= System Integrator
SPA	= Share Purchase Agreement
SEO	= Search Engine Optimisation
SFLG	= Small Firms Loan Guarantee Scheme
SLA	= Service Level Agreement
SSO	= Single Sign-on
T&Cs	= Terms and Conditions
TLA	= Three Letter Acronym
UI	= User Interface
USP	= Unique Selling Proposition
VAR	= Value-Added Reseller
VC	= Venture Capitalist
VCT	= Venture Capital Trust
VP	= Vice President - an American job title usually adopted by international software businesses
Unicorn	= A start-up technology company valued at more than a billion dollars

Appendices

As noted in the foreword, I've written two appendices which provide by way of background, a narrative of the two companies which I set-up and ran. 'The CDC Story' and 'The PleaseTech Story' offer a business overview of the development of the two companies based on publicly available data. They are an integral part of the narrative in so far as they are the basis of my experience and provide real examples of the development of two successful software businesses. They are not included in the book to save on printing costs and the eBook size (for which authors are charged per MB). They are available from the website (www.softwarecompanybook.com) as a free download.

Website

I'll be putting up a website associated with this book - www.softwarecompanybook.com. In addition to the appendices, this contains further information that I couldn't fit in the book. I discuss risk, the personal characteristics I believe that are necessary for success, and company culture. I also include my travel tips and I will, I'm sure, add to it from time to time.

Reference Links

I've given references throughout this book and the links mostly use TinyURL.com. I've used TinyURL.com for many years without an issue. For those who want the full URLs, they are available on the website. Simply go to the reference links page and use your browser's find function to locate the TinyURL (or part thereof – just the seven digit code will be fine) and you'll find the full link. If a reference link is broken or completely removed (as one or two have been over the last two years) please let me know and I'll update the site to note this and provide a replacement if possible.

Discussion and Feedback

If you'd like to argue with me/agree with me/ask a question, please feel free to come on over and join the LinkedIn Software Company Book Group where I will happily enter into dialogue, respond to points of order and encourage others to weigh in with their tuppence ha'penny worth.

Self-publishing

Having researched the topic, I've decided it will be fun to go down the self-publishing route. It's an area that is growing rapidly with increasingly sophisticated tools to assist. I'm planning to update the website with my experiences.

I guess we will soon find out if I'm any good at marketing books!

Index

In self-publishing there are a lot of decisions to take. One decision is whether to have an index. I've decided not to include an index despite the 'experts' on the web suggesting that it is essential in non-fiction books. Well, I disagree! The book has a comprehensive Table of Contents and, if you can't find what you are looking for from that, then I'm not sure how an index would help!

Cartoons

You'll note that I've invested in cartoons to illustrate the book! My thanks Mark Wood who can be found via www.markwoodcartoonist.co.uk.

Printed in Poland
by Amazon Fulfillment
Poland Sp. z o.o., Wrocław